FOCUS

0	**0.1** p.4 Grammar: Imperatives Vocabulary: Alphabet; Classroom language	**0.2** p.5 Grammar: *to be*; Subject pronouns Vocabulary: Numbers; Countries and nationalities; Age	**0.3** p.6 Grammar: Demonstrative pronouns; Plural nouns Vocabulary: Colours; Adjectives; Objects
1 Family and friends	**Vocabulary** pp. 12–13 Free time and routines; Collocations Reading: Descriptions of free-time activities	**Grammar** p. 14 Present Simple: affirmatives and negatives	**Listening** p. 15 People's typical weekends Exam Focus: Multiple choice Pronunciation: The letter *c* Vocabulary: Prepositions
2 Food	pp. 24–25 Food; Supermarket; Collocations Listening: An interview in a supermarket	p. 26 Countable and uncountable nouns	p. 27 Food and recipes Exam Focus: Gap fill Pronunciation: /iː/ and /ɪ/ Vocabulary: Cooking verbs
3 Work	pp. 36–37 Jobs; Collocations with *job* and *work*; Prepositions Listening: Descriptions of jobs	p. 38 Present Continuous	p. 39 Peace Corps volunteers Exam Focus: True/False Pronunciation: Silent letters Vocabulary: Collocations – *learn* and *teach*
4 People	pp. 48–49 Appearance; Personality; Adjective order Reading: Descriptions of appearance and personality	p. 50 Comparative and superlative adjectives	p. 51 The most important events in people's lives Exam Focus: Multiple choice Pronunciation: Numbers Vocabulary: Collocations – life events
5 Education	pp. 60–61 Schools; Phrases about school; *do/get/be* Reading: An unusual school	p. 62 *must/mustn't; should/shouldn't*	p. 63 Different parts of a school Exam Focus: Gap fill Pronunciation: /ð/ and /θ/ Vocabulary: Parts of a school
6 Sport and health	pp. 72–73 Types of sport; Verb collocations Listening: Sports	p. 74 Past Simple: affirmatives	p. 75 Expressing an opinion Exam Focus: Multiple choice Pronunciation: The letter *a* Vocabulary: Likes and dislikes
7 Travel	pp. 84–85 Holiday and transport; Accommodation; Collocations Reading: Types of holiday	p. 86 Present Perfect with *ever/never*	p. 87 Travel conversations Exam Focus: Multiple choice Pronunciation: The letter *o* Vocabulary: Travel
8 Nature	pp. 96–97 Landscape; Wildlife; Environmental problems Reading: Wonders of nature	p. 98 Future with *will*	p. 99 The weather Exam Focus: Matching Pronunciation: Predicting the weather Vocabulary: Weather nouns and adjectives

Focus review Unit 1 pp. 22–23 Unit 2 pp. 34–35 Unit 3 pp. 46–47 Unit 4 pp. 58–59 Unit 5 pp. 70–71 Unit 6 pp. 82–83

pp. 108–119 Grammar Focus

WORD STORE pp. 1–17 Word practice and Word stores 0–8 pp. 18–20 Prepositions

0.4 p.7 Grammar: Possessive adjectives; Possessive 's Vocabulary: Family	**0.5** p.8 Grammar: can/can't; Vocabulary: Common verbs	**0.6** p.9 Grammar: Prepositions; there is/there are Vocabulary: Rooms and furniture	**0.7** p.10 Grammar: have got Vocabulary: Gadgets	**0.8** p.11 Vocabulary: Days of the week; Months and seasons; Times; Ordinal numbers

Reading	Grammar	Speaking	Writing
pp. 16–17 Family life **Exam focus:** Multiple choice **Vocabulary:** Nouns, verbs and adjectives; Verb collocations	p. 18 Present simple: yes/no and wh- questions	p. 19 Preferences	pp. 20–21 An informal email
pp. 28–29 Unusual restaurants **Exam focus:** Matching **Vocabulary:** Food adjectives	p. 30 Articles	p. 31 Ordering food	pp. 32–33 An email of invitation
pp. 40–41 Dream jobs **Exam focus:** Information transfer **Vocabulary:** Nouns, verbs and adjectives; Collocations – money	p. 42 Present Simple and Present Continuous	p. 43 Describing a photo	pp. 44–45 An email of request
pp. 52–53 Clothes and personality **Exam focus:** Gapped text **Vocabulary:** Appearance and personality adjectives; Clothes	p. 54 have to/don't have to	p. 55 Shopping for clothes	pp. 56–57 A personal profile
pp. 64–65 A different kind of school **Exam focus:** Right/Wrong/Doesn't say **Vocabulary:** Nouns, verbs and adjectives; Compound nouns	p. 66 Past Simple: was/were, could	p. 67 Organising a trip	pp. 68–69 A personal email
pp. 76–77 Challenges some sportspeople face **Exam focus:** Gapped text **Vocabulary:** Nouns, verbs and adjectives; Sportspeople	p. 78 Past Simple questions and negatives	p. 79 Advice	pp. 80–81 A description of an event
pp. 88–89 A fundraising adventure **Exam focus:** Multiple choice **Vocabulary:** Nouns, verbs and adjectives; Collocations	p. 90 Present Perfect with just/already/yet	p. 91 Asking for and giving directions	pp. 92–93 An email of enquiry
pp. 100–101 Different texts about nature **Exam focus:** Right/Wrong/Doesn't say **Vocabulary:** Nouns and adjectives	p. 102 be going to	p. 103 Agreeing and disagreeing	pp. 104–105 Expressing an opinion; Presenting arguments

Unit 7 pp. 94–95 Unit 8 pp. 106–107

pp. 120–127 Word lists

p. 21 Phrasal verbs, days of the week and months   p. 22 Pronouns and numerals   p. 23 Irregular verbs   p. 24 Key to phonetic symbols

3

0.1 In class

Grammar: Imperatives
Vocabulary: Alphabet • Classroom language

1 **CD·1.2 MP3·2** Listen and repeat the alphabet.

A B C D E F G H I J K L M N O P Q R S T U V W X Y Z

2 **CD·1.3 MP3·3** Complete the letters for the sounds in the table. Then listen, check and repeat.

/eɪ/	/iː/	/e/	/aɪ/	/uː/	/əʊ/	/ɑː/
A, H	B, C	F, L	I	Q	O	R

3 **CD·1.4 MP3·4** Listen and circle the word you hear.

1 a pin   b pen
2 a book   b back
3 a disc   b desk

4 Read the classroom language and translate the verbs in red.

1 **Think** of a sport. **Tell** the group your idea. **Speak** in English.

2 **Read** the text and **choose** the correct answers. **Don't use** a dictionary.

3 **Work** in pairs. **Ask** and **answer** the questions.

4 **Listen** to the conversation and **complete** the table.

5 **Tick** (✓) / **Underline** the answers.

6 **Look** at the photos. **Don't look** at the board.

7 **Put** the words in the correct order. Then **write** the answers.

8 **Match** the words with opposite meanings. Then listen, **check** and **repeat**.

5 Read REMEMBER THIS. Then find more examples of the imperative in Exercise 4.

REMEMBER THIS
You use the **imperative** to give instructions.
✓ **Use** a dictionary.   ✗ **Don't use** a dictionary.

Grammar Focus page 108

6 Write sentences. Use the correct form of the imperative.

1 ✓ work in groups of three / ✗ speak in your language
2 ✗ use a pen / ✓ use a pencil
3 ✓ write in your notebooks / ✗ write in the book
4 ✗ talk / ✓ read the text
5 ✓ repeat the words / ✗ repeat the sentences

1 Work in groups of three.

7 Read REMEMBER THIS.

REMEMBER THIS
You use **let's** to make suggestions.

Let's read the text.

No, **let's** match the verbs with the photos first.

Grammar Focus page 108

8 Complete the conversations with *let's* and the verbs in the box.

[~~ask~~   do   finish   listen   read   use]

1 A: I don't know this word. *Let's ask* the teacher.
  B: No, _____ a dictionary.
2 A: _____ Exercise 2 now.
  B: No, _____ Exercise 1 first.
3 A: _____ the conversation.
  B: _____ to the conversation before we read it. OK?

9 In pairs, take turns to make suggestions.

A: *Let's go to the cinema today.*
B: *Let's …*

4

0.2 I'm from …

Grammar: to be • Subject pronouns
Vocabulary: Numbers • Countries and nationalities • Age

Caledonia School of English, Edinburgh

Students' page
We're students at the Caledonia School of English.

A I'm **Andrea**. I'm nineteen years old. I'm Spanish. I'm from Valencia.

B **Lukas** is twenty-one. He's German. He's from Frankfurt.

C **Boris** and **Daria** are Russian. They're from St. Petersburg.

D **Mei** is Chinese. She's twenty-three. She's from Beijing.

E **Andrew** isn't a student. He's a teacher. He's Scottish. He's thirty-four years old.

---

1 Write the numbers.
  1 nineteen – _19_
  2 twenty-one – _____
  3 twenty-three – _____
  4 thirty-four – _____

WORD STORE page 22

2 [CD•1.5] [MP3•5] Listen and repeat the numbers.

3 Read the website. Then match the people in the photos with the countries.
  1 Spain 2 Scotland 3 Germany 4 Russia 5 China

WORD STORE 0.2 page 1

4 [CD•1.6] [MP3•6] Complete WORD STORE 0.2. Complete the tables with the nationalities in the box. Then listen and repeat.

5 Complete REMEMBER THIS with the short forms. Use the website to help you.

REMEMBER THIS

to be

+
I am = ¹_____
you are = ² _you're_
he is = ³_____
she is = ⁴_____
it is = it's

we are = ⁵_____
you are = you're
they are = they're

−
I am not = I'm not
you are not = you aren't
he is not = he isn't
she is not = she isn't
it is not = it isn't

we are not = we aren't
you are not = you aren't
they are not = they aren't

?
Am I …?
⁶_____ you …?
Is he/she/it …?

Yes, I am./No, I'm not.
Yes, you are./No, you aren't.
Yes, he/she/it is./No, he/she/it isn't.

---

6 Ask and answer in pairs. Use the nationalities in the box.

American   Brazilian   German   Swiss
Portuguese   Russian   ~~Spanish~~

  1 Penelope Cruz
  2 Paolo Coelho
  3 Cristiano Ronaldo
  4 Angela Merkel
  5 Garry Kasparov
  6 Roger Federer
  7 Dakota and Elle Fanning

A: _What nationality is Penelope Cruz?_
B: _She's Spanish._

7 Read REMEMBER THIS. Then ask and answer in pairs.

REMEMBER THIS

You can say I'm nineteen years old or I'm nineteen.

  1 How old are you?
  2 How old is your brother/sister?
  3 How old is your best friend?
  4 How old are your parents?

Grammar Focus page 108

5

0.3 Favourites

Grammar: Demonstrative pronouns • Plural nouns
Vocabulary: Colours • Adjectives • Objects

1. In pairs, match the words in the box with the colours. Then name other colours you know.

   black   blue   brown   green   grey
   orange   pink   purple   red   yellow

2. In pairs, match an adjective from A with the opposite in B.

   A | beautiful   ~~big~~   fantastic   fast   new   old
   B | old   slow   ~~small~~   terrible   ugly   young

   big – small

3. Look at Amy and Mike. Which things do you think they have got?

   photos, watch, beanbag, T-shirt, sunglasses, comics, headphones, skateboard

   Amy   Mike

4. CD·1.7 MP3·7 Listen and tick the things that belong to Amy.

5. CD·1.7 MP3·7 Listen again and complete the sentences with the names of the correct objects.

   1. This is my _beanbag_. It's old and brown. I love it!
   2. These are my _____. They're beautiful.
   3. That's my new _____ on the table over there. It's my favourite thing.
   4. Those are my _____ over there, too. They're expensive. They're great.

6. Read REMEMBER THIS.

   ### REMEMBER THIS

   Singular demonstrative pronouns

   This is my beanbag. It's old.

   That is my watch. It's new.

   Plural demonstrative pronouns

   These are my holiday photos. They're great.

   Those are my headphones. They're expensive.

   Grammar Focus page 108

7. CD·1.8 MP3·8 Complete the text with *this*, *that*, *these* or *those*. Then listen and check.

   Look at ¹_these_ comics. My favourite is *Spider-Man*. And ²_____ is my favourite T-shirt. It's really old, but I love it! ³_____ are my sunglasses over there. They're cheap, but they're really cool. And ⁴_____ is my skateboard under the sunglasses. It's expensive and it's really fast. It's great!

8. CD·1.9 MP3·9 Complete the sentences with *it's* or *they're*. Then listen and check.

   1. Look at those posters over there. _They're_ terrible!
   2. Listen to this CD. _____ fantastic!
   3. 'Are your headphones blue?' 'No, _____ red.'
   4. 'What is that over there?' 'I think _____ a bicycle.'
   5. Look at this skateboard. _____ really cool!
   6. These are my holiday photos. _____ great.

   ### REMEMBER THIS

   - You add *-s/-es* to make nouns plural (e.g. *skateboard* – *skateboards*, *watch* – *watches*). Some words don't have a singular form (e.g. *sunglasses*, *headphones*).
   - Some nouns have irregular plural forms.
     man – men   woman – women   child – children

   Grammar Focus page 108

9. Draw four things that are yours and two things that are not yours. Then, in pairs, take turns to describe your things to your partner. Can he/she guess which are not yours?

   A: These are my headphones. They're blue. That is my beanbag. It's big and heavy. This is my favourite comic. It's old.
   B: I think 'the beanbag' is not your beanbag.
   A: Wrong! It's my beanbag!

0.4 My family

Grammar: Possessive adjectives • Possessive 's
Vocabulary: Family

1 Complete the table with the words in the box. What other names of family members do you remember?

brother   cousin   daughter   ~~father~~   grandfather   uncle   wife

♀	♂
mother/mum	¹ father/dad
2 _____	son
sister	3 _____
4 _____	husband
aunt	5 _____
grandmother	6 _____
7 _____	cousin

2 Read the text and complete Lara's family tree.

Hi, I'm Lara and this is my family tree. **My** sister's name is Suzanne. She's twenty years old. My brother's name is Damien. He's fourteen. **Our** parents' names are Elaine and Paul. My grandfather's name is Michael and my grandmother is Sarah. My mum's sister is Louise and **her** husband is Alex. **Their** children are my cousins, Fiona and Charles. We're a great family!

3 Complete REMEMBER THIS with the pronouns in blue in the text in Exercise 2. Then complete the cartoon caption.

REMEMBER THIS

I	¹ my
you	your
he	his
she	2 _____
it	its
we	3 _____
they	4 _____

Hi, ⁵_____ name's Mark. What's ⁶_____ name?

Grammar Focus page 109

4 **CD•1.10 MP3•10** Complete the sentences. Then listen and check.

1 Dave is good at music. That's **his** guitar.
2 Is this _____ pen? Or is it Kate's pen?
3 We love football. _____ favourite team is Arsenal.
4 This skateboard is Marta's. It's a present from _____ parents.
5 _____ brothers' names are Simon and Rob. They are fourteen and eighteen years old, but _____ birthday is on the same day!
6 _____ favourite pop group is London Grammar. What's _____ favourite group?

5 Read REMEMBER THIS. Then find more examples of the possessive 's in the text in Exercise 2.

REMEMBER THIS

Possessive 's: singular
My mum**'s** sister is Louise.
My dad**'s** sisters aren't in the photo.
Charles**'s** dog is Rover.

Possessive s': plural
Our parents**'** names are Elaine and Paul.
My grandparents**'** car is blue.

Note:
My mother**'s** English.   **'s** = is
My mother**'s** car is old.   **'s** = possessive

Grammar Focus page 109

6 Choose the correct options.

1 This is Carlos / (Carlos's) house. Carlos / Carlos's from Spain. Carlos / Carlos's mum is English and he / his dad is Spanish. He's / His from Madrid.
2 My friends / friends' / friend's names are Lucy and Kevin. They / Their favourite sports are football and tennis. Kevin / Kevin's favourite sport is football and Lucy / Lucy's favourite sport is tennis. She / Her favourite tennis star is Roger Federer. My friends / friends' / friend's are crazy about sports.
3 Lucy's / Lucys' father's from Ireland. Her / His mother's Polish. She's / She from Poznań. His / Her name is Magda. Magda's / Magda forty years old. She's / She my Maths teacher.

7 Ask and answer the questions in pairs.

1 What's your mum's name?
2 What colour is your dad's car?
3 What's your best friend's favourite band?
4 What are your friends' favourite sports?
5 Who are your cousins' favourite singers?
6 What are your grandparents' names? What are their favourite colours?

7

0.5 Abilities

Grammar: can/can't
Vocabulary: Common verbs

1. In pairs, match the verbs in the box with the photos in the questionnaire in Exercise 5 and complete the questions.

   cook   dance   paint   roller-skate
   ~~sing~~   speak   swim

2. **CD·1.11 MP3·11** Listen. Tick (✓) what Jon and Mia can do and cross (✗) what they can't do.

	roller-skate	speak a foreign language	sing	dance
Jon	✓			
Mia				

3. Complete the text with *can* or *can't*.

   Jon ¹*can* roller-skate. He ²____ speak a foreign language. He ³____ sing. He ⁴____ dance. Jon's sister, Mia, ⁵____ roller-skate, too. She ⁶____ speak a foreign language. She ⁷____ sing. She ⁸____ dance.

4. Read REMEMBER THIS. Then complete the cartoon captions.

   REMEMBER THIS

   can

+	I/You/He/She/We/They **can** sing.
–	I/You/He/She/We/They **can't** sing.
?	**Can** you sing? Yes, I **can**./No, I **can't**.

   ¹*Can* you sing?
   Yes, I ² ____ .
   No, she ³ ____ !

Grammar Focus page 109

5. Do the questionnaire. Answer *Yes, I can* or *No, I can't*.

   What can you do?

   1 Can you *sing*?
   2 Can you ____?
   3 Can you ____?
   4 Can you ____?
   5 Can you ____ a foreign language?
   6 Can you ____?
   7 Can you ____?

6. In pairs, ask and answer the questions in the questionnaire. Then tell the class about your partner.

   Teresa can dance, but she can't paint. She …

7. In pairs, write five questions. Use the ideas in the box or your own ideas.

   dance the tango   draw comics   play *Halo*
   run ten kilometres   ski   speak three languages
   swim a kilometre   use the Internet

   Can you dance the tango?

8. In pairs, ask and answer your questions from Exercise 7. Then tell the class about your partner.

   A: *Can you run ten kilometres?*
   B: *Yes, I can./No, I can't. Can you …?*
   A: *Maria can/can't dance the tango. She …*

0.6 At home

Grammar: Prepositions • *there is/there are*
Vocabulary: Rooms and furniture

WORD STORE 0.6 page 1

1 Complete WORD STORE 0.6. Label the picture with the words in the box.

[~~armchair~~ bath bed carpet chair cooker desk
dishwasher fridge lamp poster shower sink sofa
table toilet wall wardrobe window]

2 Where is the cat? Label the pictures with the prepositions in the box.

[behind between in in front of next to on
opposite above under]

3 Read the text and look at the photos. Can people live in this house? Why?/Why not?

The Upside Down House

This house is in Germany. In the living room there's a big sofa, a table and a picture. There are two beds in the bedrooms, but you can't sleep in them! There's a big kitchen. In the kitchen there's a cooker, a fridge, a dishwasher, a table and chairs. In the bathroom there's a toilet, a bath and a shower, but you can't use them. Everything in the house is upside down!

4 Read REMEMBER THIS. Then complete the cartoon captions with *there is* or *there are*.

REMEMBER THIS

Singular
There is a cooker in the kitchen.
There is an armchair in the living room.
there is = there's

Plural
There are four chairs in the kitchen.

¹_____ only one room in my house.

²_____ hundreds of rooms in my house!

Grammar Focus page 109

5 Complete the text with *there is* or *there are*. Then read the text again and draw the room.

My bedroom is my favourite room in the house! It's small, but I love it. ¹*There is* a bed. Next to the bed ²_____ a carpet. Opposite the bed ³_____ two small wardrobes. Between the wardrobes ⁴_____ a desk with a chair. ⁵_____ two posters above the bed. ⁶_____ a guitar under the bed. Under the window ⁷_____ a small table. ⁸_____ some CDs on the table and ⁹_____ a CD player, too.

6 In pairs, follow the instructions.
1 Draw a picture of your bedroom but don't show your partner.
2 Describe your bedroom for your partner to draw. Then listen to your partner's description and draw his/her bedroom. Ask questions to help you, e.g. *Where is the bed? How many posters are there?*
3 Compare your drawings.

7 Write five sentences about your flat/house, four true and one false. Then, in pairs, take turns to read your sentences to your partner. Can he/she guess which sentence is false?

*There are three rooms in my house/flat.
There is a living room, …*

0.7 Gadgets

Grammar: have got
Vocabulary: Gadgets

1 Which gadgets can you see in the photos? In pairs, take turns to tell your partner about your favourite gadget.

> CD player   digital camera   e-book reader
> games console   laptop   memory stick
> mobile phone   MP3 player   smartphone
> tablet

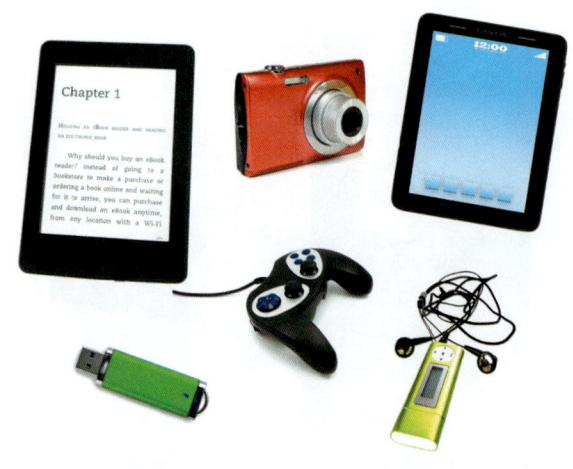

My favourite gadget is my tablet.

2 CD•1.12 MP3•12 Listen to a conversation. Are the statements true (T) or false (F)?

1 Ellen has got an old games console. **T**
2 Ellen and her brother **haven't got** the same mobile phones. ☐
3 Ellen's mobile phone hasn't got a good camera. ☐
4 Ellen **has got** a computer and a laptop. ☐
5 All the students in Ellen's class have got tablets. ☐
6 Ellen hasn't got a favourite gadget. ☐

3 Complete REMEMBER THIS with the words in blue in Exercise 2.

REMEMBER THIS

have got

+	I/You/We/They **have got** a laptop.
	He/She/It ¹_____ a laptop.
–	I/You/We/They ²_____ a tablet.
	He/She/It **hasn't got** a tablet.
?	**Have** I/you/we/they **got** a camera?
	Yes, I/you/we/they **have**.
	No, I/you/we/they **haven't**.
	Has he/she/it **got** a camera?
	Yes, he/she/it **has**.
	No, he/she/it **hasn't**.
	What gadgets **have** you **got**?

Grammar Focus page 110

4 What gadgets have they got? Read about three people and complete the table.

	digital camera	smartphone	MP3 player	tablet	laptop
Phil	✓				
Kate					
Steve					

Phil, 15

My hobby is photography. I've got a digital camera and I can also use my smartphone to take photos. I've got all my photos on ⁵my laptop.

Kate, 16

Music is great! I've got a piano and I can sing too. I'm in a band with friends. We've all got mobile phones and we can take photos ¹⁰and make videos of our music with our phones. I've got all my music on my phone!

Steve, 17

Skateboarding is my hobby! I've got a fantastic MP3 player, so ¹⁵I can listen to my favourite songs when I skateboard. I haven't got a laptop, but I can watch skateboarding videos and chat to my friends on my tablet.

5 Complete the sentences with the correct form of *have got*.

1 Phil **has got** a digital camera, but he _____ a tablet.
2 Kate _____ an MP3 player, but she _____ a mobile phone.
3 Steve _____ a digital camera, but he _____ a tablet.
4 Phil and Kate _____ mobile phones, but they _____ tablets.
5 Steve _____ an MP3 player, but he _____ a laptop.
6 Phil _____ an MP3 player, but he _____ a laptop.

6 In pairs, ask and answer questions about what gadgets you've got.

A: *Have you got an MP3 player?*
B: *Yes, I have/No, I haven't. Have you got ...*

7 Tell the class about your partner.

Igor has got an MP3 player. He hasn't got a tablet.

0.8 Times and dates

Vocabulary: Days of the week • Months and seasons • Times • Ordinal numbers

WORD STORE page 21

1 CD·1.13 MP3·13 **DAYS OF THE WEEK**
Complete the days of the week. Then put them in the correct order. Listen, check and repeat.

T_ _ _day   F_ _day   Mo_nday   S_ _day   Th_ _ _day

S_ _ _ _day   W_ _ _ _ _day

WORD STORE page 21

2 CD·1.14 MP3·14 **MONTHS AND SEASONS**
Listen and repeat the months. Then match the months with the seasons.

| January | February | March | April | May | June | July |
| August | September | October | November | December |

Spring: Autumn:
Summer: Winter:

3 CD·1.15 MP3·15 **TELLING THE TIME**
Look at the clocks. Then listen and repeat the times.

1  3:00 — three o'clock
2  6:30 — half past six
3  4:10 — ten past four
4  19:15 — quarter past seven
5  16:45 — quarter to five
6  1:40 — twenty to two

REMEMBER THIS
quarter to five = a quarter to five
quarter past six = a quarter past six

4 CD·1.16 MP3·16 What time is it? Listen and draw the times.

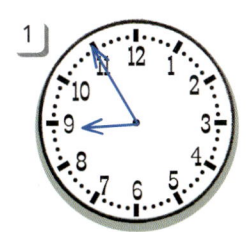

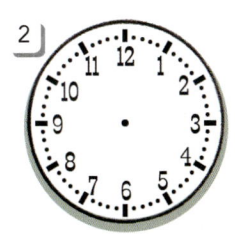

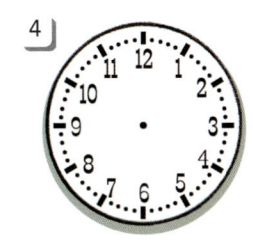

WORD STORE page 22

5 CD·1.17 MP3·17 **ORDINAL NUMBERS**
Listen and repeat the ordinal numbers.

1st 2nd 3rd 4th 5th 6th 7th 8th 9th 10th 11th 12th 13th 14th 15th 16th 17th 18th 19th 20th 21st 22nd 23rd 24th 25th 26th 27th 28th 29th 30th 31st

6 CD·1.18 MP3·18 Listen and circle the dates you hear.

1 a 10 January   (b) 1 January
2 a 16 March   b 6 March
3 a 21 May   b 20 May
4 a 12 December   b 2 December
5 a 19 July   b 9 July
6 a 13 August   b 30 August
7 a 3 April   b 23 April

7 CD·1.19 MP3·19 Read REMEMBER THIS. Then listen and write the dates.

REMEMBER THIS

Days
• You write *6 January* or *6th January*.
• You say *the sixth of January* or *January the sixth*.

Years
1863 – *eighteen sixty-three*
1900 – *nineteen hundred*
1603 – *sixteen oh three*
2014 – *two thousand and fourteen*
       or *twenty-fourteen*

8 CD·1.20 MP3·20 Say the dates. What are these dates famous for? Then listen and check.

SEPTEMBER 11 2001
JULY 4 1776
JULY 21 1969
MAY 8 1945
NOVEMBER 9 1989

9 Ask and answer the questions in pairs.

1 What's the date today?
2 When is your birthday?
3 When is your best friend's birthday?
4 When is the first day of the summer holidays?
5 When is Valentine's day?
6 When is New Year's Day?
7 When is Halloween?

11

1 FAMILY AND FRIENDS

Like father, like son.

A PROVERB

UNIT LANGUAGE AND SKILLS

Vocabulary:
- Show what you know – free-time and routine activities
- collocations – *have*, *go* and *play*
- verb + noun collocations
- verb + preposition collocations

Grammar:
- Present Simple: affirmatives and negatives
- adverbs of frequency
- Present Simple: *yes/no* and *wh-* questions

Listening:
- an interview about people's typical weekends
- multiple choice

Reading:
- a magazine article about family life
- multiple choice

Speaking:
- preferences

Writing:
- an informal email

FOCUS EXTRA

- Grammar Focus pages 110–111
- WORD STORE booklet pages 2–3
- Workbook pages 8–19 or MyEnglishLab

1.1 Vocabulary

Free time and routines • Collocations

I can talk about free time activities and routines.

SHOW WHAT YOU KNOW

1 In pairs, think of as many words or phrases as you can that start with verbs 1–6. Then compare with the class.

1 go to <u>the cinema</u> 3 play _____ 5 listen to _____
2 watch _____ 4 read _____ 6 have _____

2 Tell your partner which things from Exercise 1 you do. Find the things you both do.
We go to the cinema.

3 Read about Mike. Tick the things he does in the table on page 13.

4 Read about Mike's sister, Tina. Tick the things she does in the table on page 13. Then find four things both Mike and Tina do.

Mike

Mike

Information   Friends

👤 Information

5 In my free time I go out with friends or listen to music. In good weather we go to the park and have a picnic or just go for a walk. In bad weather we go to the gym at the sports centre or to the cinema. Sometimes we play computer games or watch DVDs. I love spending time with my friends – we always have fun. My sister Tina is different.

	Mike	Tina	You
1 go for a walk	✓		
2 **go out** with friends			
3 **go to the park/cinema/gym**			
4 **have a picnic**			
5 **have fun/a good time**			
6 listen to music			
7 **play computer games**			
8 **play the guitar**			
9 <u>read books</u>/<u>magazines</u>			
10 <u>spend time</u> at home			
11 <u>talk about</u> things			
12 <u>visit friends</u>			
13 <u>watch DVDs</u>			
14 <u>write a blog</u>			

5 Complete the table for you. Who are you more similar to, Mike or Tina?

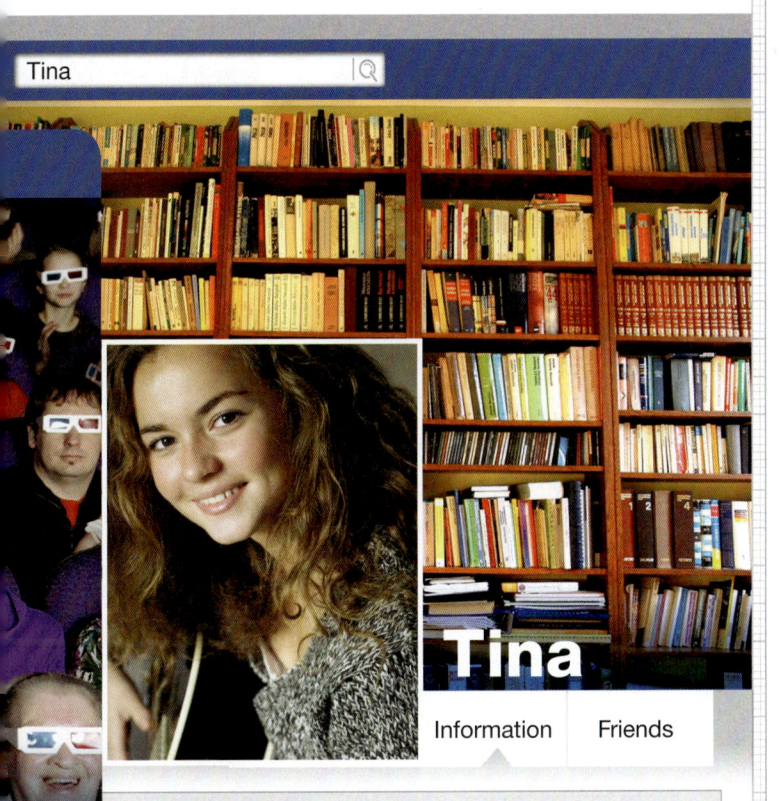

Tina

Information

When I am not at school, I visit my friends or stay at home. I spend a lot of time in my room. I read books, magazines or things on the
10 Internet. I listen to music. I also play the guitar. On Saturday morning I have a guitar lesson. I love my guitar! Sometimes my friends come over in the afternoon and we watch DVDs or play computer games. We talk about different
15 things – for example, books and films. We also write a blog about new things like CDs or DVDs. We have a good time. My brother Mike's different; he never spends time at home.

Go to **WORD STORE 1** page 3.

WORD STORE 1A

6 CD•1.21 MP3•21 Complete WORD STORE 1A with the verbs in red in the table in Exercise 3. Then listen, check and repeat.

7 Complete the sentences with *go*, *have* or *play*. Then choose the options that are true for you.

1 I *can / can't* <u>play</u> the guitar.
2 I _____ computer games / chess with my friends.
3 I _____ shopping with my friends / my family / alone.
4 I _____ to the cinema with my parents / my friends.
5 I _____ fun at the weekend / on weekdays.
6 I _____ out with my friends / my family on Sundays.

WORD STORE 1B

8 CD•1.22 MP3•22 Complete WORD STORE 1B with the <u>underlined</u> verbs in the table in Exercise 3. The first letter of each verb is given. Then listen, check and repeat.

9 Complete what Kitso says about his free time with words from WORD STORES 1A and 1B.

My name is Kitso. I'm from a small town in Botswana in Africa. In my free time, I never ¹<u>spend</u> time alone; I go ²_____ with friends. We usually go ³_____ the youth club. At the club we ⁴_____ the drums. Sometimes we go to the river for a swim and we ⁵_____ a picnic. I haven't got a computer, but I have lots of apps on my mobile phone and I can ⁶_____ games or go on the Internet. I have ⁷_____ in my free time.

WORD STORE 1C

10 CD•1.23 MP3•23 Complete WORD STORE 1C with the prepositions in the box. Then listen, check and repeat.

about   at (x2)   for   in   ~~to~~   with (x2)

11 Complete the sentences with words from WORD STORE 1C. Then tick the sentences that are true for you.

1 I stay _____ home in the evening.
2 I listen <u>to</u> music a lot.
3 I go out _____ friends every weekend.
4 My friends and I talk _____ films.
5 I spend time _____ my grandparents at the weekend.

12 In pairs, take turns to tell your partner about your free time. Use words and phrases from WORD STORES 1A, 1B and 1C.

13

1.2 Grammar

Present Simple: affirmative and negative

I can use the Present Simple to talk about facts, routines, likes and dislikes.

1 Read Jamie's blog. Are you like Ella or Jamie?

My mate Ella and me

She reads news websites on her laptop every day. I **play** computer games on my laptop every day.
I **have** a dog. She **doesn't like** dogs.
She **has** a cat.
I **go** to the park with my dog every Saturday. She **goes** shopping with her friends.
She **plays** the piano really well.
I **don't play** a musical instrument.
BUT we both like music and dancing. We're very different, but we spend a lot of time together.

2 Read GRAMMAR FOCUS 1. Then complete it with the verbs in blue in Jamie's blog.

GRAMMAR FOCUS 1
Present Simple

+ I/You/We/They ¹<u>play</u> computer games.
² _____ a dog.
³ _____ to the park.
He/She ⁴<u>plays</u> the piano.
⁵ _____ a cat.
⁶ _____ shopping.

− I/You/We/They **don't play** a musical instrument.
He/She ⁷ _____ like dogs.

don't = do not; doesn't = does not

REMEMBER THIS

Spelling rules for *he/she/it*:
- most verbs add **-s**: play → play**s**
- verbs ending in -o, -sh, -ch, -x add **-es**: go → goe**s**; relax → relax**es**
- verbs ending in a consonant + -y change y to **-ies**: study → stud**ies**
- *have* is irregular: have → **has**

3 Complete the sentences with the correct form of the verbs in brackets. Then tick the sentences that are true for you.

1 I <u>don't drink</u> (not drink) coffee.
2 My sister _____ (have) a dance class every Monday.
3 My best friend _____ (not play) the guitar.
4 My brother and I _____ (watch) DVDs together.
5 My mother _____ (not go) shopping on Saturdays.
6 My uncle _____ (live) in England.
7 I _____ (not speak) Spanish.

4 CD•1.24 MP3•24 Listen to the verbs in the box and put them in the correct column.

| <s>likes</s> | plays | watches | goes | relaxes | reads |
| loves | helps | dances | drinks | studies | |

/s/	/z/	/ɪz/
likes		

5 CD•1.25 MP3•25 Listen, check and repeat.

6 CD•1.26 MP3•26 Listen to Jamie talking about how he and his friends spend their free time. Write how often they do these things.

100% ←———————————————→ 0%
always   usually   often   sometimes   never

1 go out on weekdays — <u>never</u>
2 have fun at the weekend — _____
3 go rollerblading on Saturday afternoons — _____
4 go dancing on Saturday night — _____
5 watch music videos on Sundays — _____
6 go to the cinema on Sundays — _____

7 Read GRAMMAR FOCUS 2. Then complete the rule with *after* and *before*.

GRAMMAR FOCUS 2
Adverbs of frequency

I **always** get up early in the mornings. I am **never** late for school.
The adverb (*always, often, never,* etc.) normally comes
¹ _____ the verb. But it comes ² _____ the verb *to be*.

8 Write true sentences about you. Use the correct form of the verbs in brackets and adverbs of frequency.

1 I (get up) early in the morning.
2 My grandmother (look) for information on the Internet.
3 I (be) late for school.
4 My best friend (play) computer games before school in the morning.
5 My brother (watch) sports on TV.
6 My parents (go) shopping on Sundays.
7 My cousin (go) to parties at weekends.
8 My best friend (be) hungry.

1 <u>I always get up early in the morning.</u>

Grammar Focus page 110

1.3 Listening

Multiple choice

I can identify details in a radio interview about people's typical weekends.

A _____

B _____

C _____

1 What do you like to do at the weekend? Discuss the questions in pairs.
  1 Are you always busy or do you prefer to relax?
  2 Do you like to spend time at home or go out?
  3 Do you have a weekend job?

2 Match verbs 1–3 with words a–c to make phrases. Which person in the photos does each thing?

  1 coach ☐   a in a restaurant
  2 work ☐   b photos
  3 take ☐   c a football team

3 CD·1.27 MP3·27 Listen to three short interviews and match the speakers (1–3) with the photos (A–C).

EXAM FOCUS | Multiple choice

4 CD·1.27 MP3·27 Listen again. For questions 1–3, choose the correct answer, A, B or C.

  1 When does Simon play football?
     A   B   C

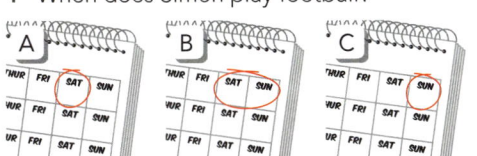

  2 What does Lena do with her photographs?
     A   B   C

  3 What does Mesut do at the restaurant?
     A   B   C

5 In your opinion, which person has the best weekend? Why?

PRONUNCIATION FOCUS

6 CD·1.28 MP3·28 In English the letter c is pronounced in different ways. Listen and repeat.

/k/	/s/	/tʃ/
des**c**ribe	**c**ity	**ch**ildren

7 CD·1.29 MP3·29 Listen and put the words in the correct column in the table in Exercise 6.

  pla**c**e   typi**c**al   exer**c**ise   wat**c**h   kit**ch**en   pi**c**ture
  coa**ch**   **c**lub   Fa**c**ebook

8 CD·1.30 MP3·30 Listen, check and repeat.

WORD STORE 1D

9 CD·1.31 MP3·31 Complete WORD STORE 1D with *at*, *in* or *on*. Then listen, check and repeat.

10 Think about your typical weekend. Make a list of your activities. Then, in pairs, talk about your weekend.

  Well, (on Friday evening/Saturday morning)
  I sometimes ...
  I often ... Then I ...

1.4 Reading

Multiple choice

I can find specific details in a magazine article about family life.

1 Look at the activities in the box. In pairs, discuss who usually does these things in your family.

> clean the house/flat   do the shopping
> look after the children   wash the car
> wash the dishes   work in the garden

2 Look at the title of the article and the photos. What do you think the article is about?

   a a typical family on a typical weekday
   b how to look after young children
   c a father who looks after his children

3 Read the article quickly. Match 1–5 with a–e to make sentences.

   1 Tom is — b
   2 Billy and Eve are
   3 Sharon is
   4 Tom works
   5 Carol works

   a Billy's teacher.
   b Carol's husband.
   c for a construction company.
   d Carol and Tom's kids.
   e as a programmer.

EXAM FOCUS Multiple choice

4 Read the article again. For questions 1–5, choose the correct answer, A, B or C.

   1 Billy and his dad
      A play together.
      B read books.
      C play computer games.
   2 Tom
      A doesn't work.
      B works at the weekend.
      C does a little work every day.
   3 The playgroup teacher thinks
      A a good mother stays at home and looks after her children.
      B a father only stays at home if his wife earns a lot of money.
      C there are different families.
   4 When Carol comes home from work,
      A she goes out to play tennis.
      B Tom goes out to play tennis.
      C Billy and Eve go to bed.
   5 In the evening, Carol and Tom
      A go out for dinner.
      B go to bed early.
      C spend time together.

CD•1.32   MP3•32

A day in the

It's eight o'clock in the morning. Tom Martin's wife gets up and gets ready for work. Tom stays at home with his kids, Billy, aged two years, and Eve, aged two months.

About 1.4 million fathers in the UK stay at home to look after their children. Tom, thirty-eight, is one of them. His wife Carol works for a construction company. After two years at home with their babies, she's happy to be back at work.

Tom, Billy and Eve have breakfast together. Then they look at picture books or Tom and Billy play ball in the park. Every day at eleven, Tom takes Billy to **playgroup** for two hours. Then he goes back home with Eve and works for an hour or two when the baby sleeps. Tom's a **programmer**, so it is easy to work at home.

life of an at-home dad

Sharon Rivers, the playgroup teacher, says 'This situation is quite **normal** these days. In some
20 families the mum **looks after** the children, but in many families, it's the dad. Some fathers want to stay at home and look after their children; some fathers stay at home because their wife **earns** more money. The important thing is that they all love
25 their children.'

When Carol comes home from work, Tom goes out for a game of tennis. In the evening, the family have dinner together. Billy and Eve go to bed at eight and then Carol and Tom can relax together and
30 talk about their day.

So, what is Tom's **advice** to young fathers?

'We have about fifty years to work and make money, but only a few years to watch our babies **grow**. Don't **miss** this important time.'

5 Look at the words in blue in the article. What part of speech are they?

1	playgroup	(noun)	verb	adjective
2	programmer	noun	verb	adjective
3	normal	noun	verb	adjective
4	look after	noun	verb	adjective
5	earn	noun	verb	adjective
6	advice	noun	verb	adjective
7	grow	noun	verb	adjective
8	miss	noun	verb	adjective

6 Complete the sentences with the correct form of the words in Exercise 5.
1 She has a good job and _earns_ a lot of money.
2 I can't go out tonight because I have to _____ my baby brother.
3 Children _____ very fast in the first years.
4 Can you give me _____ about what to see in London?
5 It's the last episode of *Sherlock Holmes* tonight and I don't want to _____ it!
6 My mum is a _____ in an international company.
7 In my family, a _____ weekday starts at 7 a.m.
8 My older sister loves small children and she works as a _____ teacher.

7 What is your opinion of at-home dads?
   I think it's a good idea because men can also look after the children.

WORD STORE 1E

8 CD•1.33 MP3•33 Complete WORD STORE 1E with the words in the box. Then listen, check and repeat.

[after   back   for   from   to (x2)   ~~up~~]

9 Complete the sentences with the correct prepositions and times to make them true for you.
1 I get _up_ at … in the morning at the weekend.
2 I come home _____ school at …
3 My father goes _____ the shops at …
4 I always go _____ bed at … on school nights.
5 My mother goes _____ home at …
I get up at 11 a.m. in the morning at the weekend.

1.5 Grammar

Present Simple: yes/no and wh- questions
I can ask questions using the Present Simple.

Seventeen-year-old rock star reaches no. 1 Grammy for musician's son

1 In pairs, look at the photo of Ryan and the headline and answer the questions.
1 Who is Ryan?
2 What does Ryan's father do?

2 CD·1.34 MP3·34 Listen to the first part of an interview with Ryan and complete it with questions a–c.
a **Does** your father **help** you?
b **Where do** you **practise** your music?
c **Do** you **live** with your parents?

Journalist: ¹_____
Ryan: Yes, I **do**.
Journalist: ²_____
Ryan: Yes, he **does**. He sometimes writes songs for me.
Journalist: ³_____
Ryan: I practise in my father's studio! When I shut the door, the neighbours can't hear anything!

3 Read the GRAMMAR FOCUS. Then complete it with the words in blue in Exercise 2.

GRAMMAR FOCUS
Present Simple questions

You use the verb **do** to form questions and short answers in the Present Simple.

- **Yes/No questions and short answers**
¹**Do** you **live** with your parents?
Yes, I ²_____ ./No, I **don't**.
³_____ your father **help** you?
Yes, he ⁴_____ ./No, he **doesn't**.

- **Wh- questions**
Where ⁵_____ you **practise** your music?

4 Put the words in the correct order to make questions.
1 parties / you / do / like?
  Do you like parties?
2 do / what kind of / like / you / music?
3 to school / your mother / does / drive / you?
4 speak / your father / English / does?
5 clothes / you / where / buy / do / your?
6 your parents / like / do / pop music ?

5 In pairs, ask and answer the questions in Exercise 4.
A: *Do you like parties?*
B: *Yes, I do./No, I don't.*

6 CD·1.35 MP3·35 Match questions 1–6 with Ryan's answers a–f. Then listen to the second part of the interview and check.
1 Where do you buy your clothes? **d**
2 What time does your day usually start? ☐
3 What kind of music do you like? ☐
4 When do you study? ☐
5 Who is your favourite rock star? ☐
6 Which stars do you follow on Twitter? ☐

a I like different kinds of music: rock, reggae, pop, jazz, classical …
b I hate Twitter. I never look at it.
c Hannah Reid in London Grammar. She's got a fantastic voice.
d At local shops in town.
e At about 7 a.m. I get up and practise the guitar.
f Early in the morning and at weekends.

7 Complete the questionnaire with the question words in the box.

[how many   what (x2)   what kind
  what time   ~~when~~   which   who (x2)]

MY LIFE
1 *When* is your birthday?
2 _____ of music do you like?
3 _____ is your best friend?
4 _____ do you wake up at the weekend?
5 _____ hours do you spend on your computer every day?
6 _____ do you like doing with your friends at the weekend?
7 _____ do you go on holiday with?
8 _____ websites do you read every week?
9 _____ is your favourite film?

8 In pairs, ask and answer the questions in Exercise 7.
A: *When is your birthday?*
B: *It's on 19 January.*

Grammar Focus page 111

1.6 Speaking

Preferences
I can ask and answer questions about likes and dislikes.

1 Read the conversation and answer the questions.

1 Does Alex like reggae a lot?
2 What is Laura's opinion of Eminem?

Alex: What kind of music do you like?
Laura: Oh, I don't know, different kinds: reggae, rock, some pop … And you?
Alex: Reggae's OK, but I prefer rap.
Laura: Who's your favourite singer?
Alex: Eminem. I like him a lot.
Laura: Eminem? He's old. My aunt and uncle listen to him.
Alex: So what? I think he's great.

2 **CD·1.36 MP3·36** Read the SPEAKING FOCUS and complete the conversations on the right. Then listen and check.

SPEAKING FOCUS

Preferences
Do you like (films/reading)?
What kind of (music/books/films) do you like?
Who's your favourite (singer/writer)?
What's your favourite (sport)?
What do you think of …?
What about you?

+ I (really) like/love …
I like … a lot.
My favourite (actor/writer) is …
(I think) He/She/It is good/great/awesome/brilliant.

– I don't like … (very much).
I hate/can't stand …
(I think) He/She/It's terrible/awful/rubbish.

+/– He/She/It's OK, but I prefer …

Conversation 1
Natalie: ¹*Do you like* reading?
Mike: Yes, I do. I read a lot.
Natalie: And ² _____ author?
Mike: Terry Pratchett, the fantasy writer. *The Colour of Magic* is my favourite. What ³ _____ ?
Natalie: I like Stephenie Meyer – you know, *The Twilight Saga*. I've got it on my tablet!
Mike: Oh no! The vampire stories? I think they're ⁴ _____ !

Conversation 2
Kate: What do you ⁵ _____ Orlando Bloom?
Jack: He's good. But my favourite actor is Martin Freeman. He's ⁶ _____ in *The Hobbit*.
Kate: So do you ⁷ _____ films?
Jack: Sure. And you?
Kate: Yes, me too. But I ⁸ _____ real-life films, not fantasy.

3 Choose the correct options.

1 **A:** Are you interested in film?
   B: Oh yes, *I really like movies.* / *I don't like movies very much.*
2 **A:** What's your favourite song?
   B: *Just The Way You Are*. I think it's *brilliant* / *rubbish*.
3 **A:** Do you like Norah Jones?
   B: She's OK, but *I don't like her.* / *I prefer Katy Perry.*
4 **A:** Who's your favourite actress?
   B: Natalie Portman. *I hate her.* / *I really like her.*

4 Complete the sentences to make them true for you.

1 My favourite film star is …
2 I like … a lot.
3 I can't stand … I think he/she is …
4 I like …, but I prefer …

5 In pairs, choose one of the topics in the box. Ask and answer about your likes and dislikes. Use expressions from the SPEAKING FOCUS.

[books   computer games   film   music   sport]

A: *Do you like …?*
B: *Yes, I do./No, I don't.*
A: *And who is your favourite …?*

1.7 Writing

An informal email

I can write to someone and tell them about me and my interests.

1 Read the information sheet about a student exchange. Who is Lorenzo?

2 Read Lorenzo's email. Tick the things he wants to know about Joe.

- age ✓
- family ☐
- favourite food ☐
- free time activities ☐
- girlfriend ☐
- home ☐
- interests ☐
- school ☐

To: joeandrews@chs.edu.uk
From: lorenzorossi17@supermail.com
Subject: Student exchange

Hi Joe,

I'm your exchange partner from Liceo Scientifico Leonardo da Vinci. Thank you for inviting me to your home. I'm seventeen years old and I'm interested in sport and film.
5 I like music, parties and new friends!

Please write and tell me about yourself. How old are you? What are you interested in? What happens on a typical schoolday? What do you usually do at the weekend?

See you in October.

10 Regards,

Lorenzo

Cotherstone High School

**Student exchange with
Liceo Scientifico Leonardo da Vinci in Italy**

Time: 12–20 October
Number of students: 14
Your exchange partners:
1. Joe Andrews – Lorenzo Rossi
2. Julia Berry – Alessi... D...
3.

---

3 Read Joe's email. Does he answer Lorenzo's questions? Is Joe a good exchange partner for Lorenzo? Why?/Why not?

To: lorenzorossi17@supermail.com
From: joeandrews@chs.edu.uk
Subject: Re: Student exchange

Hi Lorenzo,

Thank you for your email. I'm also seventeen and I also like sports, music and the cinema. My favourite actor is Andrew Garfield. He's great in the *Spider-Man* movie.

5 On a typical schoolday I get up at 7.00 (I hope that's OK for you!) and I have a BIG breakfast. School starts at 8.30. We have lunch at school at one o'clock. In the afternoon I go to the gym, do homework or relax at home.

At weekends my friends and I always play football (It's my favourite
10 sport. Do you like it?). On Saturday evenings I usually go out with friends to the cinema or to a party – or both! We can do all these things together.

Have a good trip. See you soon!

All the best,

15 Joe

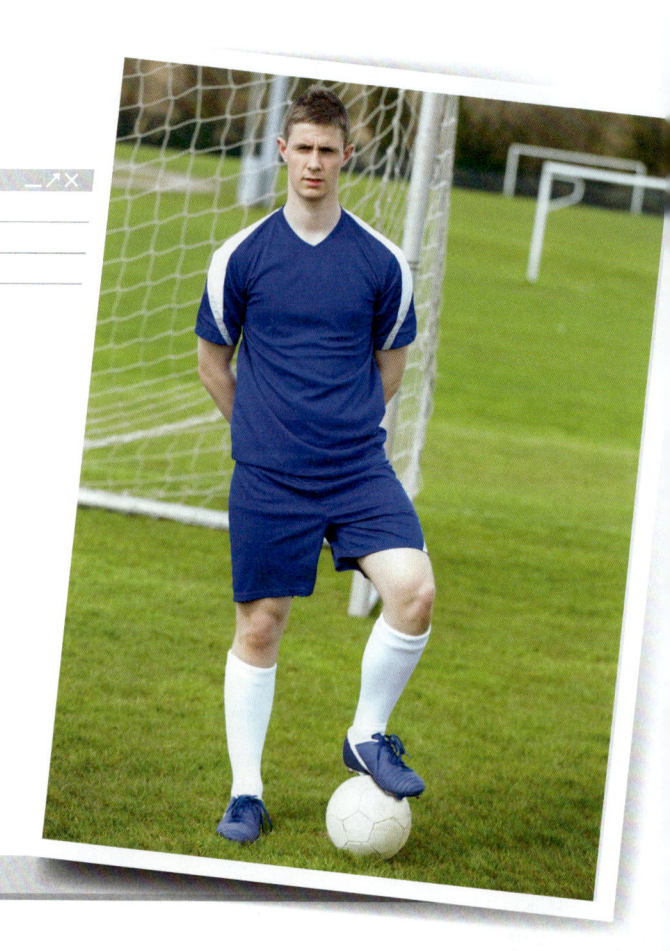

4 Write one more question for each topic Lorenzo did not ask Joe about.

What's your favourite food?

5 In pairs, exchange your questions from Exercise 4. Answer your partner's questions.

My favourite food is pizza with lots of cheese!

6 Complete the WRITING FOCUS with examples from Joe's and Lorenzo's emails.

WRITING FOCUS
An informal email
- Start the email with:
  Dear or ¹*Hi* + the person's name
- Use contractions:
  I am = ²_____   It is = ³_____
- Use phrases at the beginning of the email:
  I'm (your exchange partner).
  Thank you/Thanks for your ⁴_____ .
- Ask questions:
  What ⁵_____?   Do you ⁶_____?
- Use phrases at the end of the email:
  Write soon.   Say hello to (your parents).
  Have a ⁷_____ .   ⁸_____ soon / in October.
- Finish the email with:
  ⁹*Regards* ,   All the ¹⁰_____ ,
  Bye for now,
  Love, (if you are writing to a good friend)

7 Which exchange students in Group 2 are good for the students in Group 1?

Group 1
1 I can't stand vampire films, but I often watch real-life programmes on TV.
2 I like all music, but I prefer old bands.
3 I play the piano and I really like classical music.
4 I don't like going out. I like staying at home and reading books.
5 I go out with my friends every day after school.

Group 2
A I spend a lot of time with my friends. We go to cafés and the cinema.
B I love old music like Mozart and Beethoven.
C I enjoy watching DVDs. I especially like films about real people.
D I like relaxing at home on my own.
E I prefer music from the 1960s, like my gran's old Beatles' records!

8 Read the email from Lucy, an exchange student. Then write a reply of about 100 words, answering Lucy's questions.

To:
From: Lucy

Hi!
I'm a student at Marwell High School in England and I'm your exchange student! Write to me and tell me about yourself. How old are you? What are you interested in? What's a typical schoolday like at your school? What would you like to know about me?

---

9 Check.
✓ Have you answered all Lucy's questions?
✓ Have you given some examples?
✓ Have you started and finished your email correctly?
✓ Have you used some phrases from the WRITING FOCUS?
✓ Have you used the Present Simple correctly?

FOCUS REVIEW 1

VOCABULARY AND GRAMMAR

1 Complete the sentences with the words in the box.

[go   have   spend   visit   watch   write]

1 Do you _____ a big lunch on Sunday?
2 Two of my friends _____ a blog about music.
3 We often _____ music videos on Saturday.
4 I _____ my friends at the weekend.
5 I often _____ to bed after midnight.
6 We _____ a lot of time outdoors.

2 Complete the sentences with prepositions.

enquirer • 31 May
1 What do you usually do _____ the weekend?

musicmad • 15 minutes ago
2 I listen _____ music on my MP4 player.

katieb • 2 hours ago
3 I stay _____ home and relax.

musicmad • 15 minutes ago
4 I often go _____ a walk in the morning.

tsi18 • 1 day ago
5 I go out _____ all my friends every Saturday.

xswot • 3 days ago
6 I get ready _____ school!

moviefreak • 5 days ago
7 I always go to the cinema _____ Friday evening.

3 Complete the sentences with the Present Simple form of the verbs in brackets.

1 Ellen _____ (play) the guitar in her free time.
2 Richard _____ (watch) five films every weekend.
3 My mum _____ (not read) women's magazines.
4 We _____ (not visit) our grandparents every Sunday.
5 What _____ (you/usually/have) for breakfast?
6 _____ (your parents/listen) to pop music?
7 Where _____ (your boyfriend/live)?

4 Put the adverbs in brackets in the correct place in the conversation.

Sally: Mum, I make the coffee for the guests! Chris helps me! (always; never)
Chris: That's not true. I help you. (sometimes)
Sally: Not very often!
Chris: That's because I am tired. (often)

LANGUAGE IN USE

5 Choose the correct answer, A, B or C.

1 I usually ___ home from school at four o'clock.
  A be   B come   C stay
2 On Thursdays George sometimes ___ chess with his granddad.
  A does   B makes   C plays
3 What time do you get ___ at the weekend?
  A up   B down   C on
4 In some families fathers ___ after the children.
  A look   B see   C watch
5 What ___ does your tennis lesson start?
  A place   B time   C hour

6 Read the text and choose the correct answer, A, B or C.

My favourite day Saturday

I really like Saturdays. I get up quite late. I ¹_____ breakfast with my family at ten o'clock or later. At breakfast we talk ²_____ our week and discuss plans for the weekend. Then I do my homework and after that I relax. I often go out with my friends; we go to ³_____ or play snooker. We always ⁴_____ a good time. In the evening I ⁵_____ music before I go to sleep.

1 A have   B give   C do
2 A to   B on   C about
3 A cinema   B the cinema   C a cinema
4 A spend   B get   C have
5 A listen   B listen to   C listen of

LISTENING

7 CD·1.37 MP3·37 Listen to three people talking about celebrating their birthdays. Choose the correct answer, A, B or C.

1 Where does the boy have cake?
  A   B   C

2 What does the girl do outside on her birthday?
  A   B   C

3 What does the boy eat with his friends on his birthday?
  A   B   C

22

READING

8 Read the text and choose the correct answer, A, B or C.

Morning blues? No!

Buzzzz … it's the alarm on your phone. You wake up. You get up. You go to the bathroom, get dressed, get ready for school … Aaargh! Awful?

Linda Hurley, one of her school's champion basketball players, says the morning is not a problem for her. Today she tells us her tips for happy mornings.

- I pack my schoolbag in the evening, so I don't look for my English book at 7.45 in the morning.
- I never get up late. You need time to enjoy your morning. I get up at six every day.
- I have a shower. It wakes me up and it's fun.
- I enjoy the first drink of the day. It can be coffee, tea or orange juice. I always listen to music as I have that first drink. You can also read or watch the news.
- I sit down and have a proper breakfast – not a banana on the bus to school! It's really important. You need your breakfast.
- I usually walk to school or go for a walk with my brother's dog. I spend twenty to thirty minutes in the fresh air every morning before school – it's great!

We hope these tips help you. You too can have a happy morning – every morning!

1 Linda is
  A a teacher at the school.
  B a sporty girl.
  C a coach for a basketball team.

2 Linda gets ready for school
  A in the morning.
  B in the afternoon.
  C in the evening.

3 As she has her morning drink, Linda
  A listens to music.
  B reads.
  C watches the news.

4 Linda has breakfast
  A at home.
  B on the bus.
  C at school.

5 Before school Linda always
  A takes her dog for a walk.
  B goes for a walk with her brother.
  C spends some time outdoors.

SPEAKING

9 Complete the sentences with the correct words. The first letter of each word is given.
  1 What k_____ of music do you like?
  2 Who's your f_____ actor?
  3 What do you t_____ of Jennifer Lawrence?
  4 I like Nicholas Hoult. I think he's b_____ !
  5 What a_____ you?
  6 I don't l_____ football very much.
  7 I can't s_____ rap.

10 Imagine you are taking part in a language course in the UK. You meet someone new. In pairs, talk about the things you like and dislike.

Student A
- Say hello and introduce yourself.
- Ask B what music he/she likes.
- Reply. Ask B what films he/she likes.
- Reply. Ask B about his/her favourite sport.

Student B
- Reply and introduce yourself.
- Reply. Ask A about the same thing.
- Reply. Ask A about his/her favourite sport.
- Reply.

WRITING

11 Read the email from your new online English friend, Mark. Then write a reply of about 50–70 words, answering his questions.

To:
From: Mark

I'm very happy to be your online friend! Please write and tell me about yourself. Have you got a big family? What music do you like? What subjects do you enjoy at school?

2 FOOD

You are what you eat.

A PROVERB

UNIT LANGUAGE AND SKILLS

Vocabulary:
- Show what you know – food
- food containers
- phrases related to food
- in a supermarket

Grammar:
- countable and uncountable nouns
- singular and plural
- quantifiers – *some, any, much, many* and *a lot of*
- articles – *a/an, the* and no article

Listening:
- an interview about healthy fast food recipes
- gap fill

Reading:
- an article about unusual restaurants
- matching

Speaking:
- ordering food

Writing:
- an email of invitation

FOCUS EXTRA

- Grammar Focus pages 111–112
- WORD STORE booklet pages 4–5
- Workbook pages 20–31 or MyEnglishLab

2.1 Vocabulary

Food • Supermarket • Collocations

I can talk about the food I like and don't like.

SHOW WHAT YOU KNOW

1 Complete the table with the food words in the box. Add at least one more word to each group.

> apple   bread   carrot   cheese   chicken   egg
> ice cream   juice   ~~mushroom~~   orange   potato
> strawberry   tea   tuna   water

Fruit	
Vegetables	
Dairy	
Meat	
Fish	
Drinks	
Other	mushroom

2 In pairs, ask and answer questions to find out how similar or different you are.

A: *Do you like apples?*
B: *Yes, I do./No, I don't. Do you like …?*

3 CD•1.38 MP3•38 Listen and complete the phrases with the words in the box. Then listen again and repeat.

> bread   chocolate   ~~crisps~~   honey   ice cream
> ketchup   lemonade   milk   potatoes   tuna

1. a packet of _crisps_
2. a carton of _____
3. a bottle of _____
4. a bar of _____
5. a tub of _____
6. a loaf of _____
7. a tin of _____
8. a can of _____
9. a jar of _____
10. a bag of _____

4 **CD·1.39 MP3·39** What are they buying food for? Listen and match the people (D = Debbie, S = Sylvia, C = Chris) with the meals (1–4). There is one extra meal.

1 dinner ☐
2 an Indian meal ☐
3 a sandwich snack ☐
4 Sunday breakfast ☐

5 **CD·1.39 MP3·39** Do you remember whose shopping it is? Write *D* for Debbie, *S* for Sylvia or *C* for Chris. Then listen again and check.

a bag of onions ☐, a bar of chocolate ☐,
a bottle of oil ☐, a carton of eggs ☑,
a carton of orange juice ☐, a jar of mayonnaise ☐,
a jar of tomato sauce ☐, a loaf of bread ☐,
a packet of cornflakes ☐, a packet of spaghetti ☐,
a tin of tuna ☐, two cartons of milk ☐,
two packets of crisps ☐, a tub of ice cream ☐

Go to WORD STORE 2 page 5.

WORD STORE 2A

6 **CD·1.40 MP3·40** Complete WORD STORE 2A with the names of the containers from the lesson. Then listen, check and repeat.

7 In pairs, discuss what you usually buy in the supermarket. Do you buy the same things?

I usually buy …

WORD STORE 2B

8 **CD·1.41 MP3·41** Complete WORD STORE 2B with the phrases in red below. Then listen, check and repeat.

1 On Saturdays we **get a takeaway** from the Indian restaurant.
2 … we have ice cream **for dessert**.
3 The chocolate is for after dinner – **in front of the telly**!
4 I'm always hungry after school, so I **make a snack** when I get home.

9 Complete the sentences to make them true for you. Then compare with a partner.

1 My favourite snack is *crisps*.
2 When I eat in front of the telly, I usually have …
3 My favourite takeaway is …
4 For dessert, I love …

WORD STORE 2C

10 **CD·1.42 MP3·42** Complete WORD STORE 2C with the words in the box. Then listen, check and repeat.

[~~basket~~   checkout   shelves
shopping   trolley]

11 Complete the sentences with the words from WORD STORE 2C. Then tick the sentences that are true for you.

1 I like to push the _____ round the supermarket when we go shopping.
2 There are always a lot of people at the _____ in my supermarket. I hate it.
3 I use a *basket* when I buy only one or two things in the supermarket.
4 My brother has a weekend job in a supermarket – he fills the _____ .

25

2.2 Grammar

Countable and uncountable nouns
I can talk about quantity with countable and uncountable nouns.

How many INGREDIENTS are there on top of a typical pizza?

Well, on my favourite pizza there are five different things: there's some cheese, some tuna and a lot of tomato sauce. There are also some onions and a lot of mushrooms. But a traditional Italian pizza hasn't got many ingredients; it's got only two main ingredients – tomato sauce and mozzarella cheese; and it's also got some olive oil and some basil. There isn't any tuna and there aren't any mushrooms.

It's called a Margherita and it's delicious!

1 Read the text. Are the statements true (T) or false (F)?

1 A real Italian pizza has always got mushrooms. ☐
2 A traditional pizza has got four ingredients. ☐
3 A traditional pizza hasn't got olive oil on it. ☐

2 Read GRAMMAR FOCUS 1. Then complete it with the words in blue in the text.

GRAMMAR FOCUS 1
Countable and uncountable nouns

Countable		Uncountable
Singular	Plural	³ *cheese*
an onion	¹ *onions*	4 _____
a mushroom	2 _____	5 _____
		6 _____

Note: Uncountable nouns are always singular.

3 Think of more names of food and add them to the table in GRAMMAR FOCUS 1. Look at page 24 to help you.

4 Read GRAMMAR FOCUS 2. Then find more examples of *some* and *any* in the text.

GRAMMAR FOCUS 2
some and any

- You use **some** in affirmative sentences.
- You use **any** in negative sentences and questions.

	Uncountable nouns	Plural countable nouns
+	There is **some** cheese.	There are **some** onions.
−	There is**n't any** cheese.	There are**n't any** onions.
?	Is there **any** cheese?	Are there **any** onions?

5 Complete the conversation with *some* and *any*. What do Sue and Tom decide to have?

Sue: I'm hungry.
Tom: Me too. Let's make some sandwiches. Is there ¹ *any* bread?
Sue: Yes, there's ² _____ bread.
Tom: But there isn't ³ _____ cheese or ham in the fridge.
Sue: That's OK. I don't like cheese or ham. Are there ⁴ _____ eggs?
Tom: Yes, there are ⁵ _____ eggs.
Sue: And tuna? Are there ⁶ _____ tins of tuna? Tuna and egg sandwiches are my favourite.
Tom: No, there aren't ⁷ _____ tins of tuna.
Sue: But I can see a packet of cornflakes. Have we got ⁸ _____ milk?
Tom: No, we haven't got ⁹ _____ milk!
Sue: Oh well, let's get a takeaway. We can get ¹⁰ _____ pizzas!
Tom: Good idea!

6 Read GRAMMAR FOCUS 3. Then complete the questions below.

GRAMMAR FOCUS 3
much, many* and *a lot of

Uncountable nouns
How much cheese is there?
There is*n't much* cheese./*Not much*.
There's *a lot of* cheese./*A lot*.

Plural countable nouns
How many onions are there?
There are*n't many* onions./*Not many*.
There are *a lot of* onions./*A lot*.

1 *How much* water do you drink a day?
2 _____ pizzas do you eat a month?
3 _____ fruit do you eat a day?
4 _____ cola do you drink a week?
5 _____ milk do you drink a day?
6 _____ hamburgers do you eat a year?

7 In groups of three, ask and answer the questions in Exercise 6.

A: *How much water do you drink a day?*
B: *I drink a lot of water./A lot.*
C: *I don't drink much water./Not much.*

8 What's on your favourite pizza? Use *some*, *any* and *a lot of*.

On my favourite pizza, there's some cheese …

Grammar Focus page 111

2.3 Listening

Gap fill

I can identify specific detail in a radio programme about food and recipes.

1 Do you like fast food? Why?/Why not?

2 **CD•1.43 MP3•43** Listen to the first part of a radio programme. What is it about?
   1 unhealthy fast food
   2 healthy fast food recipes
   3 a famous fast food chef

3 **CD•1.44 MP3•44** Look at the photo of the Spanish omelette. In pairs, decide what the main ingredients are. Then listen to the second part of the programme and check.

WORD STORE 2D

4 **CD•1.45 MP3•45** Complete WORD STORE 2D with the verbs in the box. Then listen and check.

[boil   ~~chop~~   fry   mix   slice]

5 Work in pairs. How many different verbs can you use with each of these foods?
   1 eggs   3 meat
   2 potatoes   4 cheese
   1 You can boil eggs. You can fry eggs ...

6 **CD•1.46 MP3•46** In pairs, look at the photo of the fruit pancakes. Read the recipe and try to complete it. Then listen to the third part of the programme and check.

EXAM FOCUS Gap fill

7 **CD•1.47 MP3•47** Listen to the whole programme again and complete the information.
   1 The radio programme is called _____ .
   2 The Spanish omelette recipe is for _____ people.
   3 Kate suggests we eat the omelette with _____ .
   4 The presenter wants to know a healthy recipe for _____ .
   5 Kate thinks it's a good idea to eat _____ with the pancakes.

8 Which healthy fast food recipe from the programme would you like to try? Why?

9 Write the instructions for your favourite recipe.

PRONUNCIATION FOCUS

10 **CD•1.48 MP3•48** Listen and repeat.

/iː/	seat	feel	teen	heat	eat
/ɪ/	sit	fill	tin	hit	it

11 **CD•1.49 MP3•49** Listen and choose the word you hear.
   1 (seat) sit   3 teen tin   5 eat it
   2 feel fill   4 heat hit

Good for breakfast, lunch or tea

Fruit pancakes

Ingredients
- some fruit (bananas and strawberries)
- 1 cup of flour
- 1 cup of milk
- 1 egg
- some oil

Instructions
- ¹ _Chop_ the fruit.
- ² _____ the flour, milk and egg together.
- ³ _____ some oil into a pan.
- Put some of the mixture into the pan, make a pancake and ⁴ _____ it on both sides.
- Take out the pancake.
- ⁵ _____ fruit on top of the pancake.

2.4 Reading

Matching

I can find specific detail in an article about unusual restaurants.

1 In pairs, answer the questions. Use the words in the box or your own ideas.

> burger bar   kebab bar   my grandma's place
> oriental restaurant   pizza place

   1 Where do you go out for a meal with your family?
   2 Where do you go out for a meal with your friends?

2 In pairs, look at the photos and answer the questions. Then read the article and check.

   1 Which place:
   • is in the air? ☐
   • has a lot of modern technology? ☐
   • is under the water? ☐
   2 Which place would you like to go to? Why?

3 Read the article again and complete the table.

	Ithaa	Dinner in the Sky	's Baggers
1 What kind of food can you eat there?	fish and seafood		
2 How much does a meal cost?			
3 How many people can eat there?			

EXAM FOCUS Matching

4 Read the text again. Match sentences 1–8 with restaurants A–C.
   1 You choose your food from a computer screen. ☐
   2 They use only local food to prepare dishes. ☐
   3 You can see a dangerous animal when you eat there. ☐
   4 You can choose from many places in the world. ☐
   5 You can watch the world from above when you eat. ☐
   6 There are more dishes at night than during the day. ☐
   7 You can't have the same dishes in each country. ☐
   8 You can't eat there if you are 149 cm tall. ☐

5 Find the words *course*, *dish* and *meal* in the article. Then complete the sentences with the words.
   1 In my family we always have a three-<u>course</u> dinner.
   2 Breakfast is my favourite _____ of the day.
   3 I love this pasta _____ .
   4 My friends and I go out for a _____ to celebrate our birthdays.
   5 My favourite _____ is fish and chips.

6 Change the sentences in Exercise 5 to make them true for you. Then tell your partner.

   1 In my family we always have a one-course dinner.

WORD STORE 2E

7 **CD·1.51 MP3·51** Complete WORD STORE 2E. Match the words in blue in the article with the definitions. Then listen and check.

Ithaa Undersea Restaurant

Rangali Island, Maldives

A

Ithaa is the world's first undersea restaurant. It's about five metres below the sea and has fantastic views because it has glass walls. You can
5 sometimes see sharks! Visitors go to a small building and climb down some stairs to the restaurant. It's a really cool place to eat for up to fourteen people. The restaurant serves six
10 courses at night and four courses at lunch time. It's great for really **fresh** fish and seafood, but they also serve meat dishes. And the desserts are **delicious** too. A meal costs from €90 to
15 €200, but it's worth it!

28

COOL RESTAURANTS AROUND THE WORLD

Do you like trying new restaurants?
Here are some amazing ideas for a really great experience!

Dinner in the Sky

any city in the world

Dinner in the Sky organises meals in forty countries and the food is different in each place. In Hungary, for example, you can have traditional dishes like *halászlé* (fish soup) or pancakes with meat. In Spain, you can have *paella*, a traditional dish of rice with seafood. You choose a city and a menu and then Dinner in the Sky takes you fifty metres up in the sky for your meal! It's very expensive – about €30,000 for twenty-two people – but it's a wonderful experience. It doesn't matter how old you are, but you need to be at least 150 centimetres tall if you want to eat there.

's Baggers

Nuremberg, Germany

There are twelve chefs at this restaurant, but there aren't any waiters! You order your food from touch screen computers at the table. The kitchens are upstairs. The food comes to the table along long metal tracks! The food is very healthy because the chefs use only fresh local ingredients and very little fat. There are vegetarian dishes if you don't eat meat. Main courses are around €10–€20 and desserts €5–€7. Try the grilled pork with mushroom sauce or the spicy sausage (it has a hot strong taste!). And after your meal, you can rate the food and the experience from your touch screen!

2.5 Grammar

Articles
I can use the articles a/an and the with nouns.

1 Read the text and complete the table.

The Tomatina is a festival in Spain.
The festival happens every August in Buñol, on the last Wednesday in August. Buñol is a small town near Valencia. Thousands of people go to the festival every year. At the Tomatina, people go to the main square and they throw tomatoes! They squash the tomatoes first, so they don't hurt anyone. It's messy, but lots of fun!

The Tomatina Festival

What	1. a Spanish festival
Where	2. _____
When	3. _____

2 Read the GRAMMAR FOCUS. Then underline all the articles in the text.

GRAMMAR FOCUS

Articles

You use **a/an**:
- with a singular noun when it is one of many things/people:
  Buñol is **a** small town. (There are many towns in Spain.)
- when you mention something for the first time.
  It's **a** festival in Spain.

You use **the**:
- when you talk about a specific thing that everybody knows.
  People go to **the** main square. (= a specific place)
- when you mention something for the second time.
  It's **a** festival in Spain. **The** festival happens every August.

There's **no article (Ø)**:
- when you talk about something in general.
  Do you like tomatoes? I hate cheese.
- with the days of the week or months, names of places or countries.
  in Buñol   in August

3 CD·1.52 MP3·52 Read the text and choose the correct options. Then listen and check.

The Battle of the Oranges
is ¹**the /(a)** food festival. It happens every year in ²**Ø / an** Ivrea. Ivrea is ³**a / the** town in the north of Italy. At ⁴**the / a** festival, nine teams of people throw ⁵**Ø / the** oranges. Thousands of people take part! ⁶**Ø / The** oranges are not from Ivrea – they are from the south of Italy. Each year, people throw about 265,000 kilos of ⁷**Ø / the** oranges!

4 Complete the text with *a/an*, *the* or *Ø* (no article).

The Hokitika Wildfoods Festival
is ¹ **a** festival in ² _____ New Zealand. It takes place every year in ³ _____ March. ⁴ _____ festival is about ⁵ _____ wild food – food you find in the countryside. You can't buy wild food in ⁶ _____ supermarket! At ⁷ _____ festival, you can try ⁸ _____ different kinds of wild food, for example, crocodile. It's ⁹ _____ popular festival and thousands of people go!

5 Discuss the questions in pairs.
1 Which festival would you like to go to? Why?
2 Do you know any other food festivals? What happens?

Grammar Focus page 112

2.6 Speaking

Ordering food
I can order food and drink in a café.

1 [CD·1.53] [MP3·53] Look at the photo and the menu. Listen and repeat the prices.

1 twenty-five p/pence
2 thirty-five p/pence
3 two pounds forty-five
4 one pound fifty
5 seventy-five p/pence
6 two pounds ninety-nine

2 [CD·1.54] [MP3·54] Listen and tick the prices you hear. Then listen again and repeat.

1 £2.15 ✓   £2.50
2 €3.45   €2.45
3 €4.85   £4.85
4 70p   17p
5 €0.99   €0.90
6 25c   35c

3 [CD·1.55] [MP3·55] Read and listen. Then complete the conversation. What does Ben have to eat and drink?

Server: Hi. Are you ready to order?
Ben: Yes. I'd like a ¹*cheese* sandwich with ² _____ .
Server: OK. What would you like to drink?
Ben: Can I have a ³ _____ , please?
Server: Large or small?
Ben: Small, please.
Server: Anything else?
Ben: Yeah … Can I have a banana?
Server: Anything else?
Ben: No, thanks. That's it. How much is it?
Server: It's ⁴ _____ .
Ben: Here you are.
Server: Enjoy your meal.
Ben: Thanks.

4 [CD·1.55] [MP3·55] Read the SPEAKING FOCUS. Put *C* for Customer and *S* for Server next to the sentences. Then listen again and check.

SPEAKING FOCUS
Ordering food

Are you ready to order?	S
I'd like a/an/some …/Can I have a/an/some …?	
What would you like to drink?	
Large or small?	
Anything else?	
No, thanks. That's it.	
How much is it?	
It's … (+ price)	
Here you are.	,
Enjoy your meal.	

Menu:

fruit
apple 0.25
banana 0.35

sandwiches
tuna 2.99
burger 4.00
cheese & tomato 3.80

pancakes
meat 2.45

drinks
cola   small 0.75   large 1.50
lemonade   small 0.60   large 1.20
mineral water 1.30

5 Match questions 1–6 with answers a–f.

1 How much is it? — **c**
2 Are you ready to order?
3 What would you like to drink?
4 Anything else?
5 Large or small?
6 Enjoy your meal.

a A bottle of mineral water, please.
b No, thanks, that's it.
c It's four pounds sixty-five.
d Large, please.
e Thanks.
f Yes, can I have a burger?

6 In pairs, role play a conversation to order food. Use the SPEAKING FOCUS to help you.

Student A: You are the server.
Student B: You are the customer. Look at the menu and decide what you want.

31

2.7 Writing

An email of invitation
I can write an email to invite a friend to my party.

1 Discuss the questions in pairs.
1. How often do you go to parties?
2. Do you bring anything with you? If yes, what?

2 Read the email. Does Emma mention any of the things you bring to parties?

To: Anna
Subject: Invitation

[A]Hi Anna,

[B]How are you?

[C]Would you like to come to my party? [D]It's on Saturday at my house at 7.30 p.m. It's a 'bring-your-own' party – everyone makes some food and brings a drink. Then we all eat the food together! You can make any recipe you want. Your pizzas are fantastic and you always make delicious salads too. Or you can bring an interesting dessert. :-)

[E]Can you come? What can you make? Email or text me and let me know!

[F]Love,
Emma xxx

---

3 Read the email again. Match the parts of the email (A–F) with the descriptions (1–6).
1. making the invitation
2. finishing the email
3. asking for confirmation
4. giving the details (where? when? what kind of party?)
5. greeting — A
6. opening the email

4 Complete the WRITING FOCUS with the headings from Exercise 3.

WRITING FOCUS
An email of invitation

- Greeting
  Hi John,
  Hello!

- _____
  How are you?/How are things?

- _____
  Would you like to come to my party?
  Do you want to come to a party?

- _____
  It's on Friday. It's at 8 p.m./It's on Friday at 8 p.m.
  It's at my house/at Moon Club.
  It's a birthday/fancy-dress/bring-your-own/after-exams party.

- _____
  Can you come?
  Email or text me and let me know.
  I hope you can come! Let me know!

- _____
  Love,/Lots of love,
  Best wishes,

5 Read the example sentences in the tables. Then choose the correct options in the sentences below.

Subject	Verb	Article	Adjective	Object (noun)
Everyone	makes	Ø	Ø	food.
You	make	Ø	delicious	salads.
It	is	a	bring-your-own	party.

Subject	to be	Adjective
Your pizzas	are	fantastic!

1. The subject comes (before)/ after the verb.
2. The adjective usually comes before / after the noun.
3. When there is no object, the adjective comes before / after the verb *to be*.

32

6 Put the words in the correct order to make sentences.

1 fancy-dress / party / a / it's
  It's a fancy-dress party.
2 your sandwiches / delicious / are
3 listen to my / after dinner / I / music / favourite
4 the music / fantastic / is
5 make an / recipe / easy / you can

7 Complete the email with one word in each gap. Use the WRITING FOCUS to help you.

To: Jack
Subject: Invitation

Hi Jack,

¹_____ are things?

Do you ²_____ to come to a party? It's ³_____ Saturday ⁴_____ the Mayflower Club ⁵_____ 8.30. It's a birthday party. I'm seventeen! ⁶_____ a friend.

I hope you ⁷_____ come! Email or text me and ⁸_____ me know!

⁹_____ wishes,

Laura

8 Complete the replies to an invitation with the words in the box.

asking   busy   hope   I'm afraid   invitation
love   sorry

1 Thanks for your _____ . I'd _____ to come.
2 I'm really _____ , but I can't come. I'm _____ on Saturday night.
3 _____ I can't come on Saturday. Thanks for _____ me. I _____ you have a great time!

9 Imagine you are organising a party. Complete the notes.

Kind of party:
Place:
Date:
Time:
Bring:

10 Write an email of invitation of about 50–70 words to a friend. Use your notes from Exercise 9 and phrases from the WRITING FOCUS.

11 Check.
✓ Have you included all the information?
✓ Have you used phrases from the WRITING FOCUS?
✓ Have you asked for confirmation?
✓ Have you divided your email into paragraphs?

33

FOCUS REVIEW 2

VOCABULARY AND GRAMMAR

1 Complete the sentences with the words in the box. There are two extra words.

> packet bar jar carton loaf tub tin bottle

1 We've got a _____ of ice cream for dessert.
2 I want to buy a _____ of crisps for the party.
3 Can you buy a _____ of bread at the supermarket?
4 That _____ of honey is almost empty. We need to buy a new one.
5 Please can you pass me that _____ of ketchup?
6 There's a _____ of juice on the table.

2 Complete the sentences with the correct form of the words in capitals.

1 Fruit and vegetables are good for you. They are _____ foods. HEALTH
2 Fish and chips are a _____ food in Britain. Many people eat them. TRADITION
3 The food in that restaurant is _____ . It costs a lot of money, but it's very good. EXPENSE
4 I usually have _____ fish and salad for lunch. GRILL
5 I don't eat meat. I'm a _____ . VEGETABLE
6 Curry can be very _____ – it's often too hot for me to eat. SPICE

3 Choose the correct options.

1 There isn't *much / many* bread.
2 I drink *any / a lot of* water every day.
3 There's *any / some* orange juice in the fridge.
4 How *much / many* pizzas do you eat a month?
5 Are there *any / some* mushrooms on the pizza?
6 There isn't *any / some* cheese in my sandwich.

4 Complete the sentences with *a/an*, *the* or Ø (no article).

1 Do you like _____ mushrooms?
2 Let's go out for _____ meal tonight.
3 Please can I have _____ apple?
4 Dino's is a restaurant near my house. _____ restaurant is popular with young people.
5 We always have an omelette for breakfast on _____ Sunday.
6 Cheese is _____ ingredient for pizzas.

LANGUAGE IN USE

5 Choose the correct answer, A, B or C.

1 A: Hi, Mum. I'm hungry!
  B: Good morning! Do you want sausages for ____ ?
  A tea   B breakfast   C dessert
2 A: Do you want anything from the shops?
  B: Yes, I'd like ____ bar of chocolate, please.
  A the   B Ø   C a
3 A: A mushroom pizza. Is that everything?
  B: Yes. How ____ is it?
  A: It's £6.50, please.
  A much   B many   C any
4 A: What do you want to drink?
  B: Some ____ , please.
  A honey   B ham   C juice
5 A: Can I have a sandwich?
  B: Sorry, we haven't got ____ bread.
  A some   B any   C a
6 A: Do you want to go to a restaurant tonight?
  B: No, let's get a ____ .
  A burger bar B takeaway C fast food

6 Read the text and choose the correct answer, A, B or C.

Food for summer

Salad is the perfect food for summer. It's easy to ¹_____ and it's very good for you. Salads usually have ²_____ tomatoes, onions and lettuce. But you can put any ingredients you want ³_____ your salads! For example, you can add fruit such as strawberries or apples. You can add a ⁴_____ of tuna or some ham, too. You can also make a salad with rice – it's ⁵_____ !

So next time you want to make a meal or a ⁶_____ , remember: try a salad.

1 A makes   B making   C make
2 A some   B any   C many
3 A into   B on   C at
4 A bag   B packet   C tin
5 A favourite B delicious C strong
6 A tea   B snack   C dessert

LISTENING

7 **CD·1.56 MP3·56** Listen to two friends talking about going to a restaurant. Complete the information.

1 Name of restaurant: _____
2 Price of two-course meal: _____
3 Type of food: traditional English and _____
4 Anna doesn't like: _____
5 Katy's brother's job: _____
6 Time for the meal: _____

READING

8 What does each notice say? Read the notices (A–H) and match them with the sentences (1–5). There are three extra notices.

1 You can't eat meat here. ☐
2 This is not for adults. ☐
3 Call this number to learn about a job. ☐
4 Here you can eat food from one country. ☐
5 Children do not have to pay for this. ☐

A **Loch Lomond Food and Drink Festival**
Fun for all the family! And you can try lots of local and traditional Scottish food. The last weekend in June. See you there.

B **Healthy cookery courses**
Do you want to learn from a top chef? We run classes for children and adults at weekends during the summer. Phone for details.

C **Reggie's Veggy Restaurant**
Opens on Monday 18 May. Great food for all you vegetarians out there!

D **Chefs wanted**
Our hotel is looking for a new chef to work in the evenings. Phone 020 9986 4320 for more information.

E **Forest Food Fair**
Watch people cook local food and try some food from the continental market. There's food from France, Germany, Spain and Italy. It costs £5 per person and is free for under-twelves.

F **Gary Clarke on TV**
New to Channel 3. Every Monday chef Gary Clarke shows children how to cook easy recipes. They can also read the recipes in his book. Maybe a nice birthday present?

G **Farmer's market**
Buy fresh fruit, meat and vegetables from the Farmer's market in Hardford town centre every Tuesday. It's open from 9.00 to 4.30.

H **Cookery competition**
Are you a good cook? Can you cook different meals, from burgers to seafood? Phone this number and enter our competition!
022 4357 88931

SPEAKING

9 Put *C* for Customer or *S* for Server next to each sentence.

1 How much is it? ☐
2 Anything else? ☐
3 Are you ready to order? ☐
4 No, thanks. That's it. ☐
5 Enjoy your meal. ☐
6 I'd like a small pizza, please. ☐

10 In pairs, look at the menu and the prompts and role play a conversation in a café. Student A, you are the waiter. Student B, you are the customer.

Menu

Main course		Drinks				
Chicken salad	4.50	Cola	*small*	0.60	*large*	1.45
Burger and chips	4.25	Juice	*small*	0.80	*large*	1.70
Pizza	3.75	Lemonade	*small*	0.50	*large*	1.10
Cheese omelette	3.80	Tea		1.20		

Dessert
Chocolate cake 2.50
Ice cream 1.25
Pancakes 2.45

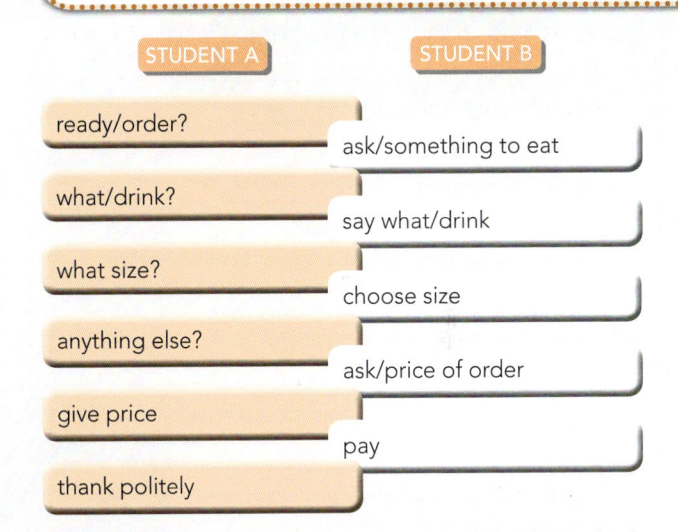

STUDENT A
- ready/order?
- what/drink?
- what size?
- anything else?
- give price
- thank politely

STUDENT B
- ask/something to eat
- say what/drink
- choose size
- ask/price of order
- pay

WRITING

11 Read the writing task. Match sentences a–d to points 1–4 in the task. Then do the task.

a Would you like to come with me?
b How are you?
c It's next weekend.
d There are chefs from different countries.

> You are going to a food festival and want to invite your friend. Write an email to him/her and include these points:
> 1 Greet him/her and ask how he/she is.
> 2 Say where and when the festival is.
> 3 Say what you can see and do there.
> 4 Invite him/her to come.
> Write your email in 50–70 words.

3 WORK

Practice makes perfect.

A PROVERB

UNIT LANGUAGE AND SKILLS

Vocabulary:
- *Show what you know* – jobs
- jobs with suffixes
- collocations – *job* and *work*
- *work* + prepositions

Grammar:
- Present Continuous
- Present Simple and Present Continuous

Listening:
- a radio programme about voluntary work
- true/false

Reading:
- an article about unusual jobs
- information transfer

Speaking:
- describing a photo

Writing:
- an email of request

FOCUS EXTRA

- Grammar Focus pages 112–113
- WORD STORE booklet pages 6–7
- Workbook pages 32–43 or MyEnglishLab

3.1 Vocabulary

Jobs • Collocations with *job* and *work* • Prepositions
I can talk about jobs and work.

SHOW WHAT YOU KNOW

1 In pairs, name as many jobs as you can in sixty seconds. Then compare with the class.

2 Label the photos with ten of the jobs in the box. Which jobs are not in the photos?

> accountant   architect   artist   builder   dentist   doctor
> engineer   factory worker   farmer   gardener   hairdresser
> journalist   lawyer   mechanic   ~~nurse~~   plumber
> receptionist   scientist   shop assistant   soldier
> sports instructor   taxi driver   teacher   vet   waiter

1 nurse

3 **CD·2.1 MP3·57** Listen and repeat the jobs. Check that you understand the words.

4 Think of five people you know. Then, in pairs, take turns to tell your partner about their jobs.
My neighbour is a builder.

> **REMEMBER THIS**
> When you talk about jobs, use the article *a/an*.
> *My mum is a scientist.*

5 **CD·2.2 MP3·58** Listen to four people talking about their jobs. Match the speakers (A–D) with four of the photos (1–10).
A [6]   B [ ]   C [ ]   D [ ]

6 **CD·2.2 MP3·58** Listen again and match the speakers (A–D) with the sentences (1–9).
1 He/She **works long hours**. [A]
2 He/She **works with children**. [ ]
3 He/She **works for an international company**. [ ]
4 He/She **works in a supermarket**. [ ]
5 He/She **works from home**. [ ]
6 He/She's got **a badly-paid job**. [ ]
7 He/She's got **a well-paid job**. [ ]
8 He/She's got **a part-time job**. [ ]
9 He/She **works in a team**. [ ]

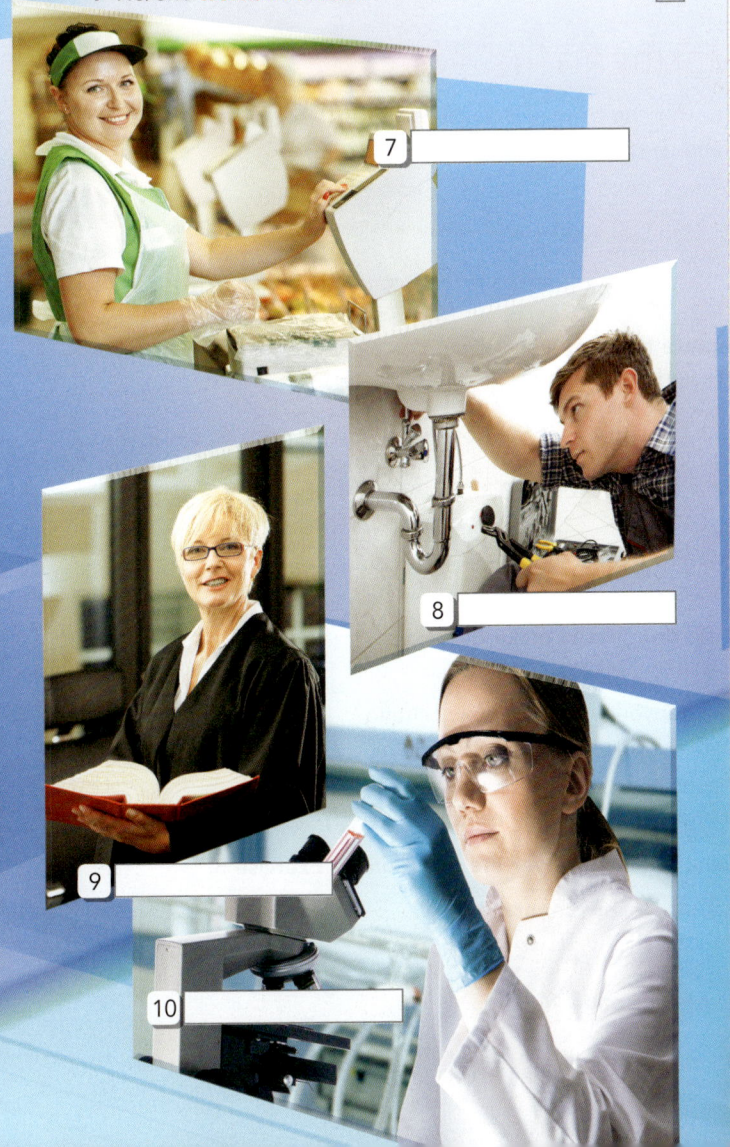

Go to WORD STORE 3 page 7.

WORD STORE 3A

7 **CD·2.3 MP3·59** Complete WORD STORE 3A with the jobs in Exercise 2. Then listen, check and repeat.

8 Complete the sentences with jobs from WORD STORE 3A.
1 You need a *mechanic* when your car doesn't work.
2 A _____ looks after people in hospital.
3 An _____ can help build roads and bridges.
4 I've got a sore tooth – I need to go to the _____ .
5 At a hotel, the _____ gives you the key to your room.
6 A _____ can repair the water pipe in the bathroom.

WORD STORE 3B

9 **CD·2.4 MP3·60** Look at Exercise 6 again. Complete WORD STORE 3B with *job* or *work*. Then listen, check and repeat.

10 Complete the sentences with names of people you know. Then tell your partner.
1 _____ works long hours.
2 _____ has got a part-time job.
3 _____ works full-time.
4 _____ has got a well-paid job.
5 _____ works hard and is badly paid.
6 _____ works nine to five.

1 *My mum works long hours.*

WORD STORE 3C

11 **CD·2.5 MP3·61** Complete WORD STORE 3C with prepositions from Exercise 6. Then listen, check and repeat.

12 Complete the questions with prepositions from WORD STORE 3C. Then ask and answer in pairs.
1 Would you like to work *for* a big company or a small company? Why?
2 Would you like to work _____ home? Why?/Why not?
3 Would you like a full-time or a part-time job? Why?
4 Do you prefer to work _____ a team or alone? Why?
5 Would you like to work _____ children? Why?/Why not?
6 Would you prefer to work _____ an office or outside? Why?

37

3.2 Grammar

Present Continuous
I can talk about actions happening at the time of speaking.

> Oh hello, Mrs Vincent. Yes, everything is fine here. The house is almost ready. **I'm standing** in the living room at the moment and it looks really good. Joey is finishing the bathroom … What **is** he **doing** exactly? Erm, he's fitting the shower. Dan and Nick **are working** too … **Are** they **working** on the roof? Yes, they are – it's almost finished … Yes, the gardener is here. He's digging a flowerbed for your roses … Joey's dog? Yes, he's here, but he **isn't playing** in the house. He**'s sleeping** … Fishing? No, we **aren't fishing**, Mrs Vincent! We're all working very hard! So, are you enjoying your holiday, Mrs Vincent? … What? Are you coming home now? Right … er … fine … see you soon then.

1 Look at the men in the picture. What are their jobs? Use the words from the box on page 36.

2 **CD•2.6 MP3•62** Read and listen to Frank's telephone conversation with Mrs Vincent, the owner of the house. Does Frank tell her the truth?

3 Read the GRAMMAR FOCUS. Then complete it with the words in blue in Exercise 2.

GRAMMAR FOCUS

Present Continuous: am/are/is + -ing
You use the **Present Continuous** to talk about actions happening at the time of speaking.

+ I ¹ *'m standing* in the living room.
   He ² _____ .
   They ³ _____ too.

− He ⁴ _____ in the house.
   We ⁵ _____ !

? What ⁶ _____ he _____ exactly?
   ⁷ _____ they _____ on the roof?
   Yes, they **are**./No, they **aren't**.

REMEMBER THIS

To form the *-ing* form of a verb:
- add *-ing* to the verb: stand → stand**ing**
- if the verb ends in *-e*, drop *-e*: make → mak**ing**
- if the verb ends in a short vowel + a consonant, double the final consonant: fit → fit**ting**

4 Complete the sentences about the picture. Use the correct form of the verbs in the box.

> drink   eat   fry   not fit   not sleep   ~~not stand~~   not work   run

1 Frank *isn't standing* in the house. He _____ a fish.
2 Dan and Nick _____ on the roof. They _____ sandwiches.
3 Joey _____ the shower. He _____ coffee.
4 The dog _____ in the house. It _____ round the garden.

5 Use the prompts to make questions.
1 doing / is / the teacher / what?
2 near / anyone / is / a window / sitting?
3 anybody / black / wearing / something / is?
4 any / writing / are / students?
5 this / are / doing / all the students / exercise?

6 In pairs, ask and answer the questions in Exercise 5.
A: *What is the teacher doing?*
B: *He/She is writing on the board.*

Grammar Focus page 112

3.3 Listening

True/False

I can identify specific detail in a radio programme about volunteers abroad.

1 Read *US TODAY* and answer the questions.

1 Which country is the Peace Corps from?
2 What does the Peace Corps do?
3 Where do the volunteers work?

US TODAY

Peace Corps is a US government programme. It sends American volunteers to work abroad. Peace Corps promotes peace and friendship in the world. Volunteers work with local people. They work with children and adults. They teach subjects such as English, Business Skills and Information Technology. They can work in health, education or agriculture.

2 What kind of information is missing in each sentence? Match the sentences (1–6) with the descriptions (a–f).

1 More than _____ Peace Corps volunteers are working around the world today. **c**
2 The first speaker, Amy, is in South _____ .
3 Amy is helping to build a new _____ .
4 Terri and her co-workers are producing fresh _____ for people in hospital.
5 Richard is learning _____ from the children.
6 Peace Corps volunteers meet people who are _____ .

a the name of a continent   d something you can learn
b a kind of food   e an adjective
c a number   f a type of building

3 CD·2.7 MP3·63 Listen and complete the sentences in Exercise 2.

EXAM FOCUS True/False

4 CD·2.7 MP3·63 Listen again. Are the statements true (T) or false (F)?

1 Peace Corps volunteers live and work in fifty-seven countries.
2 Amy likes the place where she's living.
3 Terri doesn't like physical work.
4 Some patients work in the hospital garden.
5 The children learn more than to bake bread.
6 Richard says being a volunteer is easy.

5 Would you like to work as a volunteer abroad? Which statements do you agree with? Discuss as a class.

I would like to do voluntary work abroad because:
• I love travelling.
• I want to learn about the world.
• I would like to teach in Africa.

I wouldn't like to work abroad because:
• I don't like foreign food.
• I'm rubbish at learning languages.
• I'm scared of new places.

PRONUNCIATION FOCUS

6 CD·2.8 MP3·64 Listen and circle the silent letter in each word. Then listen again and repeat.

1 plum(b)er   4 government   6 listen
2 lawyer   5 climber   7 know
3 writer

WORD STORE 3D

7 CD·2.9 MP3·65 Complete WORD STORE 3D with *learn* or *teach*. Then listen, check and repeat.

8 Complete the sentences with the correct form of *learn* or *teach*.

1 My brother <u>teaches</u> Maths in a big secondary school. He is _____ me Maths now because I have a test tomorrow.
2 This year in History, we are _____ about the French Revolution.
3 My grandmother is _____ to use the computer. Today, I'm _____ her to send emails.

3.4 Reading

Information transfer

I can find specific details in texts about dream jobs.

1 Look at the title of the article and the photos. In pairs, answer the questions.
   1 What do you think the people's jobs are?
   2 What do they do in their jobs?
   3 Which job do you think is more exciting? Why?

2 Read the article and check your ideas in Exercise 1.

3 Look at the words in blue in the article. What part of speech are they?

1 demanding	noun	verb	(adjective)
2 employer	noun	verb	adjective
3 factory	noun	verb	adjective
4 customer	noun	verb	adjective
5 earn	noun	verb	adjective
6 company	noun	verb	adjective
7 resort	noun	verb	adjective
8 responsible	noun	verb	adjective
9 salary	noun	verb	adjective

4 Look at the words in blue in text A and choose the correct answer, A, B or C.
   1 If a job is *demanding*,
      A it's difficult and you work hard.
      B it's well-paid.
      C it's easy and you don't work much.
   2 An *employer* is
      A a friend from work.
      B a worker in a shop or business.
      C a person or business people work for.
   3 A *factory* is not
      A an owner of a business.
      B a business that makes things.
      C a building where they produce things.
   4 A *customer* is
      A a shop assistant.
      B a shopper.
      C an owner of a business.
   5 When you *earn* money,
      A you use money to buy things.
      B you put money in a bank.
      C you get money for work.

5 Match the words in blue in text B with the definitions.
   1 a business that makes and/or sells things – _____
   2 money from an employer for work (usually every month) – _____
   3 having a duty or job to do something – _____
   4 popular places for tourists – _____

6 Read the article again and answer the questions. Write *E* for Ella or *T* for Tommy.
   1 Who says he/she doesn't work hard?
   2 Who travels in his/her job?
   3 Who is doing the job for a short time only?
   4 Who says his/her job can have a negative aspect?
   5 Who has a job of testing a product for sale?
   6 Who uses the money to pay for his/her education?
   7 Who needs to fill in questionnaires in his/her job?
   8 Who meets a lot of people in his/her job?

EXAM FOCUS   Information transfer

7 Read text A again and the email below. Then complete Becky's notes.

   From: Sophie
   To: Becky

   Ella's got a fantastic job this summer in The Bed Store. She only works Monday to Wednesday and she sleeps all the time! Do you want to go and watch her sleeping this afternoon?! The shop is in Grove Street. See you there at 2.30?

   place: ¹ _____
   salary: ² _____
   number of days a week: ³ _____
   address: ⁴ _____
   meet Sophie: ⁵ _____

8 Why does each person think he/she has a 'dream job'? Discuss your ideas.

9 In pairs, decide which job, A or B, these sentences are about.

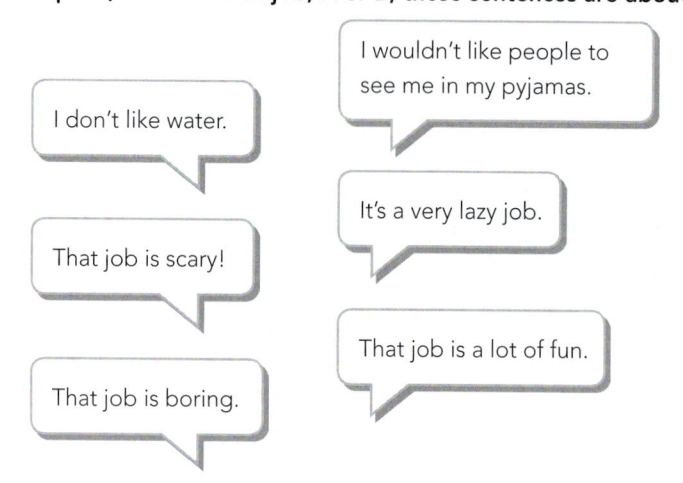

   I don't like water.
   I wouldn't like people to see me in my pyjamas.
   That job is scary!
   It's a very lazy job.
   That job is boring.
   That job is a lot of fun.

10 Tell the class which job you would/wouldn't like to do and why.

   I wouldn't like to be a waterslide tester because I can't swim.

WORD STORE 3E

11 CD•2.11 MP3•67 Complete WORD STORE 3E with a verb from the article. Then listen, check and repeat.

40

You call this WORK?

Do you sometimes dream of a job that is easy and fun? Here are some great jobs.

A DREAM JOB

⁵ **Ella, twenty-one, gets her pay for 'sleeping'.**

I work from nine to five, but my job is not very **demanding**! What do I do? Well, every day, I go to work and I sleep –
¹⁰ I sleep in a huge, comfortable bed. I know it doesn't sound like work, but my **employer** is a **factory** that makes beds. They want to test the beds and advertise the comfortable ones. So, some days, I
¹⁵ sleep in the shop window so **customers** can watch me! I write a blog about the experience. It's only for a month and I need the money for my studies. I **earn** thirty pounds a day.

²⁰ WOOSH!

Tommy, thirty, tests waterslides for a travel company.

I think I've got the best job in the world. No one believes me when
²⁵ I tell them what I do. I fly to holiday **resorts** round the world and test water slides! I write down the answers to questions like: *How high is the slide? How fast do you go? Is it fun?* And I
³⁰ ask people their opinion about the water slides, so I meet lots of people. I'm also **responsible** for testing safety. This year I'm working in Spain, Turkey, Mexico and the USA. I earn
³⁵ a good **salary** and I have lots of fun. It can be a bit unpleasant when it's cold, but apart from that, it's great. I love it!

3.5 Grammar

Present Simple and Present Continuous

I can use the Present Simple and Present Continuous to talk about present actions.

1 Read the text and answer the questions.
1 What is the girl's job?
2 What are the hotel staff doing today?

Every summer I work as a receptionist in the local hotel. I like it. It's usually quiet and I don't have a lot of work. When guests **arrive**, I **give** them their keys. At 11.00, I always **have** coffee and a cake.
But this summer everything's different. Our town **is organising** an arts festival. 100 people are staying at the hotel. Today we're preparing for a big party! At the moment, the waiters **are bringing** more tables and the manager **is telling** me to do three different jobs. I hate it when it is like this! No coffee for me today!

2 Read the GRAMMAR FOCUS. Then complete the examples with the words in blue in the text.

GRAMMAR FOCUS

Present Simple and Present Continuous

You use the **Present Simple** to talk about facts, habits and routines.
When guests ¹<u>arrive</u>, I ²_____ them their keys.
At 11.00, I always ³_____ coffee and a cake.
Time expressions: *always, usually, every day/morning/summer, on Saturdays,* etc.

You use the **Present Continuous**:
- to talk about activities at the moment of speaking.
  The waiters ⁴_____ more tables. The manager ⁵_____ me to do three different jobs.
- to talk about temporary actions.
  Our town ⁶_____ an arts festival. (this summer)
  Time expressions: *at the moment, now, right now, today, this month, this summer,* etc.

REMEMBER THIS
We don't use these verbs in the Present Continuous:
believe, hate, know, like, love, mean, need, prefer, understand, want.

3 Complete the sentences with the Present Simple or Present Continuous form of the verbs in brackets.
1 I __work__ (work) as a mechanic for SuperCars.
2 Jane _____ (work) as a waitress in a café this summer.
3 Please don't talk to me now. I _____ (finish) an email.
4 I _____ (finish) work at five.
5 We _____ (go) to the cinema on Saturdays, but today we _____ (go) to the theatre.

4 Complete Emily's email with the Present Simple or Present Continuous form of the verbs in brackets.

Hi Freddie,

Guess where I am. At the moment, I ¹<u>'m looking</u> (look) at the Atlantic!

I've got a holiday job as an au pair with a Spanish family. They're on holiday in Vigo just now and I ²_____ (look) after the children.

I usually ³_____ (play) with the kids, but at the moment they ⁴_____ (sleep). It's their siesta. I usually ⁵_____ (relax) too, but today I ⁶_____ (write) to you.

My 'working' day ⁷_____ (start) early; I ⁸_____ (take) the children for a swim. They ⁹_____ (love) the water! After dinner, I ¹⁰_____ (read) stories to them. It's so quiet now. The sun ¹¹_____ (shine) and life ¹²_____ (be) perfect! I ¹³_____ (believe) I've got the best job in the world!

What about you? How's your holiday job going?

Love,
Emily

5 Write true sentences. Use the Present Simple or Present Continuous.
1 I / do / a lot of sports
  I do/don't do a lot of sports.
2 I / learn / to play a musical instrument / at the moment
3 my best friend / live / near me
4 my parents / work / in a big company
5 we / go / on holiday abroad / every year
6 my English teacher / talk / at the moment

6 Write questions for the sentences in Exercise 5. Then ask and answer in pairs.
A: *Do you do a lot of sports?*
B: *Yes, I do./No, I don't.*

Grammar Focus page 113

3.6 Speaking

Describing a photo

I can describe the people in a photo and say what they are doing.

1 Look at Photo A and answer the questions. Then compare your answers in pairs.

  1 Who is in the photo?
  2 Where are they?
  3 What are they doing?

2 **CD·2.12 MP3·68** Listen to a student describing Photo A. Compare his answers with yours.

3 **CD·2.12 MP3·68** Listen again and tick the questions the student answers.

  1 What are the people wearing? ☐
  2 How old are they? ✓
  3 Are they working alone or in a team? ☐
  4 Is the work hard? ☐
  5 How are they feeling? ☐
  6 What are they thinking? ☐
  7 Do you think they like their job? ☐

4 **CD·2.12 MP3·68** Read the SPEAKING FOCUS. Then listen again and underline the phrases you hear.

SPEAKING FOCUS

Who? Where? What are they doing?
The photo shows (a person/people) in a (place).
In the photo there is/there are (a person/people) in a (place).
He/She is …/They are … + -ing

Details of the picture
On the left/right …
In the background …
We can also see …
He's/She's wearing …

What you think
Perhaps/Maybe …
I think he/she is …/they are …

REMEMBER THIS

You use the **Present Continuous** to say what people are doing in a photo.

5 Work in pairs. Student A, describe Photo B. Student B, describe Photo C. Follow the instructions below and use the phrases in the SPEAKING FOCUS.

  1 Say who is in the photo and where they are.
  2 Say what the people are doing.
  3 Try to say more. Use some of the questions in Exercise 3 to help you.

6 Would you like to do the job in your photo? Why?/Why not?

3.7 Writing

An email of request
I can write an email to ask someone to do something.

1 CD·2.13 MP3·69 Listen to the conversation between Rose and her boss, Jeremy. What does Jeremy want Rose to do? Complete the notes.

> - phone a ¹<u>restaurant</u>
> - order ² _____ for ³ _____ people (for the meeting)
> - remember to order something for ⁴ _____
> - need lunch by ⁵ _____
> - prepare bags of ⁶ _____ for customers

2 What is Rose's problem and how do you think she decides to solve it?

3 Read the first email. What is wrong with it?

1. There is not enough information. ✓
2. There is too much information. ☐
3. The message is not clear. ☐
4. The request is not polite. ☐
5. The message is too long. ☐

To: Greg Sutter
From: Rose Orton
Subject: Tomorrow's meeting

Greg,
Phone a restaurant and order lunch for the people at the meeting. Order something for vegetarians too. Prepare bags of presents for everyone. Use the pens in my desk.
Rose

---

4 Read the second email. Why is it better?

To: Greg Sutter
From: Rose Orton
Subject: Tomorrow's meeting

Greg,
[A]I've got a problem and I need your help with tomorrow's meeting. I've got an exam in half an hour and I haven't got the time to do this.
[B]Please could you phone a good restaurant and order lunch for twelve people for tomorrow's meeting at 12.30? Could you order some vegetarian dishes, too? Also, we need to prepare bags of presents for the customers. There are twenty expensive pens in a box in my desk and you could use those. The receptionist has got company bags to put them in.
[C]Sorry to bother you, but I just don't have the time.
Thanks a lot,
Rose

---

5 Read the second email again and match the parts (A–C) with the descriptions (1–3).

1. Rose asks Greg to do some things. ☐
2. Rose introduces her problem. A
3. Rose thanks Greg and says she's sorry for the trouble. ☐

6 Complete the WRITING FOCUS with words and phrases from the second email.

WRITING FOCUS
An email of request

- **Introduction**
  I've got a ¹<u>problem</u>.
  I need your/some ² _____ .
  Could you help me?
  Could you do me a favour?

- **Requests**
  Please ³ _____ you …?
  Could you please …?
  Do you think you could …?
  Could you also …?

- **Conclusion**
  (So) Sorry to ⁴ _____ you.
  Thanks ⁵ _____ ./Thank you very much.

7 Number the sentences in the correct order to make another email from Rose.

Jack,
a Could you please finish the report for me?
b Thank you very much.
c So sorry to bother you.
d Can you do me a favour?
e Could you also check some of the information about the sales?
f I'm writing a report and I have to go to a meeting now.
Rose

8 Put the words in the correct order to make sentences.
1 need / problem / help / got / I / a / some / I've / and
2 me / you / favour / do / could / a?
3 you / please / could / me / help?
4 think / do / please / could / you / me / you / help?
5 you / much / very / thank
6 to / you / bother / sorry

9 Rewrite the sentences as polite requests. Use the words in brackets.
1 Take this letter to the post office. (could/please)
   Could you please take this letter to the post office?
2 Phone the plumber. (think/could)
3 Give these papers to Mr Flynn. (could/please)
4 Ask him to sign them. (also/please)

10 Write requests for these things. Try to use a different way to make a request for each one.

You'd like Dave to:
1 help you with a report.
2 email you a file.
3 get you a sandwich from the café.
4 get you a coffee.

11 Read the information and write an email of about 100 words to a colleague. Ask him/her to do the things you cannot do.

You work in a small music shop. You don't feel well and you're going home.

Things you haven't got time to do:
- Send the three CDs on the desk to Mr L. Henderson (the address is on a piece of paper with the CDs).
- Email Mrs Young and tell her we've got the old Beatles LP for her.
- Phone the computer man. The system isn't working well.

12 Check.
✓ Have you included all the points in the question?
✓ Have you used language from the WRITING FOCUS?
✓ Have you introduced your requests correctly?
✓ Have you included an appropriate conclusion?
✓ Have you organised your email well?

FOCUS REVIEW 3

VOCABULARY AND GRAMMAR

1 Read the descriptions and complete the jobs.
   1 This person helps people who aren't well. n_ _ _ _
   2 You tell this person what you want to eat in a restaurant. w_ _ _ _ _
   3 This person repairs cars. m_ _ _ _ _ _ _
   4 You ask this person for help in a shop. s_ _ _ a_ _ _ _ _ _ _ _
   5 This person works in an office and has lots of clients. l_ _ _ _ _
   6 This person gives you your keys in a hotel. r_ _ _ _ _ _ _ _ _ _

2 Complete the second sentence so that it has the opposite meaning to the first sentence.
   1 He's got a well-paid job.
     His job is _____ paid.
   2 She works part-time.
     She's got a _____ job.
   3 Their working day is quite short.
     They work long _____ .
   4 She's got a demanding job.
     Her job is _____ .
   5 He works in an office.
     He works from _____ .

3 Complete the text with the Present Continuous form of the verbs in the box.

   [have   not work   order   phone
     prepare   serve   talk]

   Dan's café is very busy today. A big group of people
   ¹_____ a party. One of them ²_____ food for the
   whole group. The waiters ³_____ drinks. The chef
   ⁴_____ desserts. Dan, the manager, ⁵_____ on
   the phone. He ⁶_____ a plumber because the toilet
   ⁷_____ .

4 Complete the sentences with the Present Simple or Present Continuous form of the verbs in brackets.
   1 Matt's got a good job. He _____ (earn) a lot of money.
   2 Alex and Rachel are engineers. They _____ (work) for an electronics company. They _____ (work) on a new smartphone at the moment.
   3 I _____ (travel) a lot in my job. This week I _____ (travel) to South Africa.
   4 Lucy _____ (love) her job. She _____ (believe) it's perfect.
   5 I _____ (send) about a hundred emails every day. This is the last one I _____ (send) today.
   6 Sarah _____ (hate) her job and she _____ (want) to find a different one.

LANGUAGE IN USE

5 Read the text and choose the correct answer, A, B or C.

   My cousin Helena has a good job. She ¹__ in a computer shop. She knows a ²__ about computers and she ³__ help customers to choose the right one. Her boss likes her very much. He says that she works well ⁴__ a team and she's good at selling. She ⁵__ a lot of computers every week! At the moment her young sister, Magda, ⁶___ in the same shop. But it's only a summer job for her. Magda ⁷___ work long hours. She starts at 9.30 and finishes at 12.30. Today Helena is teaching Magda about ⁸___ new computers they have in the shop.

   1 A does work   B works   C is working
   2 A much   B lot   C many
   3 A is   B does   C can
   4 A on   B at   C in
   5 A is selling B sell   C sells
   6 A works   B working   C is working
   7 A doesn't   B isn't   C don't
   8 A some   B any   C many

6 Choose the correct answer, A, B or C, to complete both sentences.
   1 We all ____ long hours at the end of the month.
     Journalists often ____ from home.
     A write   B do   C work
   2 An au pair looks ____ children.
     Karen was late today; she came to the office ____ the first meeting.
     A at   B after   C in
   3 Paul's got a part-time ____ .
     I'm looking for a holiday ____ .
     A work   B salary C job
   4 Would you like to work ____ an international company?
     I'm responsible ____ answering the phone.
     A in   B for   C to
   5 A photographer is coming today to ____ photos of all the staff.
     As an au pair, I ____ children to their after-school activities.
     A take   B make   C go

LISTENING

7 **CD·2.14 MP3·70** Listen to two friends talking about Charlie's new job. Are the statements true (T) or false (F)?
   1 Charlie works for a newspaper. ☐
   2 The job is interesting. ☐
   3 Charlie works part-time. ☐
   4 His job is well-paid. ☐
   5 Charlie likes his co-workers. ☐

46

READING

8 Read the advertisement and the email below. Then complete Dave's notes.

Summer jobs

Are you looking for a summer job? Here are some ideas.

If you like being outside and can do physical work, there are always jobs in agriculture in the summer. The work is hard but healthy. You can pick strawberries in July and apples in August – yummy! We work with many farms in the south of England. We have our own buses too. Contact John Jones at teenjobs.com or on 07023354129.

From: Gary
To: Dave

How's this for a summer job for you and me? I'm in the USA in July, but can do the next month. Sounds fun! Can you phone and ask about pay?

Summer job

job in: *agriculture*

month: 1 _____

fruit: 2 _____

transport: 3 _____

speak to: 4 _____

ask about: 5 _____

SPEAKING

9 Describe the photo. Use the words in the box and the prompts.

> buy   clothes shop   customer   help   pay for
> shop assistant   smile

The photo shows …
They are in …
The man/woman is …

WRITING

10 Read the information and write an email of about 100 words to a colleague. Ask him/her to do the things you cannot do.

> You are working in an office during your summer break. You have to go to the dentist this afternoon. Things you'd like your colleague to do while you are away:
> - Photocopy a report to give to a customer.
> - Phone a customer to arrange an appointment for tomorrow morning.
> - Google a good local restaurant and book a table for the boss tomorrow.

47

# 4 PEOPLE

If you want a friend, be a friend.

A PROVERB

UNIT LANGUAGE AND SKILLS

Vocabulary:
- Show what you know – describing a face
- appearance
- adjective order
- personality adjectives

Grammar:
- comparative and superlative adjectives
- *have to/don't have to*

Listening:
- people talking about important events in their lives
- multiple choice

Reading:
- a magazine article about clothes and personality
- gapped text

Speaking:
- shopping for clothes

Writing:
- a personal blog

FOCUS EXTRA

- Grammar Focus pages 114–115
- WORD STORE booklet pages 8–9
- Workbook pages 44–55 or MyEnglishLab

48

4.1 Vocabulary

Appearance • Personality • Adjective order

I can describe what people look like and say what they are like.

SHOW WHAT YOU KNOW

1 Label the photo with the words in the box.

| ear | eye | eyebrow | eyelashes | forehead | hair |
| head | lip | mouth | neck | nose | |

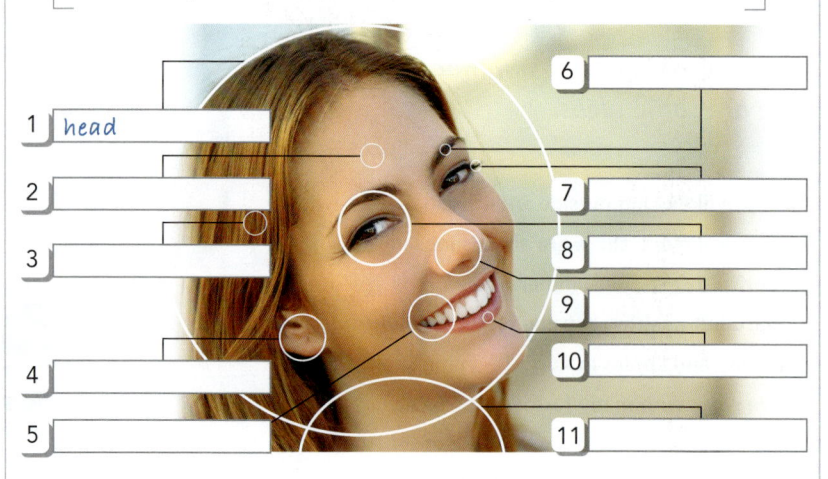

1 head
2 ___
3 ___
4 ___
5 ___
6 ___
7 ___
8 ___
9 ___
10 ___
11 ___

2 Write sentences to describe your face.

I've got red hair and big green eyes. My ears are small.

Twins

We usually think that twins are similar, but they can be very different! Read about James and Daniel.

James   Dan

3 Read about James and Daniel and complete the table.

	James	Daniel
Hair	short curly black	
Eyes		
Height	tall	
Build and looks	well-built	

4 In pairs, answer the questions.
 1 Do you know any twins? Are they similar of different?
 2 Who are you like: Daniel or James? Explain why.

James

What does he look like?
5 He's got short curly black hair and brown eyes.

What is he like?
He's very **sociable** and he's got lots of friends. He's **clever** too. He's studying for A levels* at school and he wants to go to university. He's
10 **confident** and **funny** – he's got a great sense of humour and he often tells jokes. He's a very **positive** person.

Daniel

What does he look like?
He's got short curly blond hair and brown eyes.
15 **What is he like?**
He's **shy**, so he doesn't like big groups of people, but he's got some good friends. He's **serious** and thinks a lot about things. He's **kind** too and always helps his friends. He isn't
20 at school any more – he's got a job and he's learning to be an engineer.

So have the twins got anything in common?
Yes! They're both tall, good-looking and well-built. They're also young, fit and sporty and
25 they've both got good friends. They're both **interesting** people.

*A levels – exams that students take when they are eighteen in England, Wales and northern Ireland

---

Go to WORD STORE 4 page 9.

WORD STORE 4A

5 CD·2.15 MP3·71 Complete WORD STORE 4A with the underlined adjectives in the text. Then listen, check and repeat.

WORD STORE 4B

6 CD·2.16 MP3·72 Analyse the order of adjectives in WORD STORE 4B. Then listen and complete sentences 1–4.
 1 Sally's tall and she's got _____ black hair.
 2 Jack is young and _____ . He's got medium-length _____ _____ hair.
 3 Jess is _____ and fit and she's got _____ eyes.
 4 Tom is _____ and _____ . He's got _____ eyes.

7 Put the adjectives in brackets in the correct order.
 1 She's got long straight black (black, long, straight) hair and _____ (brown, small) eyes.
 2 He's got _____ (very big, green) eyes and _____ (wavy, brown, medium-length) hair.
 3 He's got _____ (short, red, wavy) hair and _____ (blue, beautiful, big) eyes.
 4 She's got _____ (fair, medium-length) hair and _____ (small, blue) eyes.
 5 He's bald and he's got _____ (big, black) eyes.
 6 She's got _____ (grey, curly, short) hair and _____ (brown, big) eyes.

8 Write about a classmate. Use WORD STORE 4A and 4B. Read your description to the class. Can they guess who you described?

He's tall, slim, fit and well-built. He's got short curly black hair and beautiful big brown eyes.

WORD STORE 4C

9 CD·2.17 MP3·73 Complete WORD STORE 4C with the adjectives in red in the text. Then listen, check and repeat.

10 Complete the sentences with adjectives from WORD STORE 4C.
 1 My mother never thinks bad things can happen, she's very positive .
 2 I always believe in myself. I'm really _____ .
 3 My father never smiles. He always looks _____ .
 4 My best friend loves people. He/She is very _____ .
 5 My best friend is doing well at school because he/she is _____ .
 6 My brother loves telling jokes. He's _____ !
 7 I don't like going to parties. I'm a little _____ .

11 Which sentences in Exercise 10 are true for you? Tell your partner.

4.2 Grammar

Comparative and superlative adjectives
I can use adjectives to make comparisons.

1 In pairs, choose one of the people from the photos below and answer the questions.
   1 What does he/she look like?
   2 What do you think he/she is like?

2 Read the text. What is important to Natalie, Martin and Danny? Who do you agree with most?

WHAT'S THE MOST IMPORTANT THING?

Natalie, 16
Money is not the most important thing! I like nice clothes and I love my new mobile phone, but they're just things. Money is less important than your family or friends. I think people are happier when they spend time with their friends and family.

Martin, 18
Sports! I love playing and watching sports. I also like hanging out with my friends. For me, my friends are more important than my family. Health is important too. I hate being sick! It's worse than exams!

Danny, 21
A good job is the best thing. Then you can buy everything you need. I don't think the poorest people in the world are happy. Their lives are harder than ours.

3 Read the GRAMMAR FOCUS. Then look at the words in blue in the text and complete the examples.

GRAMMAR FOCUS
Comparative and superlative adjectives

	Adjective	Comparative	Superlative
Short	hard	¹hard**er**	the hard**est**
	nice	nic**er**	the nic**est**
	big	big**ger**	the big**gest**
	happy	²happ___	the happ**iest**
Long	important	³_____ important	the ⁴_____ important
Irregular	good	better	the ⁵_____
	bad	⁶_____	the worst
	far	further	the furthest

My friends are more important ⁷_____ my family.

4 Complete the sentences with the comparative form of the adjectives in brackets.
   1 My best friend is **kinder** (kind) than me.
   2 I'm _____ (thin) than my father.
   3 I'm _____ (intelligent) than my brother/sister.
   4 I'm _____ (funny) than all my other friends.
   5 My mother is _____ (slim) than her sister.
   6 My sister is _____ (good) at Maths than me.
   7 My best friend is _____ (pretty) than me.

5 Guess which sentences in Exercise 4 are true for your partner. Then ask and answer in pairs.
   A: *Is your best friend kinder than you?*
   B: *Yes, he/she is/No, he/she isn't.*

6 Complete the quiz with the superlative form of the adjectives in brackets. Then, in pairs, guess the correct answers.

Record breakers!*

1 How tall is the **tallest** (tall) person in the world?
   A 2 m 72 cm   B 2 m 60.3 cm   C 2 m 51.4 cm

2 What nationality is Skye Broberg, the ____ (flexible) person in the world?
   A American   B Australian   C English

3 Chanel Tapper has got the ____ (long) tongue in the world. How long is it?
   A 6.75 cm   B 8.75 cm   C 9.75 cm

4 What is the ____ (difficult) language to learn?
   A Arabic   B Japanese   C Chinese

5 How old is the ____ (old) university student in Britain?
   A 70   B 83   C 91

6 Who are the ____ (famous) people in the world?
   A film stars   B pop stars   C sports stars

* in 2013

7 CD•2.18 MP3•74 Listen and check your answers to Exercise 6.

8 Complete the sentences with the correct form of the adjectives in brackets. Then finish the sentences to make them true for you.
   1 The **most expensive** (expensive) thing I have is …
   2 The _____ (fit) person I know is …
   3 The _____ (old) person I know is …
   4 I'm _____ (serious) than my …
   5 I think … is a _____ (good) actor than ….
   6 I think … is the _____ (good) sportsperson in the world.

9 Write questions for the sentences in Exercise 8. Then, in pairs, ask and answer.
   What is the most expensive thing you have?

Grammar Focus page 113

4.3 Listening

Multiple choice

I can identify specific detail in short monologues about important events in life.

1 **In pairs, label the four life events in the photos with phrases from the box.**

1 fall in love
2
3
4

buy your first flat	~~fall in love~~	get married
get your first job	go on your first date	
learn to drive	leave home	

2 **When do the life events from Exercise 1 happen in your country? Discuss in pairs.**

People usually leave home when they are twenty.
You can learn to drive when you are …

3 CD·2.19 MP3·75 **Listen to four people and tick the life events they talk about.**

	Sara	Mike	Grace	Simon
1 buy your first flat				
2 fall in love				
3 get married				
4 get your first job				
5 go on your first date				
6 learn to drive				
7 leave home	✓			

4 CD·2.19 MP3·75 **Listen again and match the speakers (1–4) with the sentences (a–f). There are two extra sentences.**

1 Sara ☐   3 Grace ☐
2 Mike ☐   4 Simon ☐

a thinks learning to drive helps you get a better job.
b wants to get married now.
c says getting your first job is less important than leaving home.
d would like to leave home next year.
e wants to use the money from his/her job to learn to drive.
f is in love, but doesn't want to get married yet.

EXAM FOCUS Multiple choice

5 CD·2.19 MP3·75 **Listen again and choose the correct answer, A, B or C.**

1 Sara thinks the best age to leave home is
   A sixteen.   **B eighteen.**   C twenty.
2 Mike wants to learn to drive because
   A his parents never collect him from friends' houses.
   B he needs to drive for his job.
   C then he can come home later.
3 Grace says it's better to get married when you are about
   A thirty.   B thirteen.   C eighteen.
4 Simon has got
   A his own car.
   B a job in a shop.
   C a lot of money.

6 **What is the most important life event for you? Discuss in pairs.**

PRONUNCIATION FOCUS

7 CD·2.20 MP3·76 **Listen and repeat the numbers.**

1 sixteen – **sixty**
2 seventeen – seventy
3 eighteen – eighty
4 thirteen – thirty
5 fourteen – forty
6 thirteen – fourteen – fifteen
7 thirty – forty – fifty

8 CD·2.21 MP3·77 **Listen and circle the numbers you hear in Exercise 7.**

WORD STORE 4D

9 CD·2.22 MP3·78 **Complete WORD STORE 4D with the verbs in the box. Then listen, check and repeat.**

buy   fall   get   go   learn   ~~leave~~

51

4.4 Reading

Gapped text
I can understand the structure of a text.

WORD STORE 4E

1 **CD·2.23 MP3·79** Complete WORD STORE 4E with the words in the box. Then listen, check and repeat.

> boots   a coat   a dress   a hat   a jacket
> jeans   jumper   a scarf   a shirt   ~~shoes~~   a skirt
> socks   a suit   a tie   a top   a tracksuit
> trainers   trousers   a T-shirt

2 In pairs, ask and answer questions about your favourite clothes.

What clothes do you:
- most often/sometimes/never wear?
- wear when you go out with friends?
- wear when you go to school?

3 Look at the photos on page 53 and describe what the celebrities are wearing.

Who do you think is:
1 a casual dresser?
2 an original dresser?
3 a smart dresser?

4 Read the article and check your answers to Exercise 3.

5 Read the article again and answer the questions.
1 What clothes do casual dressers wear? *comfortable*
2 What kind of people usually wear casual clothes?
3 What kind of clothes do original dressers wear?
4 Why do you think Lady Gaga wears crazy clothes?
5 What kind of clothes do smart dressers wear?
6 What kind of clothes does People Tree make?

6 Read the sentences. What do the <u>underlined</u> pronouns refer to?
1 John is my friend. <u>He</u> lives in Chicago. <u>His</u> house is big.
   He = John   His = John's
2 Tom and Marie work in a hospital. <u>Their</u> jobs are interesting. <u>They</u> are doctors.
3 Kate is a teacher. <u>She</u> enjoys sport. <u>Her</u> favourite sport is basketball.
4 The fashion is new. <u>It's</u> really popular at the moment. <u>Its</u> fans are usually teens.

7 <u>Underline</u> all the pronouns in sentences a–e. Then complete gaps 1–3 in the article with the sentences. There are two extra sentences.
a She always wears great outfits and her clothes look fantastic.
b It's one of the most interesting fashions at the moment.
c He often wears an open shirt on top of his T-shirt.
d He is making a new film in Australia at the moment.
e They are sociable and fun.

8 Match the pictures with the <u>underlined</u> adjectives in the article.

1  _____   2 _____

3  _____   4 _____

5  _____   6 _____

9 Complete the second sentence with the adjectives in Exercise 8 and the adjectives in blue in the article.
1 She always has lots of good ideas.
   She's very <u>creative</u>.
2 He gives thousands of euros to charity.
   He's very _____ .
3 They're always calm and never worried.
   They're _____ .
4 She works for a big company now but she wants to start her own business.
   She's very _____ .
5 My brother never puts his clothes and things in his cupboards – his bedroom is very _____ .
6 Sarah can play the guitar, the piano and the violin and she can sing – she's very _____ .
7 I help my parents in their shop on Saturdays because they are always very _____ at weekends.
8 Her clothes are very unusual and crazy.
   She looks _____ .

10 Discuss the questions in pairs.
1 Which of the celebrities in the article has the best style? Why?
2 Clothes say a lot about a person's personality. Do you agree?

WHAT DO YOUR CLOTHES SAY ABOUT YOU?

Do you ever look at someone and think, 'I bet he's a fun person,' or 'She's a creative person'? Well, you could be right! It seems our clothes say a lot about our personality.

Casual dressers love comfortable clothes. They live in jeans and a T-shirt and they often wear tracksuits and trainers because they are sporty and energetic; they often go jogging or spend time in the gym. Casual dressers are usually relaxed, positive people and it's easy to spend time with them. They are often kind and generous with their time and money. Robert Pattinson is a typical casual dresser. [1]____ He says James Dean (an actor and teen style icon from the 1950s) inspires his look.

Lady Gaga

Original dressers like clothes that make people look at them, like a crazy hat, a fun skirt or a mad jacket! They love having people around them. [2]____ They love to be the centre of attention. They are usually talented and creative people. Lady Gaga is one of the most original dressers in the world. She uses wigs, make-up and all kinds of materials such as feathers, beads, shells and even pieces of meat to make her clothes. Her costumes are usually outrageous!

Smart dressers like formal clothes such as suits. Smart clothes are well-designed and fit well; the material is good quality and never looks untidy. Smart dressers are usually clever, confident and busy people. They can be very ambitious – they want to be successful.
Emma Watson is a smart and stylish dresser. [3]____ She also designs and models clothes for the fair trade eco-fashion label, People Tree. People Tree supports poorer farmers in Africa and India by buying organic materials from them to make their clothes.

Robert Pattinson

Emma Watson

53

4.5 Grammar

have to/don't have to

I can talk about obligation with have to and don't have to.

1 In your country, can you do these things when you are sixteen?

[get married   leave school   learn to drive]

2 Read UK TODAY. At what age can you do the things in Exercise 1 in the UK?

UK TODAY

Young people have to be in education until they are eighteen years old. They have to stay at school until they are sixteen years old, but after sixteen, they don't have to stay at school; they can train for a job as an apprentice.

A young person can get married when he or she is sixteen, but he or she has to get permission from his or her parents.

You can learn to drive a car when you are seventeen. You don't have to have lessons at a driving school; your parents can teach you! You don't have to be seventeen if you want to ride a moped – you can start learning when you are sixteen years old.

3 Read the GRAMMAR FOCUS. Then find examples of *have to/has to* and *don't have to/doesn't have to* in UK TODAY.

GRAMMAR FOCUS

have to/don't have to

You use **have to/has to** to talk about:

- laws and obligation.
  You **don't have to** be seventeen to drive a moped.
  She **has to** stay at school until she's sixteen.
- necessity.
  He **doesn't have to** do homework today – it's for next week.

+	I/You/We/They **have to** go to school. He/She **has to** go to school.
−	I/You/We/They **don't have to** go to school. He/She **doesn't have to** go to school.
?	**Do** I/you/we/they **have to** go to school? Yes, I/you/we/they **do**. / No, I/you/we/they **don't**. **Does** he/she **have to** go to school? Yes, he/she **does**. / No, he/she **doesn't**. **What do** you **have to** do? **Where does** she **have to** go?

4 Complete the text with the correct form of *have to*.

Did you know?

Read our FAQs about eighteen-year-olds to find out more!

- An eighteen-year-old ¹<u>doesn't have to</u> ask his/her parents for permission to buy a house. It's not the law.

- An eighteen-year-old can ride a motorbike above 125cc* with an L-plate, but he/she ²_____ get a licence within two years.

- Can you vote in an election? Yes, but you ³_____ vote. You decide.

- Can you drive a bus? No, you ⁴_____ be twenty-one years old to do that.

- ⁵_____ (you) get your parents' permission to have a tattoo? No, you ⁶_____ .

- Can you buy an alcoholic drink in a pub when you are eighteen? Yes, but you ⁷_____ show your identity card if the owner asks.

*cc = cubic centimetres (engine size)

5 Which of these things do your parents say you have to or don't have to do?

- make your bed
- do the washing-up
- be home by 11 p.m. at the weekend
- tell your parents who you are going out with
- go to bed by 10 p.m. during the week
- babysit your younger brother or sister

I have to …/I don't have to …

6 In pairs, ask and answer questions about the activities in Exercise 5.

A: *Do you have to make your bed?*
B: *Yes, I do./No, I don't.*

7 Tell the class about your partner.

Olga has to make her bed, but she doesn't have to …

Grammar Focus page 114

54

4.6 Speaking

Shopping for clothes
I can go shopping for clothes.

1 Read the statements. Which ones are true for you?

- Shopping for clothes is really boring!
- I love wearing all the latest fashions.
- My mum buys all my clothes.
- I hate trying on clothes in the shop; I buy all my clothes online!
- I usually go shopping for clothes with a friend.

2 **CD·2.25 MP3·81** Read and listen to two conversations. Then answer the questions.
1 What do Simon and Rosie want to buy?
2 Who is successful?

Conversation 1
Assistant: Can I help you?
Simon: I'm looking for a new pair of jeans.
Assistant: Do you want slim fit or loose fit?
Simon: Loose fit, please.
Assistant: How about this pair? They're the fashion this year.
Simon: Yes, they're great. They're exactly what I'm looking for.
Assistant: What size are you?
Simon: I'm a 30.
Assistant: Here you are. Would you like to try them on? The changing rooms are over there.
Simon: Thanks. … Yes, these are perfect. How much are they?

Conversation 2
Rosie: Excuse me, could you help me, please?
Assistant: Yes, sure.
Rosie: Have you got this T-shirt in small or medium?
Assistant: What colour are you looking for?
Rosie: Black.
Assistant: We've only got black in large or extra large. How about red?
Rosie: No, thanks! It's not really what I want. I don't like red.

3 Read Conversation 1 and put the shop assistant's phrases in the SPEAKING FOCUS in order.

4 Read the conversations and complete the customer's phrases in the SPEAKING FOCUS.

SPEAKING FOCUS
Shop assistant
- [1] Can I help you?
- [ ] The changing rooms are over there.
- [ ] What size are you?
- [ ] How about (this pair/these)?/What about this one?
- [ ] Do you want slim fit or loose fit jeans?
- [ ] Would you like to try it/them on?
- [ ] They're the fashion this year.

Customer
Excuse ¹ *me* , could you help me, ² _____ ?
I'm looking for a new pair of ³ _____ .
They're exactly what I'm ⁴ _____ for/want/need.
I'm a (size) 30.
⁵ _____ you got this T-shirt in small/medium/large?
Have you got these in black/a different colour?
It's/They're great/fantastic/perfect.
It's ⁶ _____ really what I want.
Where are the changing rooms?

5 Match the questions with the answers.
1 Can I try this on? — d
2 Have you got this in medium?
3 What size are you?
4 Excuse me, can you help me?
5 Are you looking for a specific colour?
6 How about these trainers?

a I'm a 10 or 12.
b I'm not sure … green or blue.
c Yes, of course.
d Yes, the changing rooms are over there.
e No, they're not really what I want.
f No, sorry. We've only got it in large.

6 In pairs, choose one of the situations below. Use the SPEAKING FOCUS to role play a conversation about shopping. Take turns to be the shop assistant and customer.
1 You want to buy some blue trainers in size 39.
2 You are looking for black or brown trousers. You see trousers you like, but they are green.
3 You want a white T-shirt in medium or large.

4.7 Writing

A personal profile

I can write a personal profile on a blog.

1 Match the information people sometimes give about themselves in a personal profile (1–5) with the extracts from an email (a–e).

1 information about your family
2 a physical description
3 information about your favourite band
4 a description of your personality
5 a list of your ambitions

a They play rock and I'd love to see them in concert.
b One day I'd like to be a teacher.
c I've got five cousins, but I don't often see them.
d I'm quite a creative person.
e I'm not very tall and I've got medium length hair.

2 Read Emily's profile. Match three of the points (1–5) in Exercise 1 with the paragraphs (A–C).

Hi! I'm Emily.

[A] I'm sixteen years old. I'm quite tall – I'm 1.65 m and I'm slim. I've got long wavy brown hair and blue eyes.

[B] I'm a positive person and I'm very sociable – I've got lots of friends. I like going out with my friends and having fun. I really enjoy sports (especially tennis). But I'm not very fit. I also spend quite a lot of time shopping for clothes! And of course, I love fashion (that's why I'm writing this blog!). My friends say I'm kind and I've got a good sense of humour. I like laughing a lot. 🙂

[C] I've got a brother and a sister. My brother is fourteen, but he's taller than me. He's got short dark hair and blue eyes. He's really funny! My sister is ten. She's quite tall, but she isn't taller than me. She's very clever. She's got long straight blond hair and green eyes.

So now you know all about me!

3 Read Emily's profile again and complete the table.

	Emily
Age	
Height	1.65 m
Build	slim
Hair and eyes	
Personality	
Interests	
Family	

4 Complete the WRITING FOCUS with examples from Emily's profile.

WRITING FOCUS
A personal profile

- Start your profile with a physical description:
  1 *I'm quite tall.*
- Write about your personality:
  2 _____
- Write about your family and friends:
  3 _____
- Use adverbs (*really, quite, very, not very, not really,* etc.) to make your writing more interesting:
  - with adjectives:
    4 _____
  - with *like/enjoy*:
    5 _____

Notice the position of adverbs with adjectives and with verbs: *very clever, really enjoy.*

- Don't use *not* with *quite* + personality adjective.

5 Rewrite the sentences with the adverbs in brackets in the correct place.

1 He's got short red hair. (very)
   He's got very short red hair.
2 I'm serious. (not very)
3 I like computer games. (quite)
4 I enjoy watching films. (not really)
5 I've got long blond hair. (really)
6 My best friend is fit. (very)

6 Rewrite the sentences with the adjectives and adverbs in brackets in the correct place.

1 I've got black hair (wavy, short).
   I've got short wavy black hair.
2 I've got wavy hair (beautiful, blond).
3 He's got eyes (blue, big).
4 I'm tall (not very), but I'm well-built (quite).
5 She's got brown hair (curly, long) and a smile (big, lovely).

56

7 Look at the photos of Rob, Emily's boyfriend, and complete his personal profile.

Hi! I'm Rob.

I'm seventeen years old.

I've got ¹_____ _____ hair and I'm slim. I usually wear a T-shirt and blue ²_____ .

I love spending time hanging out with ³_____ or ⁴_____ films!

I'm learning ⁵_____ _____ and soon I hope to pass my test. I'm writing this blog about it!

So that's me!

8 Choose the correct options to complete Emily's comment on Rob's blog.

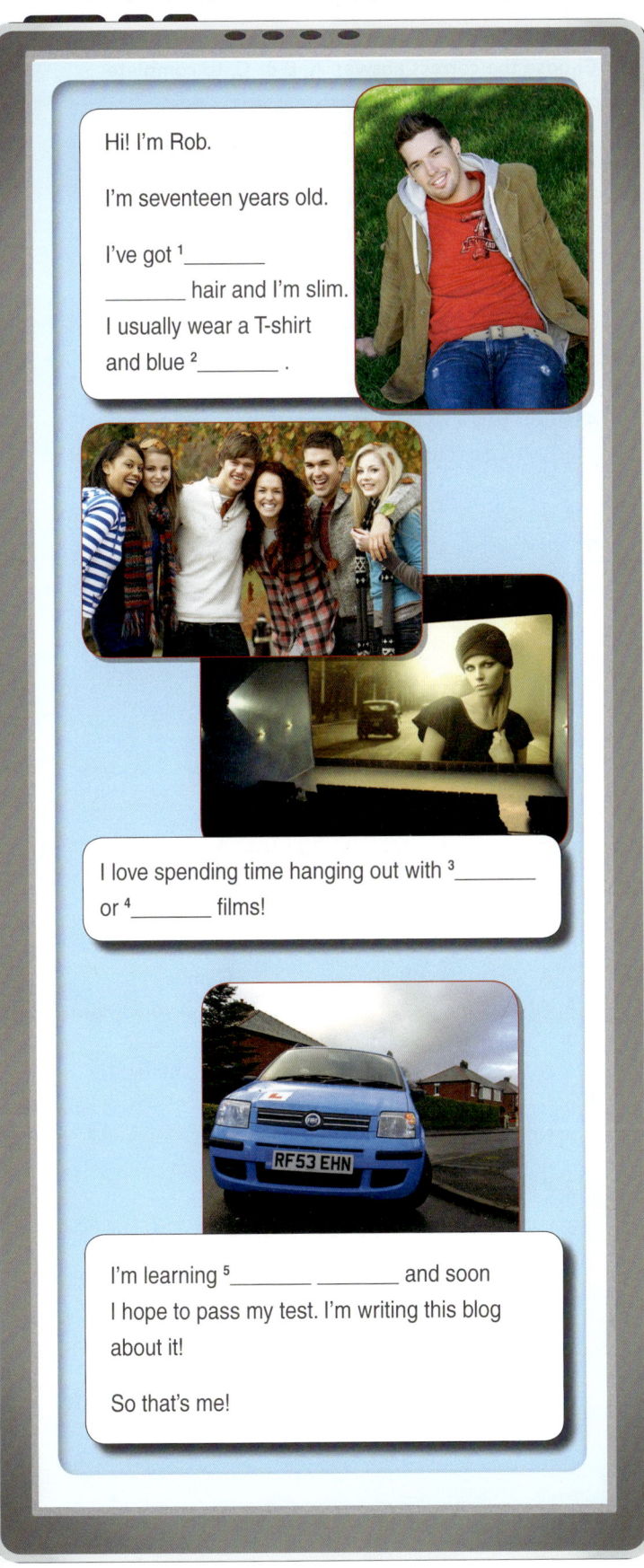

Emily 5.53 p.m.

Look at those clothes! You are SO ¹*unfashionable / unkind*, Rob!

You should try not to be so ²*serious / confident*. You're always studying. And you never come to parties with me – you're really ³*unsociable / generous*! But I love you!

9 In pairs, complete the sentences to make them true for you and your partner.
1 I've got long dark hair, but … has got …
2 … is … than me.
3 … and I both like …
4 I enjoy … , but … likes …

10 Complete the table for you and your best friend.

	You	Your best friend
Age		
Height		
Build		
Hair and eyes		
Personality		
Interests		
Family		

11 Read the writing task and write your post in about 100 words.

Tell us about you and your best friend! Are you the same or different? Do you look similar? Do you have similar ambitions? Are your personalities similar? Post a comment below.

12 Check.
✓ Have you answered all the questions in the task?
✓ Have you used phrases from the WRITING FOCUS?
✓ Have you used paragraphs?
✓ Have you checked your grammar and spelling?

FOCUS REVIEW 4

VOCABULARY AND GRAMMAR

1 Choose the correct options.
1 Jane has got curly *hair / eyes*.
2 My grandma doesn't like wearing *trainers / trousers*. She usually wears a skirt or dress instead.
3 I can walk a long distance in those boots. They're really *successful / comfortable*.
4 He's forty-five years old on his next birthday – he's *middle-aged / medium-length*.
5 Simon has got beautiful green *ears / eyes*.
6 Ruth wears great clothes. She's very *organic / stylish*.

2 Read the descriptions and complete the adjectives.
1 This describes someone who helps other people. k _ _ _
2 This describes someone who wants to get a very good job. a _ _ _ _ _ _ _ _
3 This describes someone who has a good imagination and can make things. c _ _ _ _ _ _ _
4 This describes someone who likes going out and meeting people. s _ _ _ _ _ _ _
5 This describes someone who does well in tests. c _ _ _ _ _

3 Complete the sentences with the correct form of the adjectives in brackets.
1 I think Roger Federer is the _____ (good) tennis player in the world.
2 Rob is _____ (tall) than me.
3 Do you think films are _____ (interesting) than books?
4 Sarah is the _____ (funny) person in our class.
5 Katie is one of the _____ (successful) people I know.
6 Matt is usually _____ (calm) than his brother.

4 Complete the sentences with the correct form of *have to*.
1 Steve _____ make his bed because his mother always makes it for him.
2 I _____ get home by eleven o'clock during the week, but I can stay out later at the weekend.
3 Tim _____ tidy his room every week, but he likes it and he's happy to do it.
4 In many countries you _____ vote. You can decide if you want to vote or not.
5 _____ you _____ wear a helmet when you ride a motorcycle in your country?
6 If you are fourteen years old, you _____ go to school. You can finish school when you're sixteen in the UK.

LANGUAGE IN USE

5 Choose the correct answer, A, B or C, to complete both sentences.
1 Tina exercises a lot. She's very ____ .
   These trousers ____ me. I'll take them.
   A slim   B well   C fit
2 The wig is on ____ of the table.
   I like your skirt and ____ . Are they new?
   A top   B shirt   C boots
3 John is ____-built. He's very strong.
   I'm not feeling very ____ . I think I'll go to the doctor's.
   A medium   B slim   C well
4 Jack is only 1.60 m – he's quite ____ .
   I don't wear that skirt in winter. It's ____ , so my legs get cold.
   A short   B ugly   C stylish
5 I don't want to ____ married until I'm in my thirties.
   I'm having lessons because I want to ____ my driving licence.
   A be   B get   C take
6 We usually ____ pizza on Friday evening.
   I like Pete because we always ____ fun together.
   A eat   B have   C make

6 Choose the correct answer, A, B or C.
1 A: What does Jamie look like?
   B: He's ____ . Everyone says he's very attractive.
      A ugly   B good-looking   C energetic
2 A: What have you got on your feet?
   B: Two pairs of ____ . My boots are a bit big.
      A socks   B trainers   C shoes
3 A: Why are there clothes and books all over your room?
   B: It's ____ because I'm studying for my exams.
      A untidy   B outrageous   C comfortable
4 A: Is that John's friend Mark over there?
   B: No, Mark has got blond ____ .
      A lips   B hair   C ears
5 A: Sally is very ____ .
   B: Yes, she always says good things about everyone.
      A talented   B relaxed   C positive
6 A: Do you fancy going to the ____ ?
   B: No, I'm not very sporty.
      A cinema   B gym   C restaurant

58

READING

7 What does each notice say? Read the notices (A–F) and match them with the sentences (1–4). There are two extra notices.

1. You can get fit with this. ☐
2. You don't always have to pay here. ☐
3. You need to send information here. ☐
4. You can learn about the history of fashion in this class. ☐

A **Diana's Clothes Shop**
Lots of casual clothes at cheap prices this Saturday. Come and buy all your T-shirts and jeans for the year!

B Love clothes? Join our course: 500 years of clothes. Monday and Wednesday evenings at Hardbrick College.

C **Your website!**
We want to know your opinions about new beauty products. Email us and we can put them on the school magazine website.

D Creative person wanted to join fashion design team. Please apply online to angelafashion.com.

E **Hair Affair**
Are you bored with your hair? We can help change your look. Good prices and an experienced, creative team! Come on a Monday evening and you can get a free haircut with our new apprentice, Shona.

F **Jogging Club**
Don't jog alone! Meet at 7.30 every morning in the park and jog for half an hour with other people. It's much more fun.

LISTENING

8 [CD·2.26] [MP3·82] Listen to Hayley talking to a friend about her sister, Sara, and choose the correct answer, A, B or C.

1. How many brothers and sisters does Hayley have?
   A two   B three   C four
2. Sara's birthday is in
   A March.   B June.   C November.
3. Sara's hair is
   A short and dark.   B long and blond.
   C short and blond.
4. Hayley and Sara do not both like the same
   A music.   B jokes.   C sports.
5. Where does Sara go with Hayley?
   A to the shops   B to the cinema   C to parties

SPEAKING

9 Choose the correct reply, A, B or C.

1. Can I help you?
   A Yes, I'm looking for a dress.
   B No, it's not really what I want.
   C I'm not sure. Red or green.
2. What size are you?
   A I want loose fit.
   B No, thanks.
   C I'm a 14, I think.
3. Can I try this on?
   A I'm looking for that.
   B Sure, the changing rooms are there.
   C Yes, it's perfect.
4. Have you got this in small?
   A No, I don't like blue.
   B No, sorry. Only in medium.
   C Yes. It's in large.
5. How much is this?
   A It's medium.
   B It's green.
   C It's £20.

10 In pairs, use the notes to role play the conversation in a shop. Student A, you are the shop assistant. Student B, you are the customer.

STUDENT A	STUDENT B
what/look for?	
	choose jeans/a jumper/a jacket
what/size?	
	give size
what/colour?	
	give colour
want/try on?	
	agree to try on
	ask price
give price	

WRITING

11 Your brother is going to stay in London with your English friend, Joe. Write an email of about 50–70 words to Joe and tell him about your brother's:
- appearance
- personality
- interests.

59

5 EDUCATION

Learn to walk before you run.

PROVERB

UNIT LANGUAGE AND SKILLS

Vocabulary:
- Show what you know – classroom objects, school subjects and people at school
- schools
- phrases about school
- collocations – *do*, *get* and *be*

Grammar:
- *must/mustn't*
- *should/shouldn't*
- Past Simple: *was/were*
- Past Simple: *could*

Listening:
- a conversation about parts of a school
- gap fill

Reading:
- a text about an unusual school
- right/wrong/doesn't say

Speaking:
- organising a trip

Writing:
- a personal email

FOCUS EXTRA
- Grammar Focus pages 115–116
- WORD STORE booklet pages 10–11
- Workbook pages 56–67 or MyEnglishLab

5.1 Vocabulary

Schools • Phrases about school • *do/get/be*

I can talk about schools.

SHOW WHAT YOU KNOW

1 Put the words in the box under the appropriate heading. Then add more words to each group.

> ~~blackboard~~   Chemistry   coursebook   desk   Geography
> head teacher   IT (Information Technology)   form teacher
> IWB (interactive whiteboard)   Maths   PE (Physical Education)
> Physics   pupil   Science

Classroom objects	Subjects	People
blackboard		

2 Complete the sentences to make them true for you. Then, in pairs, compare your answers.

1 My favourite subject is …
2 My worst subject is …
3 The best thing about my school is …
4 The worst thing about my school is …

3 Read the text and answer the questions.

1 Why do some children have to leave school at eleven?
2 Why do many children in Bangladesh miss school for four months of the year?
3 Do the children go to boat schools at the weekend?
4 How do the children feel about the floating schools?

BOAT SCHOOLS BEAT THE FLOODS

The United Nations says that every child has the right to an education. But millions of children around the world don't go to school. The government in their country doesn't have the money to build **state schools**. In some places there
5 is a **primary school** for children up to eleven years old, but there is no **secondary school**, so students have to leave school when they are still very young. In some countries, like Bangladesh in South Asia, a lot of children miss school between July and October because of all the rain.

10 But now a non-profit organisation in Bangladesh is solving the problem. When schools on land close because of the floods, the organisation runs free 'floating schools'. Twenty special boat schools travel up and down the rivers and pick up children from all the villages. They are **mixed schools**
15 for boys and girls. Each school has one classroom for thirty students and a teacher. Children go to their boat schools for two or three hours a day, six days a week.

The students are very proud of their floating schools. They never miss a class and they are always on time for lessons!
20 They do their homework and try very hard to get good marks because they want to do well and pass the exams.

Boat schools mean that children in South Asia now have a chance to get an education and even go to **university**.

Go to **WORD STORE 5** page 11.

WORD STORE 5A

4 CD•2.27 MP3•83 Complete WORD STORE 5A with the words in red in the text. Then listen, check and repeat.

5 Complete the text with words from WORD STORE 5A.

In Britain children go to ¹*nursery* school when they are three or four and then they go to ²____ school from age five to eleven. Some students go to ³____ school from eleven to thirteen, but most students go to ⁴____ school from twelve to sixteen or eighteen. Some parents pay for their children to go to ⁵____ schools, but most students go to ⁶____ schools.

After school, students go to ⁷____ or they can learn a skill like building at ⁸____ or they can try and get a job. Most state schools are ⁹____ – they are for boys and girls – but some are ¹⁰____ schools for either boys or girls only.

WORD STORE 5B

6 CD•2.28 MP3•84 Complete WORD STORE 5B with the underlined phrases in the text. Then listen, check and repeat.

7 Complete the sentences with phrases from WORD STORE 5B.
1 You have to work hard if you want to *do well* in the exams.
2 Sarah loves Maths and always gets _____ in the Maths tests.
3 I work hard, but I still do _____ in the English tests.
4 I am always _____ for lessons – I am never late!
5 In England children usually _____ school at the age of five and they can _____ after the age of sixteen.
6 My brother doesn't work hard, but he always _____ his exams.
7 I love Biology and I always try not to _____ a class.

WORD STORE 5C

8 CD•2.29 MP3•85 Read the text in Exercise 3 again and complete WORD STORE 5C with *be*, *do* or *get*. Then listen, check and repeat.

9 Complete the text with the correct form of *be*, *do* or *get*.

In Guatemala many children don't ¹*get* an education because there is no school in their village. But now many students, like Carlos, are building their own schools. They fill old plastic bottles with rubbish and then use them as 'eco-bricks' to make walls. Carlos ²____ very proud of his new 'bottle school'. He ³____ always on time. He never ⁴____ bad marks because he wants to ⁵____ well in the exams.

61

5.2 Grammar

must/mustn't, don't have to, should/shouldn't
I can talk about rules and give advice.

1 Do you know any unusual schools? What do people learn there?

2 Look at the photos and read the school rules. Which school are they for, A or B?

Unusual schools

A   B

1 You must start learning when you are two years old.
2 You must practise every day.
3 You mustn't sit very close to the snakes.
4 You must learn to play music for the snakes.
5 You mustn't touch the snakes when the teacher is not there.

3 Read GRAMMAR FOCUS 1. Then complete the rules for becoming a stunt performer with *must* or *mustn't*.

GRAMMAR FOCUS 1
must/mustn't

- You use **must** to say that something is a rule or is necessary.
- You use **mustn't** when you want to say, 'don't do this'.
    + I/You/He/She/We/They **must** practise.
    − I/You/He/She/We/They **mustn't** touch the snakes.

Note: To say that something is not necessary, we use **don't have to**, NOT ~~mustn't~~.
He **doesn't have to** practise if he doesn't want to. (It's not necessary.)
It's late. He **mustn't** practise at this time of night. (It's not allowed.)

To be a stunt performer,

1 you _must_ be very fit and love outdoor activities.
2 you _____ be very good at different kinds of sports.
3 you _____ be able to work in a team.
4 you _____ be afraid of danger.
5 you _____ take risks.

4 CD•2.30 MP3•86 Listen and check.

5 Complete the sentences with *must*, *mustn't* or *don't have to* to make them true for you. Then compare your answers in pairs.

1 I _____ be at school before eight.
2 I _____ wear a school uniform.
3 I _____ use my mobile phone during lessons.
4 I _____ be at home after nine in the evening.

6 Read the conversations. Does B give good advice?

1 A: I'm good at sports and I'm not afraid of danger. Where **should** I study?
   B: You **should** go to a stunt school.

2 A: I love films and TV, but I'm not very fit and I hate danger. **Should** I go to a stunt school?
   B: No, you **shouldn't**! You **should** go to a film school.

7 Read GRAMMAR FOCUS 2. Then complete the conversations with *should* or *shouldn't* and the words in brackets.

GRAMMAR FOCUS 2
should/shouldn't

You use **should/shouldn't** to give advice.

+ I/You/He/She/We/They **should** go to a film school.
− I/You/He/She/We/They **shouldn't** go to a stunt school.
? **Should** I study there?
  Yes, you **should**./No, you **shouldn't**.
  Where **should** I go?
  You **should** go to a film school.

1 A: I want to be an actor. [1] _Should I leave_ (I/leave) school now and go to Hollywood?
   B: No, you [2] _____ (leave) school yet. You [3] _____ (go) to theatre school after you finish school.
2 A: I love working with animals. My parents want me to get an office job. What [4] _____ (I/do)?
   B: Well, you [5] _____ (work) in an office! You [6] _____ (train) to become a vet.
3 A: I'm scared of heights. [7] _____ (I/go) walking with the class this weekend?
   B: Yes, you [8] _____ , but you [9] _____ (tell) the leader and you [10] _____ (climb) any mountains.

8 Complete the sentences to make them true for you. Use the ideas in the box.

> be friendly and helpful   cheat in exams
> do extra activities   do your homework
> run inside the school   wear a uniform
> use a mobile phone in class   use a tablet

At my school:
1 you must _____ .
2 you mustn't _____ .
3 you don't have to _____ .
4 you should _____ .
5 you shouldn't _____ .

Grammar Focus page 114

62

5.3 Listening

Gap fill
I can identify specific detail in conversations about schools.

1 Which parts of a school can you see in the photos?

canteen   classroom   corridor   gym   hall   library
playground   science lab   sports field   staff room

A B C D E F

2 **CD·2.31 MP3·87** Jane is showing Mark round the school. Listen to the first part of their conversation. Where are they? How do you know?

3 Read the conversation. What kind of information is missing in each gap? Match the gaps (1–3) with the descriptions (a–c).

Jane: There is a lot of special ¹_____ here. Students do ²_____ in Chemistry and Physics lessons. You mustn't touch anything until the teacher tells you to.
Mark: What are all those books?
Jane: We keep all the Science books here so everyone can use them in the lessons. You have to wear an ³_____ in here too, over your school uniform, to protect it.

a something you wear on top of your clothes
b something students do in Science classes
c something students use in Science classes

4 **CD·2.31 MP3·87** Complete the conversation in Exercise 3 with the words in the box. Then listen again and check.

equipment   experiments   overall

5 **CD·2.32 MP3·88** Listen to the second part of the conversation. What three other places does Jane describe? Don't worry about words you don't understand.

EXAM FOCUS Gap fill

6 **CD·2.32 MP3·88** Listen again and complete the information.
1 Price of cola: _____
2 Jane eats in: _____
3 Borrowing time for CDs: _____
4 Number of teachers in school: _____
5 Lesson in _____ : drama

7 Complete the sentences with the correct form of the words in the box.

borrow   do   give   ~~have~~   meet   use

1 Let's *have* a meeting to discuss our summer holiday.
2 I want to _____ *Lord of the Rings* from the school library, but I have to give it back after three days.
3 On Thursdays we _____ **experiments** in our Science lesson.
4 Do you _____ **computers** in your English classes?
5 I'm going to _____ **a speech** about students' rights in front of the whole school.
6 I always _____ **my friends** for a drink in the canteen during the eleven o'clock break at school.

PRONUNCIATION FOCUS

8 **CD·2.33 MP3·89** Listen to the /th/ sound and put the words in the box in the correct column.

/ð/	/θ/
the	think

three   then   bathroom   they   thin
together   mother   thousand   thing
tooth   there   those   author   this
thanks   other   Thursday   father

9 **CD·2.34 MP3·90** Listen again and check.

WORD STORE 5D

10 **CD·2.35 MP3·91** Complete WORD STORE 5D with the words in Exercise 1. Then listen, check and repeat.

5.4 Reading

Right/Wrong/Doesn't say

I can find specific detail in an article about a different kind of school.

1 In pairs, discuss the questions about your school.
   1 How many students are there?
   2 What courses can students study?
   3 What activities can students do?
   4 Are there any compulsory (something that you have to do) activities?
   5 Do students take part in any volunteer programmes?

2 Read the title and the introduction of the article. Choose the phrase that describes what the article is about.
   a learning to sail a tall ship
   b a school on a sailing ship
   c sailing around the world

3 In which paragraph can you find this information? Read the article and match the paragraphs (A–F) with the information (1–6).
   1 the courses — C
   2 the students
   3 the school on the ship
   4 activities on the boat
   5 volunteer projects
   6 activities in the ports the students visit

EXAM FOCUS   Right/Wrong/Doesn't say

4 Read the text again. Are the statements right (R), wrong (W) or does the text not say (DS)?
   1 Students must know how to sail before they join the ship.
   2 Students come from different parts of the world.
   3 All the students do the same courses.
   4 Students don't have to speak English well.
   5 Besides studying, students also have to do jobs on the ship.
   6 Students go home to their parents for the holidays.
   7 Students don't usually meet any local people when they stop in ports.

5 In pairs, answer the questions in Exercise 1 for Class Afloat. Then compare Class Afloat with your school.

   In my school there are ... students. Class Afloat has up to sixty students.

CD·2.36 MP3·92

School Ahoy!

Imagine sailing to over twenty different ports around the world while you are studying subjects you love! Impossible? Well, that is exactly what the students in Class Afloat do.

A **Class Afloat** is a Canadian school on a tall ship! The ship is sixty-four metres long and nine metres wide and it can take up to sixty students. The classrooms are well-equipped and comfortable and there's even a library! It isn't necessary to know anything about sailing – students can learn on the ship.

B Not all the students are Canadian – there's usually a mix of nationalities. This year, there are also students from Mexico, the USA, Germany and Turkey. There's a mix of ages too. There are secondary school students – usually they're sixteen to eighteen years old – first year university students and students who are doing a gap year programme.

C The teachers design special study programmes for each student. Because the school is a ship, you can do some exciting courses – for example, Marine Biology (studying the animals and plants in the sea) and History or Geography courses about the places you visit. Students also learn all about sailing! All the classes are in English, so you must have a good level of English.

D Students don't just study. They must also clean, cook and sail the ship. In their free time, students can rest, read or watch a film. In the evenings, they relax with friends, have club meetings and sometimes they have a karaoke night.

E Every sixteen to twenty days, the ship stops in a port for three to six days. In port there's lots to do – home stays, camping trips, museum tours, cultural events, hiking, etc. They also go snorkelling and do other water sports. Parents can meet up with the students in one port every term.

F Students also participate in two volunteer programmes in Senegal and the Dominican Republic. They help local families in different ways, for example, with basic health matters or starting a business. Students learn how, with just a little money and time, they can make changes that improve other people's lives.

64

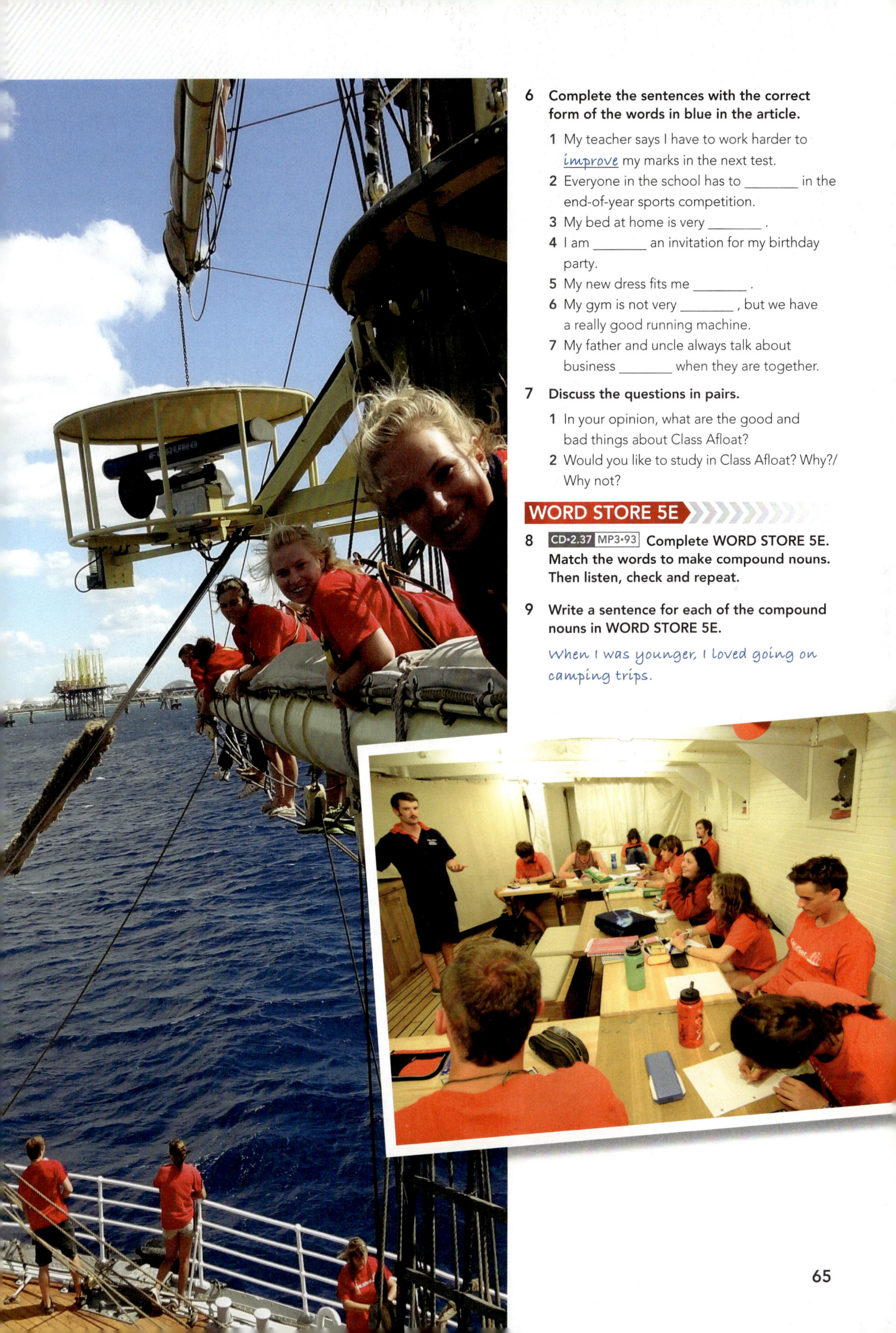

6 **Complete the sentences with the correct form of the words in blue in the article.**

1 My teacher says I have to work harder to _improve_ my marks in the next test.
2 Everyone in the school has to _____ in the end-of-year sports competition.
3 My bed at home is very _____ .
4 I am _____ an invitation for my birthday party.
5 My new dress fits me _____ .
6 My gym is not very _____ , but we have a really good running machine.
7 My father and uncle always talk about business _____ when they are together.

7 **Discuss the questions in pairs.**

1 In your opinion, what are the good and bad things about Class Afloat?
2 Would you like to study in Class Afloat? Why?/Why not?

WORD STORE 5E

8 [CD·2.37] [MP3·93] Complete WORD STORE 5E. Match the words to make compound nouns. Then listen, check and repeat.

9 Write a sentence for each of the compound nouns in WORD STORE 5E.

When I was younger, I loved going on camping trips.

65

5.5 Grammar

Past Simple: was/were, could

I can talk about the past with the verbs be and can.

1 In pairs, look at the photo in text A and answer the questions. Then read text A and check.

1 Who is the person in the photo?
2 What do you know about him?
3 What is he most famous for?

THE STARS AND SCHOOL

A **JOHNNY DEPP** is a famous film star now, but what was he like at school? **Was** he a good student? School **wasn't** a good experience for Johnny. The problem was that he **was** at over twenty different schools and often the students **weren't** very friendly. So school was often a lonely place for Johnny. His two favourite things **were** music and acting. He **couldn't** play the piano, but he **could** play the guitar. He could also sing very well and he was in a band called The Kids. His dream was to be a musician after school. His band was successful, but they couldn't get a record deal. Luckily, Johnny was also a great actor.

B **KRISTEN STEWART** is a famous actress. But when she ¹was / were younger, things ²wasn't / weren't always easy. She ³wasn't / weren't happy at high school because she ⁴could / couldn't talk to other kids her age. They ⁵was / were interested in different things and so they ⁶wasn't / weren't very friendly to her. They ⁷were / weren't often jealous because Kristen ⁸could / couldn't act really well.

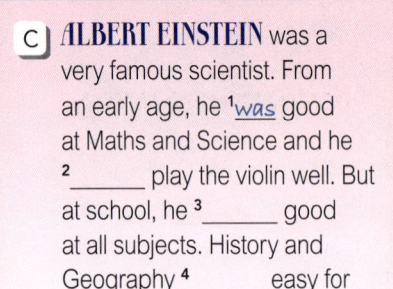

C **ALBERT EINSTEIN** was a very famous scientist. From an early age, he ¹was good at Maths and Science and he ² _____ play the violin well. But at school, he ³ _____ good at all subjects. History and Geography ⁴ _____ easy for him and he ⁵ _____ good at foreign languages. But Einstein ⁶ _____ a genius and scientists are still studying his brain to help them understand about intelligence.

2 Read GRAMMAR FOCUS 1 and 2 and complete the examples with the verbs in blue in text A. Then find more examples in the text.

GRAMMAR FOCUS 1

Past Simple: be

+	I/He/She ¹<u>was</u> a good student. You/We/They ² _____ good students.
–	I/He/She ³ _____ a good student. You/We/They ⁴ _____ good students.
?	⁵ _____ I/he/she a good student? Yes, I/he/she was./No, I/he/she wasn't. Were you/we/they good students? Yes, you/we/they were./No, you/we/they weren't. What was he good at? What were they good at?

Note:
- You also use **was/wasn't** with **it**: *It was lonely for him.*
- wasn't = was not, weren't = were not

GRAMMAR FOCUS 2

Past Simple: can

+	He ⁶<u>could</u> play the guitar.
–	He ⁷ _____ play the piano.
?	Could he play the piano?

Note:
- **Could** is the same for all persons (I, you, he, she, it, we, they).
- couldn't = could not

3 Read text A again and correct the sentences.

1 School was fun for Johnny.
   School wasn't fun for Johnny. It wasn't a good experience.
2 The other students were always nice.
3 Johnny was always happy.
4 Johnny's favourite things were Maths and History.
5 Johnny couldn't sing well.
6 The band wasn't very successful.

4 CD•2.38 MP3•94 Read text B and choose the correct options. Then listen and check.

5 CD•2.39 MP3•95 In pairs, complete text C with *was/wasn't, were/weren't* or *could/couldn't*. Then listen and check.

6 Complete the questions with *was, were* or *could*. Then ask and answer in pairs. Write down the answers.

When you were at primary school:
1 <u>were</u> the other students friendly?
2 _____ your teacher nice?
3 _____ you speak English?
4 _____ you good at Science?
5 _____ you understand everything?
6 _____ you quiet or noisy?
7 _____ school fun?
8 _____ you good at sports?

7 Tell the class about your partner.

When Ricardo was at primary school, the other students were friendly. His teacher was ...

Grammar Focus page 115

5.6 Speaking

Organising a trip
I can ask for information to organise a school trip.

1 Read the information below about the Eden Project and Shakespeare's house. Which is the best place to visit on a school trip? Why?

2 **CD·2.40 MP3·96** Ben is organising a trip for his class. Read and listen. Which place do they want to visit?

Clerk: Good morning. <u>Can I help you?</u>
Ben: Good morning. I'd like some information.
Clerk: Certainly, what would you like to know?
Ben: <u>What are your opening times?</u>
Clerk: We're open from ¹_____ a.m. to ²_____ p.m.
Ben: And how much does it cost to get in?
Clerk: For adults it costs ³_____ and for children it costs ⁴_____. <u>There are also discounts for groups.</u>
Ben: Can I book online?
Clerk: Yes, you can. There's a discount if you book online.
Ben: Are there any guided tours?
Clerk: No, but you can download an app to your phone. It's got lots of great information.
Ben: And where is the house exactly?
Clerk: It's on Henley Street, near the train station.
Ben: OK, thanks very much.
Clerk: You're welcome.

3 **CD·2.40 MP3·96** Complete the conversation in Exercise 2. Then listen again and check.

4 Read the conversation in Exercise 2 again and complete the SPEAKING FOCUS with the <u>underlined</u> phrases.

SPEAKING FOCUS

Asking for information
I'd like some information.
¹_____
How much does it cost to get in?
How much are the tickets?/How much is (a family) ticket?
Can I book online?
Are there any guided tours?
Is there an app?
Where is the (park/museum/attraction) exactly?
Thanks very much.

Giving information
² <u>Can I help you?</u>
What would you like to know?
Tickets are (£10) for adults and (£5) for children.
Children under (5) are free.
³_____
A family ticket costs (£20).
The (museum/park) opens at (9 a.m.) and closes at (5 p.m.).
It's in/on (Green Street).
You're welcome.

5 Put the words in the correct order to make questions. Then answer the questions about a place you visited on a school trip.

1 how / cost / much / it / to / in / does / get?
   How much does it cost to get in?
2 any / there / are / tours?
3 book / online / I / can?
4 is / where / exactly / it?
5 there / is / app / an?

6 In pairs, role play a conversation asking for information about the Eden Project.

Eden Project — Cornwall

Explore the rainforest, walk through the Mediterranean area, have fun in the education centre and learn about plants. There are also fantastic concerts and the longest zip wire in England!

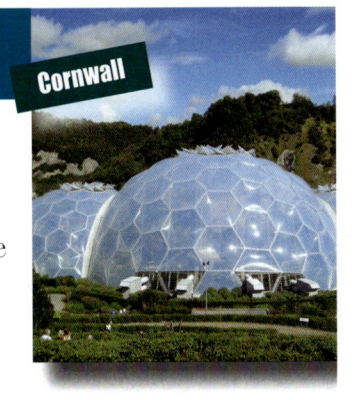

Opening times: 9.30 a.m.–6 p.m., 7 days a week all year
Tickets: Adults: £23.50 (£19.95 online)
Children 5–16 years old: £13.50
(£11.50 online)
Children under 5: free
Students: £11.50
Discounts for groups of ten or more – contact 01726811911
Guided tours: Choose from three different tours – £100–£125

Shakespeare's house — Stratford upon Avon

See where Shakespeare was born and lived for over twenty years. Explore the gardens, visit the shop or do a workshop. Download the Eye Shakespeare app to your phone to get the most from your visit!

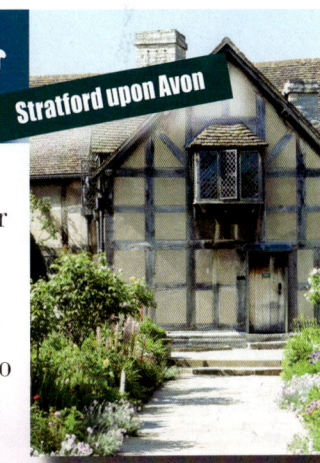

Opening times: 9.00 a.m.–5 p.m.
Tickets: Adults: £15.90 (10% discount online)
Children 5–16 years old: £9.50
(10% discount online)
Family: £41.50
Students: £14.90
Discounts for groups of ten or more – contact 01789204016

5.7 Writing

A personal email
I can write to someone and tell them news about school.

1 Which of these topics would you *not* write about in an email to a friend about a new school?
- the other students
- activities you are doing
- your favourite film
- your news
- school sports teams

2 Read the email. Which topic does Jen *not* write about?

[A] Hi Mark,

[B] How are you? I hope you're fine and not too busy!

[C] I'm getting on OK at my new school. It's great because everyone's very friendly. I don't know my way round the school yet. I get lost all the time, but someone always helps me find the right place. What else? The trials for the hockey team are next week. I'd love to be in the team, so I have to practise really hard. My other news is that I'm in a band! There are six of us in the band. I play the guitar (of course!) and it's great fun.

[D] How about you? Are you still in the volleyball team? What are your plans for this weekend? Do you want to come and stay soon?

[E] Write soon! I can't wait to hear all your news! I miss you all! 🙂
Love,
Jen

3 Read the email again. Match the parts of the email (A–E) with the descriptions (1–5).
1 asking about the other person — D
2 giving your news ☐
3 signing off ☐
4 greeting ☐
5 asking how someone is ☐

4 Complete the WRITING FOCUS with the expressions in purple in the email.

WRITING FOCUS
A personal email

- Asking about someone
  1 How are you?/How are things?
  I hope you're fine!/I hope you're not too busy!
  How's everyone?

- Giving your news
  I'm getting on OK/fine/well.
  What else?
  I'd love to …
  2 _____

- Asking about the other person
  What are you up to?
  3 _____
  What are your plans for this weekend/the holidays?
  How's life?
  What's your news?

- Signing off
  Write soon!
  4 _____
  I hope to hear from you soon!
  I miss you!/I miss you all!

5 Complete the email with one word in each gap.

¹Hi Sandy,
How are you? How's ² _____ ? I hope they're all well.
I'm ³ _____ on fine at school at the moment. We've got a new teacher for Maths. What ⁴ _____ ? I won my swimming competition!
What are you ⁵ _____ to at the moment? What's your ⁶ _____ ? Are you doing anything interesting?
I hope to ⁷ _____ from you soon.
I ⁸ _____ you all!
Bye for now,
Maddy

6 Read examples A–D. Then choose the correct options.

A I hope you're fine! I hope you're not too busy! →
I hope you're fine **and** not too busy!
B I get lost all the time. Someone always helps me. →
I get lost all the time, **but** someone always helps me.
C It's great **because** everyone is very friendly.
Everyone is very friendly, **so** it's great.
D The trials are next week. I have to practise hard. →
The trials are next week, **so** I have to practise hard. →
I have to practise hard **because** the trials are next week.

1 I'm learning to play the guitar *and / but* the drums.
2 I'm really angry *because / so* I can't go to the concert on Saturday.
3 It's my best friend's birthday today, *because / so* we're going to a club later.
4 We have to play hockey in sports lessons now *and / but* I don't like it!

7 Complete the text with *and*, *but*, *because* or *so*.

I want to get fit, ¹ __so__ I'm doing a lot of sport this year. I'm in the football team ² _____ I'm in the badminton team, ³ _____ I'm not in the hockey team. I'm also in a theatre group. We've got a show next week, ⁴ _____ we have to practise hard. What else? We've got a new History teacher ⁵ _____ she's really nice! I'm learning a lot ⁶ _____ she's a great teacher.

8 Read the email from your English friend, Carrie. Then write a reply of about 100 words, answering Carrie's questions.

From: Carrie
To:

How's your new school? Have you got any new friends? Are there any interesting clubs? Do you do the same subjects? Tell me all your news!

9 Check.
✓ Have you answered all the questions?
✓ Have you used phrases from the WRITING FOCUS?
✓ Have you started and finished your email correctly?
✓ Have you checked your grammar and spelling?

FOCUS REVIEW 5

VOCABULARY AND GRAMMAR

1 Complete the sentences with the words in the box. There are two extra words.

[book cheat do get have miss pass]

1 To _____ the most from school, you should study hard.
2 Let's _____ a meeting to organise the party.
3 I have to _____ my homework before I can watch TV.
4 You can _____ online before you go to the museum.
5 It's not a good idea to _____ in exams.

2 Choose the correct options.

1 My parents pay for me to go to a *state / private* school.
2 I'm *proud / afraid* of passing all my exams. My parents were very happy too.
3 I love water sports, especially *diving / riding*.
4 Please write the answers on the *desk / blackboard* so everyone can see.
5 Pupils usually *start / leave* school when they are five years old.
6 I like learning about the past, so I enjoy *Maths / History*.

3 Complete the second sentence with the verbs in the box.

[doesn't have to must mustn't should shouldn't]

1 It's not necessary for Joanne to help me.
   Joanne _____ help me.
2 My advice is to talk to your parents about your problem.
   I think you _____ talk to your parents about your problem.
3 The school rules say: 'No mobile phones in class.'
   You _____ use mobile phones in class.
4 I don't think it's a good idea to invite Jack to your party.
   You _____ invite Jack to your party.
5 At our school all students wear a uniform. It's the rule.
   At our school you _____ wear a uniform.

4 Complete the sentences with the correct form of the verbs in brackets.

1 I _____ (be) shy as a child, but now I'm not shy.
2 Simon _____ (not can) swim when he _____ (be) four years old.
3 Where _____ (be) you yesterday?
4 They _____ (can) sing very well when they were at school.
5 I _____ (not be) at school last week. It _____ (be) a holiday.
6 _____ (can) you play the guitar when you _____ (be) at primary school?

LANGUAGE IN USE

5 Complete the email with one word in each gap.

Hi!

Thanks for your email.

Tell me more about your school. What age ¹_____ you start school in your country? We start when we're five years old, but when my mum ²_____ young, the children could start at six. Now we ³_____ to stay at school until we're seventeen, but my mum ⁴_____ leave school at fifteen! I enjoy school and I never ⁵_____ lessons! Do you like school? What are your favourite subjects? I like History, so I always ⁶_____ well in History tests! I usually pass my exams and ⁷_____ good marks. Maths isn't the same! I should work harder for that!

That's all for now! I ⁸_____ do my Maths homework! Ugh!

Marcus

6 Choose the correct answer, A, B or C.

1 Sarah is nervous because she's got to ____ a speech.
   A do   B give   C have
2 My cousin is three years old. She goes to ____ school every morning.
   A nursery   B high   C primary
3 I hope I don't ____ the test.
   A do badly   B fail   C get lost
4 We play football on the sports ____ .
   A hall   B gym   C field
5 Matt ____ to go to school by bus.
   A has   B must   C should
6 I ____ play the piano when I was six years old.
   A can   B could   C should

LISTENING

7 CD•2.41 MP3•97 Listen to Emily talking to her friend about the teachers in her school photo. Match the teachers (1–5) with the subjects they teach (a–h). There are three extra subjects.

1 Mr Banks ☐   4 Miss Finlay ☐
2 Mr Jacobs ☐   5 Mr Smith ☐
3 Miss Rowe ☐

a English   e Spanish
b Science   f PE
c Maths   g History
d IT   h Drama

70

READING

8 Read the text. Are the statements right (R), wrong (W) or does the text not say (DS)?

1 Green School is completely environmentally friendly.
2 All the school's energy comes from the sun.
3 Adults can study at the Green School in the evenings.
4 At Green School, students also learn about growing food.
5 There aren't any rules about how many students must be from Bali.
6 Now some students live in green houses near the school.

Green School

Green School in Bali is an unusual school.

It was an experiment in 2010 by John and Cynthia Hardy. Their idea was to make a school that was totally environmentally friendly. Everything in the school is 'green' – that means it's good for the environment. The classrooms are made of bamboo wood and the light is from the sun. The school uses solar power and water power from their river.

The Hardys' experiment was successful and there are now 160 students from more than twenty-five countries – and it goes from kindergarten up to age eighteen. The students at Green School don't only learn subjects such as English and Maths; they also learn to grow organic vegetables and other foods such as rice in the huge school gardens. They look after the plants and learn to cook them. The school also has a cow, some pigs and a buffalo. The students also study building, making furniture and traditional art and dance.

The Hardys want the local community to be a part of Green School. They have a rule that twenty percent of the students must be from Bali because they want local children to learn about protecting the environment. The children are often poor, so people from all over the world pay for them to go to the school. The idea of green living is becoming more popular and now people are building green houses near the school so their children can walk to school. The Hardys' dream is that one day all the schools in the world will be green.

SPEAKING

9 Work in pairs. Student A, you work at the museum. Student B, you want to visit the museum. Use your information to role play the conversation.

STUDENT A

Clothes Museum

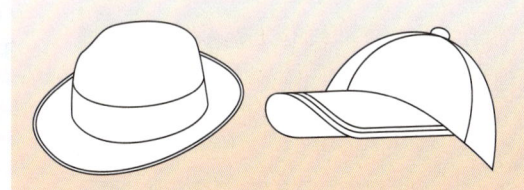

- Learn all about the history of fashion.
- Special exhibition of 1920s clothes showing now!
- Buy books and posters in our shop.

Open Monday–Saturday, 9.30 a.m.–5.30 p.m.
Tickets: Adults: £10
Students: £5
Special discounts for groups!
Book online to get extra discount at clothesmuseum.com or phone 020 3456 75284.

STUDENT B

- when/open?
- what/see/now?
- shop?
- ticket prices?
- book/online?

WRITING

10 Read the email from your English friend, Carl. Then write a reply of about 100 words, answering Carl's questions.

I'm sure you're in your new house now! How are you and what's your new school like? Do you do the same lessons? Are the teachers nice?

6 SPORT AND HEALTH

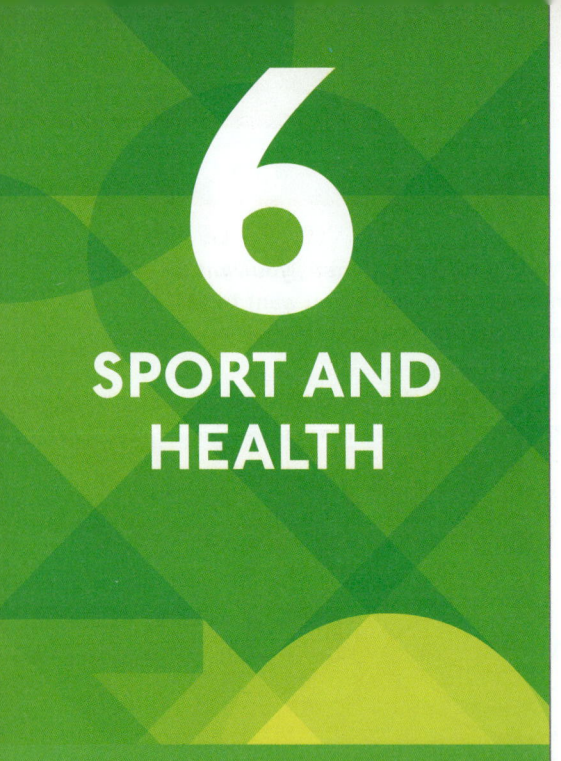

Health is better than wealth.

A PROVERB

UNIT LANGUAGE AND SKILLS

Vocabulary:
- *Show what you know* – sports
- types of sport
- collocations – *do, go* and *be*
- collocations – sport and health

Grammar:
- Past Simple: affirmatives (regular and irregular verbs)
- Past Simple: questions and negatives (regular and irregular verbs)

Listening:
- a conversation about Physical Education
- multiple choice

Reading:
- an article about two sportspeople
- gapped text

Speaking:
- asking for and giving advice

Writing:
- a description of an event

FOCUS EXTRA
- Grammar Focus pages 116–117
- WORD STORE booklet pages 12–13
- Workbook pages 68–79 or MyEnglishLab

6.1 Vocabulary

Types of sport • Verb collocations

I can talk about sport and health.

SHOW WHAT YOU KNOW

1 In pairs, add as many sports as you can to the table in sixty seconds.

Summer sports	skateboarding,
Winter sports	hockey,
Both	basketball,

2 Which sports do you like? Which don't you like? Tell your partner.

3 In pairs, look at the photos of Harry, Sally and Luke. What sports are their favourite? Choose from the words in the box.

badminton   cycling   football   ice skating   jogging
karate   kayaking   kung fu   sailing   skiing   swimming
table tennis   tennis   volleyball   yoga   Zumba

Harry: _____   Sally: _____   Luke: _____

4 In pairs, look at the icons for each photo and guess what other sports Harry, Sally and Luke do.

Harry: badminton , _____ , _____
Sally: _____ , _____ , _____
Luke: _____ , _____ , _____

5 CD·3.1 MP3·98 Complete the sentences with *Harry*, *Sally* or *Luke*. Then listen and check.

1 Harry goes ice skating on Monday evenings.
2 _____ goes jogging before school three times a week. After jogging he has a healthy breakfast.
3 _____ plays table tennis for a team. Her team often wins.
4 In summer, _____ goes swimming and kayaking. He has a very healthy lifestyle.
5 _____ and his/her friends go skiing in winter. They go to the gym to play volleyball twice a week, to keep fit.
6 _____ plays tennis or badminton every week.
7 _____ plays football at the weekend with his friends.
8 _____ takes part in karate competitions.

Go to WORD STORE 6 page 13.

WORD STORE 6A

6 CD·3.2 MP3·99 Complete WORD STORE 6A with the sports in Exercises 1 and 3. Then listen, check and repeat.

WORD STORE 6B

7 CD·3.3 MP3·100 Look at the phrases in red in Exercise 5 and complete WORD STORE 6B with *go*, *play* or *do*. Then listen, check and repeat.

8 In pairs, follow the instructions.
1 Make a list of at least six sports you or your friends do.
2 For each sport on your list write *go*, *play* or *do*.
3 Tell your partner about the sports you do, when you do them and who you do them with.

In winter I go skiing with my family.
I play tennis with my friend Daniel on Mondays.

WORD STORE 6C

9 CD·3.4 MP3·101 Look at the underlined phrases in Exercise 5 and complete WORD STORE 6C. Then listen, check and repeat.

10 Complete the questions with the verbs in WORD STORE 6C. Then ask and answer in pairs.
1 Do you have a healthy breakfast? What do you have?
2 What do you do to ____ fit?
3 Do you ____ for a sports team? What sport do you play?
4 Do you ____ a healthy lifestyle? What do you do?
5 How often do you ____ to the gym?
6 Do you ____ part in any sports competitions? What kind?

11 Complete the text with one word in each gap. Use WORD STORES 6B and 6C to help you.

EXAMS AND YOUR HEALTH

- Don't study all night. You learn better when you're not tired.
- Try to have a ¹healthy diet. A healthy ²____ first thing in the morning gives you energy for the whole day.
- Exercise is important. You're never too busy to ³____ jogging or swimming. If you don't have time to ⁴____ tennis or football, walk or cycle to school. Or ⁵____ to the gym for an hour.
- If there isn't a gym near your home, ⁶____ exercises for ten minutes every morning.
- And take regular breaks when you're studying.

12 In pairs, find these things in the text in Exercise 11.
- two things you already do
  I have a healthy diet.
- two things you'd like to do
  I'd like to do more exercise.

6.2 Grammar

Past Simple: affirmatives

I can use the Past Simple to describe events in the past.

PASSION OR MADNESS?

When you look at mountains like this, do you think, 'I'd love to climb that!' or are you one of those people who say, 'Anyone who wants to climb that is mad!'?
[5] These are Trango Towers (6,286 m) in the Karakoram in Pakistan. British climber Martin Boysen tried to climb them in 1975 and nearly died. In 1976 he tried again and became the first climber to reach the top.
In 1990 Japanese climber Takeyasu [10] Minamiura climbed to the top of one side of the mountain. But that wasn't his main aim. He wanted to paraglide to the bottom.
On 9 September Minamiura jumped off the top of Trango Towers, but his paraglider hit [15] the wall and he fell forty-five metres until the glider caught on a piece of rock and saved his life. And there he hung. The fall broke his glasses, but [20] he was OK. When his hands stopped shaking, he took his radio and contacted his friends. He asked them to send a helicopter to rescue him.

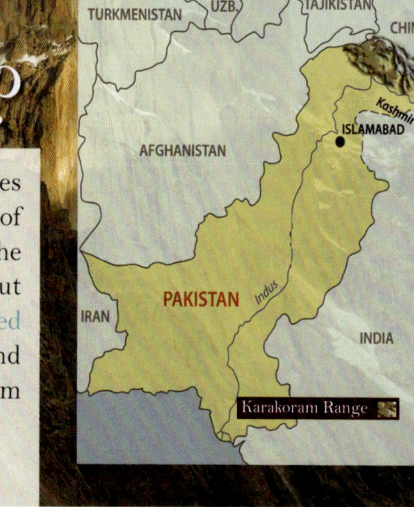

1. Read the first part of a story. Who was the first person to climb Trango Towers?

2. Read GRAMMAR FOCUS 1 and look at the verbs in blue in the story. Then write the Past Simple form of the verbs below.

GRAMMAR FOCUS 1
Past Simple: regular verbs
To form the **Past Simple** of regular verbs:
- add -ed to the end of the verb.
  jump → jump**ed**
- add -d to the end of regular verbs that end in -e.
  save → save**d**
- double the final letter and add -ed if the verb ends with a single vowel and a consonant.
  stop → stop**ped**
- for a verb that ends in a consonant + -y, change the -y to -i and add -ed.
  try → tr**ied**

1 look – looked	7 ask – _____
2 climb – _____	8 shout – _____
3 want – _____	9 help – _____
4 like – _____	10 save – _____
5 stay – _____	11 cry – _____
6 decide – _____	12 start – _____

3. **CD•3.5 MP3•102** Listen and put the Past Simple form of the verbs in Exercise 2 in the correct column.

/t/	/d/	/ɪd/
look**ed**	climb**ed**	want**ed**

4. **CD•3.6 MP3•103** Listen, check and repeat.

5. **CD•3.7 MP3•104** Read GRAMMAR FOCUS 2 and complete it with the underlined verbs in the article. Then listen, check and repeat.

GRAMMAR FOCUS 2
Past Simple: irregular verbs
1 become – became   4 catch – _____   6 break – _____
2 hit – _____   5 hang – _____   7 take – _____
3 fall – _____

6. Complete the sentences with the Past Simple form of the verbs in the box.

> break drink fall ~~go~~ have say run take

1 We went swimming yesterday afternoon.
2 We _____ part in a Zumba competition.
3 'I have to train really hard,' _____ the champion.
4 Sarah _____ a lot of homework, so she stayed home to do it.
5 Jake _____ 100 metres in forty seconds.
6 I _____ a lot of water during the tennis match.
7 The man _____ off his bike and _____ his leg.

7. Read the second part of the story about Minamiura. Complete it with the Past Simple form of the verbs in brackets.

Two of his friends [1]walked (walk) twelve miles to a Pakistani army base to get help and they [2]_____ (fly) to Trango Towers. They [3]_____ (see) Minamiura, but winds [4]_____ (stop) the helicopter from landing. The two friends [5]_____ (plan) a daring rescue – they [6]_____ (go) to Trango Glacier and [7]_____ (look) for Boysen's fourteen-year-old ropes to help them climb the glacier.
Minamiura [8]_____ (spend) six days without food and water before his friends [9]_____ (reach) him and [10]_____ (bring) him down the mountain. They [11]_____ (arrive) back on 18 September, forty-nine days after Minamiura [12]_____ (start) his adventure on Trango Towers.

Grammar Focus page 116

6.3 Listening

Multiple choice
I can find specific details in conversations.

1. What can you remember? In pairs, think of as many sports as you can for each group in sixty seconds.
   1. team sports
   2. individual sports
   3. martial arts
   4. water sports

2. In pairs, look at the photo and answer the questions.
   1. Do you have PE at school?
   2. What kinds of activities do you do?
   3. Do you enjoy it? Why?/Why not?

3. Read the questions in Exercise 4. Match the underlined words and phrases with the ones with a similar meaning in a–f below.
   - a wants
   - b hates
   - c likes
   - d PE is necessary
   - e has fun in
   - f thinks it isn't important

4. **CD·3.8 MP3·105** Listen to two students discussing PE. Tick the correct speaker for each question.

Who:	Alfie	Millie
1 can't stand team sports?		
2 doesn't care about winning?		
3 enjoys PE lessons?		
4 likes Science more than PE?		
5 thinks all students need PE?		
6 thinks they shouldn't get grades for PE?		
7 is into individual sports at school?		
8 would like to do kung fu at school?		

EXAM FOCUS Multiple choice

5. **CD·3.8 MP3·105** Listen again and choose the correct answer, A, B or C.
   1. Which sport does Alfie dislike most?
      A basketball B rugby C football
   2. Alfie doesn't like team sports because he doesn't like
      A his team. B losing. C competition.
   3. Millie likes PE because
      A she likes competition.
      B she likes team games.
      C she thinks it's relaxing.
   4. Millie thinks PE is important because
      A students don't have enough time after school.
      B students can get good grades.
      C students need exercise during the day.
   5. Alfie thinks that at school there should be
      A less sport.
      B better instructors.
      C different sports.

6. Look at the questions in Exercise 4. Who do you agree with – Alfie or Millie? Discuss in pairs.

   I agree with … I also …

PRONUNCIATION FOCUS

7. **CD·3.9 MP3·106** In English the letter *a* is pronounced in many ways. Listen and repeat.

/ɔː/	/æ/	/eɪ/	/ɑː/
water	badminton	skating	martial arts

8. **CD·3.10 MP3·107** Listen and put the words in the correct column in the table in Exercise 7.

   [ball bat game hard last match play talk]

9. **CD·3.11 MP3·108** Listen, check and repeat.

WORD STORE 6D

10. **CD·3.12 MP3·109** Complete WORD STORE 6D with words and phrases from Exercises 3 and 4. Then listen, check and repeat.

11. Complete the sentences to make them true for you. Then compare your answers with a partner.
    1. I like _____ more than tennis.
    2. I hate _____ .
    3. I prefer swimming to _____ .
    4. I'm into _____ and _____ but I can't stand _____ .
    5. I _____ winning.

6.4 Reading

Gapped text

I can understand the structure of a text.

1 In pairs, look at the photos and discuss the questions.
   1 Who are the people?
   2 What do you know about them?

2 Read the article. Are the statements true (T) or false (F)?
   1 Lionel Messi is from Brazil. **F**
   2 Lionel Messi had a health problem when he was a child.
   3 Lionel Messi started to play for Barcelona's first team at the age of nineteen.
   4 Lionel Messi helps children in need.
   5 Natalia Partyka has got one leg.
   6 Natalia Partyka's older brother played table tennis.
   7 Natalia Partyka didn't play in the Paralympics in Beijing.
   8 Natalia Partyka won a silver medal at the Paralympics in London in 2012.

3 Read the sentences in Exercise 4 and look at the underlined words and phrases. Then match statements 1–7 below with sentences A–D.
   1 The sentence before is probably about a man. **D**
   2 The sentence before is probably about a woman.
   3 The sentence before is probably about two or more people.
   4 Something was expensive.
   5 Perhaps the person did or said something unusual.
   6 The sentence before probably says something like 'one (person)' or 'the first one'.
   7 The sentence before is probably about a bad result.

EXAM FOCUS Gapped text

4 Read the article again. Complete gaps 1–3 with sentences A–D. There is one extra sentence.

   A <u>Her</u> parents <u>weren't surprised</u> and they helped her from the start.
   B It was <u>the worst result</u> in their career.
   C <u>The other one</u> was the South African swimmer Natalie du Toit.
   D It <u>cost too much</u> for <u>his</u> family and even for the local football club.

CD•3.13 MP3•110

A little

'All kids need is a little help, a little hope and somebody who believes in them.' Magic Johnson, the American basketball player, said this about children in sport. But what if a child is born without an arm or with a serious *illness*? Is there still hope for them? What kind of help do they need? Here are the stories of two children who had someone who believed in them.

Lionel ('Leo') Messi started playing football at a local club in Rosario, Argentina, at the age of five. When he was eleven he stopped growing. Doctors discovered he had a hormone problem. He needed expensive *treatment*. ¹_____ Then the director of FC Barcelona noticed the boy and invited him to move to Spain. The club promised to pay for his treatment. So Lionel and his father moved to Europe. Messi grew and trained. He started playing for the Barcelona first team before he

5 Complete the sentences with the words in blue in the article.
   1 The Paralympics is an international sports competition for *disabled* athletes.
   2 Wimbledon is the oldest tennis _____ in the world.
   3 Many _____ became champions because someone believed in them.
   4 The Leo Messi Foundation pays for the _____ of poor Argentinian children with serious health problems.
   5 The American swimmer Michael Phelps _____ eight gold medals at the 2008 Olympic Games in Beijing.
   6 Tennis star Venus Williams couldn't play in the 2011 US Open because of her _____ .

76

help, a little hope

How can a girl born without a hand become a table tennis star? When **Natalia Partyka** was seven, she wanted to play Ping-Pong like her older sister. ² _____ Six months after she started training, Natalia took part in the first national tournament for disabled players. After that she never looked back. The Polish table tennis player won her first international medal at the age of ten. When she was fifteen, she won gold and silver medals at the Paralympics in Athens in 2004. Four years later, in Beijing, she was one of only two athletes who took part in the Olympics and the Paralympics at the same time. ³ _____ . At the 2012 Paralympics in London Natalia won gold and bronze.

was eighteen. Then, at the age of nineteen, he became the youngest Argentinian to play in the World Cup. Soon he was one of the most famous footballers in the world. In 2007 Messi started a foundation which pays for medical help for poor children.

6 Complete the sentences with prepositions from the article.
1 The Brazilian footballer Pelé first played in the World Cup Final _at_ the age _____ seventeen.
2 Great South American football players often move _____ Europe early in their careers.
3 The largest stadium _____ the world is the Rungrado May Day Stadium in Pyongyang, North Korea.
4 Not many athletes take part _____ both the Olympics and the Paralympics.
5 A good coach believes _____ his players.
6 Most sportspeople need sponsors to pay _____ their equipment.
7 In football, when someone scores a goal, everyone shouts _____ the same time.

7 Discuss the questions in pairs.
1 What sport were you interested in when you were a child?
2 Who is your favourite athlete? What sport does he/she do?
3 Would you like to be a professional sportsperson? Why?/Why not?

WORD STORE 6E

8 [CD·3.14] [MP3·111] What do you call different sportspeople? Complete WORD STORE 6E with more examples from the lesson. Then listen, check and repeat.

77

6.5 Grammar

Past Simple: questions and negatives
I can make questions and negatives in the Past Simple.

1 ▶ CD•3.15 ▶ MP3•112 In pairs, do the quiz. Then listen and check.

WHAT DO YOU KNOW ABOUT THE ANCIENT OLYMPIC GAMES?

1 Where did the first Olympic Games take place?
  A in Rome   **B** in Greece   C in Egypt

2 Which god did the people honour at the Olympics?
  A Apollo   B Athena   C Zeus

3 What did an athlete win at the ancient Olympics?
  A a gold medal
  B a silver cup
  C a crown of olive leaves

4 Did competitors in the ancient Olympic Games wear clothes?
  A Yes, they did.
  B No, they didn't.
  C They did at first, but not after the year 720BC.

5 Women didn't take part in Olympic events, but in 396BC the Spartan princess Cynisca won the horse chariot race. How did that happen?
  A She dressed up as a man.
  B She was the winner because she owned the horses.
  C She could take part because she was a king's daughter.

CROWN OF OLIVE LEAVES

HORSE CHARIOT

---

2 Read the GRAMMAR FOCUS. Then complete the examples with the verbs in blue in the quiz.

GRAMMAR FOCUS

Past Simple questions and negatives

Questions: **did + subject + infinitive**
- Yes/No questions
  ¹<u>Did</u> competitors in the ancient Olympics Games <u>wear</u> clothes?
  Yes, they **did**./No, they **didn't**.
- Wh- questions
  Where ² _____ the first Olympic Games take place?
  What did an athlete ³ _____ at the ancient Olympics?

Negatives: **didn't + infinitive** (didn't = did not)
Women ⁴ _____ part in Olympic events.

---

3 Complete the questions with the Past Simple form of the verbs in brackets.

Modern Olympics

1 The International Olympic Committee organised the first modern Olympic Games in 1896. Where <u>did they take</u> (they/take) place?

2 _____ (women/take) part in the first modern Olympics?

3 Which sports _____ (women/do) at first?

4 When _____ (the first disabled athlete/win) an Olympic medal?

5 When and where _____ (the first Winter Olympics/take) place?

6 The Olympics _____ (not take) place in 1940 or 1944. Why not?

7 When _____ (the triathlon/become) an Olympic sport?

4 ▶ CD•3.16 ▶ MP3•113 Match the answers (a–g) with the questions (1–7) in Exercise 3. Then listen and check.

a Because of World War II.
b In Athens.
c In 1924 in Chamonix, France.
d In 2000.
e No, they didn't. Women first took part in the Olympics in 1900.
f Tennis, golf, croquet and sailing in 1900, then swimming in 1912.
g In 1904. Fifty-six years before the first Paralympics, George Eyser, a German-American gymnast with one leg, won six medals at the St Louis Olympics.

5 Complete the sentences to make them true for you. Use the affirmative or negative form of the verbs in brackets.

1 I _____ (learn) to swim when I was a little child.
2 I _____ (like) PE lessons in primary school.
3 I _____ (go) skiing last year.
4 I _____ (take) part in a competition last month.
5 I _____ (try) bungee jumping during my last holiday.
6 I _____ (watch) the 2012 London Olympics on TV.

6 Write questions for the sentences in Exercise 5. Then ask and answer in pairs.

A: *When did you learn to swim?*
B: *When I was six years old.*

Grammar Focus page 116

6.6 Speaking

Advice

I can ask for and give advice about a healthy lifestyle.

1 In pairs, look at the photo and answer the questions.
  1 Who are the two people?
  2 Where are they?
  3 What do you think is happening?

2 Who says each phrase, the doctor or the patient?

- How are you feeling today?
- I have a headache every morning.
- I feel terrible.
- I feel dizzy.
- Everything seems fine.
- Tell me a bit about your lifestyle.

3 CD·3.17 MP3·114 Read and listen to the conversation. Check your answers to Exercises 1 and 2. Then find the advice the doctor gives Tony.

Tony: Good morning, Doctor.

Doctor: Good morning, Tony. How are you feeling today?

Tony: I feel terrible, Doctor. I'm always tired, I have a headache every morning, I feel dizzy.

Doctor: OK. Let me examine you … Well, everything seems fine. Tell me a bit about your lifestyle. Are you getting enough sleep?

Tony: Well, I have exams in two weeks' time, so I'm working hard. I stay up late to study and get up early to go to university. At the weekend, I sleep late, but sometimes I stay up all night – there are a lot of parties at the moment.

Doctor: Well, it's important to get eight hours of sleep every night. Tell me, what sports do you do?

Tony: I play Ping-Pong sometimes. And I watch a lot of football on TV!

Doctor: That's not *doing* sports, Tony! You <u>must do</u> some kind of sport regularly. Exercise is very important.

Tony: So <u>should I start</u> jogging in the park?

Doctor: Good idea. <u>It's important to spend</u> some time outdoors. And you <u>should also eat</u> a lot of fresh fruit and vegetables.

Tony: I do, Doctor. I like fruit.

Doctor: OK, that's good. <u>Make sure</u> you <u>eat</u> well … and Tony, you <u>really shouldn't stay up</u> all night. You need your sleep!

Tony: OK, Doctor. Thanks. Goodbye.

4 Complete the SPEAKING FOCUS with the <u>underlined</u> phrases in the conversation.

SPEAKING FOCUS

Asking for advice

What **should I** do/eat/wear?

¹<u>Should</u> I start jogging in the park?

Giving advice

+ You (really) ² _____ do some kind of sport regularly.
  It's ³ _____ to spend some time outdoors.
  Make ⁴ _____ you always do some stretching exercises.
  You ⁵ _____ also eat fresh fruit and vegetables.

− You (really) ⁶ _____ stay up all night.

5 Complete the advice with one or two words in each gap. Tick (✓) the things you should do. Cross (✗) the things you shouldn't do.

1 <u>Make</u> sure you do an hour of exercise every day. ☐
2 You _____ eat five kinds of fruit and vegetables a day. ☐
3 You really _____ train too hard at the beginning. ☐
4 It's _____ to have a healthy diet. ☐
5 You _____ eat so much sugar. It's bad for your teeth. ☐
6 It's _____ to get enough sleep every day. ☐

6 In pairs, role play a conversation. Use the SPEAKING FOCUS to help you.

Student A: You want to prepare for a sporting event. Ask your coach for advice on these points:
• diet • training • rest • equipment

Student B: You are the coach. Give Student A advice on the four points he/she asks about.

6.7 Writing

A description of an event
I can write a simple description of a sports event.

1 Read David's blog and answer the questions.
1 What event did David take part in?
2 Did he complete it?
3 What else did he achieve?

A day to remember

Yesterday I ran the London Marathon!

I dressed up as a mouse to raise money for the charity WellChild.

My group started at 9.45. **At first**, it was impossible to run fast because there were so many runners. A lot of the runners were in weird costumes – one runner wore a Dracula outfit, there was a woman in a wedding dress and lots of runners came in different animal costumes.

After half an hour I had more space around me. I remembered to run at the same speed and to take a drink of water every fifteen minutes. After twelve miles I was really tired. **Suddenly**, I saw my mum and my sister in the crowd near Tower Bridge. **And after that** I felt much better!

Then I just concentrated on running. I reached the finish line in three hours and forty-two minutes. **Finally**, I got my medal. I was really pleased. They told me I raised £1,000!

2 Complete the WRITING FOCUS with the phrases in purple in David's blog.

WRITING FOCUS
A description of an event
- The beginning
  ¹*At first*, it was impossible to run fast.
- The middle
  ²_____ half an hour/a few minutes, I had more space around me.
  ³_____ I felt much better!
  ⁴_____ I just concentrated on running.
  ⁵_____ , I saw my mum.
- The ending
  In the end/⁶_____ , I got my medal.

3 Match the sentence halves.
1 I dressed up as — **d**
2 I wanted to raise money for
3 It was impossible to
4 I couldn't run fast because
5 I remembered
6 Suddenly, I saw a group of my friends and
7 I concentrated on
8 I was really pleased that

a to take regular drinks of water.
b after that I felt much better.
c I completed the race.
d a strawberry.
e my breathing.
f the charity Children in Need.
g find my friends in the crowd.
h my feet were so sore.

4 Choose the correct options.

Yesterday our school played a rugby match against Brompton High School. ¹*At first* / *Then* our team played really well. We scored ten points in the first twenty minutes. ²*After that* / *At first* the Brompton players started trying much harder. In the second half they scored several times. In the last minute our best player, Terry, ran towards the goal line with the ball, but ³*suddenly* / *after a few minutes*, he slipped and fell. We couldn't believe it! ⁴*In the end* / *Suddenly*, Brompton won 16–12.

5 Put the events (a–l) in the correct order (1–12).

a Suddenly, I heard people shout my name. `9`
b My dad drove me to the pool.
c They called my name and I went to the start.
d We had to wait a long time for the prizes.
e My mum gave me a big breakfast.
f I swam faster, passed my friend and won the race. `10`
g I swam for about ten minutes to warm up before the race. `5`
h I was very excited when I woke up because of the swimming competition that day. `1`
i My friend passed me and I knew he was winning.
j I changed into my swimming trunks.
k Finally, at half past three, I received my prize and we all went home.
l At first I swam quite fast, but then I got tired and I slowed down. `7`

6 Read the email from your English friend, Olly, and the list of possible points to include below. Which three are not important to include?

To:
From: Olly

In your last email you told me about a sports event. Did you take part? What was it like? Did you win?

Possible points to include
- what the event was
- where the event was
- what the weather was like
- how many people there were
- how you felt
- if your friends won their races too
- what you did later that day
- what training you're going to do next week

7 Write an email of about 100 words to Olly, answering his questions.

8 Check.
✓ Have you answered all the questions?
✓ Have you included some points from Exercise 6?
✓ Have you used phrases from the WRITING FOCUS?
✓ Have you checked your grammar and spelling?
✓ Have you organised your email well?

81

FOCUS REVIEW 6

VOCABULARY AND GRAMMAR

1 Complete the sentences with the words in the box.

> basketball   ice skating   sailing   skiing
> table tennis   volleyball   yoga   Zumba

1 Natalie plays _____ , _____ and _____ .
2 She often goes _____ , _____ and _____ .
3 She also does _____ and _____ .

2 Complete the sentences with the words in the box.

> feel   get   stay   take   win

1 I want to _____ part in a swimming competition next month.
2 If you want to run a marathon, you must _____ enough sleep!
3 Do you think Chris can _____ a medal?
4 You were ill last week, weren't you? Do you _____ better today?
5 Don't _____ up late the night before the match!

3 Complete the sentences with the Past Simple form of the verbs in brackets.

1 The match _____ (take) place in the largest stadium in the country. A million people _____ (watch) it on television.
2 During the holidays we _____ (spend) a lot of time outdoors. We _____ (play) beach volleyball and other games.
3 Bob _____ (want) to win the tournament, so he _____ (train) hard every day.
4 I _____ (feel) dizzy, so I _____ (go) to see the doctor.
5 The skier _____ (fall) and _____ (break) her leg.

4 Complete the conversation with the Past Simple form of the verbs in brackets.

Mia: Hi, Ben. How ¹_____ (the match/be)?

Ben: We ²_____ (win) 3–1. It's a pity you ³_____ (not see) it!

Mia: So ⁴_____ (you/score) any of the goals?

Ben: Yes, ⁵_____ ! In the fifteenth minute!

Mia: Congratulations! ⁶_____ (George/play)?

Ben: No, ⁷_____ . He's ill.

Mia: How about Tom?

Ben: He ⁸_____ (play) really well, but he ⁹_____ (not score).

Mia: Too bad. So, ¹⁰_____ (the coach/be) happy?

Ben: Yes, ¹¹_____ ! He ¹²_____ (say) we ¹³_____ (be) a fantastic team!

LANGUAGE IN USE

5 Choose the correct answer, A, B or C.

1 My brother ___ three different team sports.
  A makes
  B takes
  C does
2 Mel wants to take ___ in a bicycle race in the summer.
  A break
  B part
  C place
3 Christine ___ stand water sports.
  A can't
  B doesn't
  C isn't
4 Dave started playing football ___ the age of five years and six months.
  A in
  B on
  C at
5 ___ you do a lot of sports during your last holidays?
  A Are
  B Do
  C Did

6 Choose the option, A, B or C, which has a similar meaning to the underlined words.

1 I really like skiing.
  A am into
  B believe in
  C support
2 Kevin returned without a medal.
  A doesn't win
  B didn't win
  C don't win
3 It's a good idea to do a sport regularly.
  A You should
  B You can
  C You have to
4 Jack took part in the marathon, but he didn't complete it.
  A run
  B win
  C finish
5 I've got a really great swimming instructor.
  A swimmer
  B swimming coach
  C swimming champion

82

READING

7 Read the email and the advert below. Then complete Kenny's notes.

From: Jess
To: Kenny

It's Dave's swimming competition on Saturday. Do you want to go? His race is in the morning. We can get the train – it's only twenty minutes. I'll be in the station café at 9.30. And bring some sandwiches. We can have lunch in the park after the competition! See you on Saturday.

Swimming competition
Stokewood Pool
10.30–5.30 Saturday, 5 February

Tickets: Morning or afternoon session: **£2.50**
All day: **£5.00**

Swimming competition
place: Stokewood Pool
date: ¹ _____
travel by: ² _____
meeting place: ³ _____
ticket price: ⁴ _____
take: ⁵ _____

LISTENING

8 CD·3.18 MP3·115 Listen to a conversation and complete the information.
1 David's new sport: _____
2 An expensive sport: _____
3 David wants a sport that is: _____
4 Length of a sailing course: _____
5 Time of dancing lessons: _____

SPEAKING

9 In pairs, role play a conversation. Student A, you want to do a new sport. Student B, recommend a sport.

STUDENT A	STUDENT B
recommend/new sport?	
	recommend a sport
why?	
	say why
equipment?	
	give advice on equipment
training?	
	give advice on training

WRITING

10 Read the email from your English friend, Cathy. Then write a reply of about 100 words, answering Cathy's questions.

I hear you spent a day at the Olympics last month! Wow! What did you see? What was it like? Did anything interesting happen? Tell me all about it!

7 TRAVEL

The first step is the hardest.

A PROVERB

UNIT LANGUAGE AND SKILLS

Vocabulary:
- *Show what you know* – forms of transport and travel verbs
- types of holiday and transport
- collocations – journeys and holidays
- accommodation

Grammar:
- Present Prefect with *ever/never*
- Present Perfect and Past Simple
- Present Perfect with *just/yet/already*

Listening:
- recordings in various places related to travelling
- multiple choice

Reading:
- an article about a fundraising adventure
- multiple choice

Speaking:
- asking for and giving directions

Writing:
- an email of enquiry

FOCUS EXTRA
- Grammar Focus pages 117–118
- WORD STORE booklet pages 14–15
- Workbook pages 80–91 or MyEnglishLab

84

7.1 Vocabulary

Holiday and transport • Accommodation • Collocations

I can talk about different kinds of holidays and transport.

SHOW WHAT YOU KNOW

1 In pairs, put the words in the box under the appropriate heading.

> ~~bike~~   boat   bus   car   coach   cycle   drive   ferry   fly
> motorbike   plane   sail   ship   ride   train   tram
> underground

Forms of transport	bike
Travel verbs	

HOME   CONTACT US   TYPE OF HOLIDAYS

HARVEY'S HOLIDAYS

Use the search bar to find your perfect holiday.
Book today for fantastic savings!
For more information, to <u>book a flight</u> or to <u>book a holiday</u>, click HERE .

Our top offers:

Beach holidays ★★★

If you want **a beach holiday**, we can offer you a choice of some of the most beautiful beaches
5 in the world. Why not experience the soft white sand and clear water of St Vincent in the Caribbean? The beaches are perfect,
10 the water is warm and you can relax at your luxury hotel.

Tours ★★★

Do you fancy **a tour** of some great cities? Try
15 our Essential Europe Tour! It includes two nights in Rome, Venice, Lucerne, Paris and London. You travel by **plane** and by
20 **coach** and we <u>make all the arrangements</u> for you. You stay in three-star hotels, eat in fantastic restaurants and <u>visit</u> all
25 the top tourist sights and <u>museums</u> with an experienced guide.

2 Read the website. On which holiday can you do these things?
   1 visit local towns – <u>activity holidays</u>
   2 eat at good restaurants – _____
   3 travel on two continents – _____
   4 travel round by car – _____
   5 relax by the sea – _____
   6 go to museums – _____

Activity holidays ★★★

If you prefer to be active when you are on holiday, then try
30 **an activity holiday**. This fantastic holiday offers you a chance to go mountain biking, hiking, climbing and kayaking in Sardinia, Italy. You stay in
35 a friendly guesthouse and eat fresh local food. You can also <u>book excursions</u> into nearby towns to <u>visit the sights</u> and <u>local markets</u>.

Backpacking holidays ★★★

40 If you prefer to stay in youth hostels or bed and breakfasts (B & Bs) on **a backpacking holiday**, we can plan your trip and <u>book all your transport</u>
45 and <u>accommodation</u>. With an InterRail card, you can travel cheaply by **train** everywhere in Europe. In America, you can go by **bus**, by plane or by train.
50 We can help you find the best solution for your budget.

Camping holidays ★★★

Go on **a camping holiday** in Denmark! You can travel round the country by **car** and
55 stay at fantastic campsites for great prices. We can book your car and campsites, provide tents, sleeping bags and cooking equipment. You
60 only need to bring some warm clothes as nights can be cold!

Go to WORD STORE 7 page 15.

WORD STORE 7A

3 CD·3.19 MP3·116 Complete WORD STORE 7A with the words in red in the website. Then listen, check and repeat.

4 In pairs, discuss which type of holiday is best for these people.
   1 Annie loves culture and good food.
   2 Peter hasn't got much money, but he wants to see the sights in Europe.
   3 James loves the outdoors, but he is tired and just wants to relax.
   4 Sue and Jane want to be independent. They have a free week and want to escape to the countryside.
   5 Sam is a great hiker and wants to learn how to rock climb.

The best type of holiday for Annie is …

5 What is the best form of transport for these journeys? Why?
   1 from home to school
   2 from home to the station
   3 on a skiing holiday to the mountains
   4 on a camping holiday
   5 on a trip abroad

WORD STORE 7B

6 CD·3.20 MP3·117 Complete WORD STORE 7B with the correct form of the <u>underlined</u> phrases in the website. Then listen, check and repeat.

WORD STORE 7C

7 CD·3.21 MP3·118 Complete WORD STORE 7C with the types of accommodation in the website. Then listen, check and repeat.

8 CD·3.22 MP3·119 Listen to four people and complete the table.

Name	Type of holiday	Who with?	Travelled by?	Where?
Mike		*Sam*		
Sally				*Europe*
Dominic			*plane*	
Magda	*beach holiday*			

9 Discuss the questions in pairs.
   1 What's your favourite type of holiday? Why?
   2 What kinds of holiday don't you like? Why?
   3 Do you prefer to stay at a youth hostel or a hotel? Why?
   4 Do you like staying at a campsite? Why?/Why not?
   5 In your family, who usually books your tickets and accommodation?

85

7.2 Grammar

Present Perfect with ever/never

I can talk about actions that happened some time in the past.

1 CD•3.23 MP3•120 Richard and Suzy are talking about where to go on holiday. Read and listen to the first part of their conversation. Are the statements true (T) or false (F)?

S: This holiday in Australia sounds fantastic! I'd love to go. You can go to a desert, a beach and a rainforest. You can even ride a camel. I bet you **haven't ridden** a camel.

R: Actually, I **have ridden** a camel and I**'ve ridden** an elephant too.

S: Really? When did you do that?

R: I rode a camel last year in the Sinai Desert when I was in Egypt. It was weird. And I rode an elephant in Thailand!

S: Wow! I've never done anything like that. **Have** you **ever walked** in a rainforest?

R: No, I haven't. I'd love to do that.

1 They are talking about a holiday in Europe. [F]
2 Suzy wants to go to Australia. [ ]
3 You can do lots of different activities on the holiday. [ ]
4 Richard rode an elephant in Egypt. [ ]

2 Read GRAMMAR FOCUS 1. Then complete the examples with the words in blue in the conversation.

GRAMMAR FOCUS 1

Present Perfect

Form: *have/has* + Past participle

+ I/You/We/They ¹*have ridden* a camel.
  He/She/It *has ridden* an elephant.

− I/You/We/They ²_____ a camel.
  He/She/It *hasn't done* anything like that.

? ³_____ I/you/we/they ever _____ in a rainforest?
  Yes, I/you/we/they *have.*/No, I/you/we/they *haven't.*
  Has he/she/it ever *been* in a desert?
  Yes, he/she/it *has.*/No, he/she/it *hasn't.*

Note:
- You often use short forms.
  I ⁴_____ ridden an elephant.
  She *hasn't* ridden an elephant.
- You often use **ever** (in questions) and **never** (in negatives).
  Have you **ever** walked in a rainforest?
  She's **never** done anything like that.

3 Complete the table.

	Infinitive	Past Simple	Past participle
Regular	¹walk		
	²chat		
	³try		
Irregular	⁴be		been
	⁵have		had
	⁶do		
	⁷go		gone/been
	⁸ride		

REMEMBER THIS

*John has **gone** to Peru.* = He is there now.
*John has **been** to Peru.* = He went there and came back.
You usually use **been** with activities.
*Have you ever **been** kayaking?* (NOT ~~gone~~)
*She's never **been** sailing.* (NOT ~~gone~~)

4 CD•3.24 MP3•121 Complete the second part of the conversation with the Present Perfect form of the verbs in brackets. Then listen and check.

S: I ¹*'ve never been* (never/be) up in a hot-air balloon, but my sister Kate ²_____ (do) it a lot. She says it's great fun.

R: ³_____ (you/ever/try) hang-gliding?

S: No, I ⁴_____ . I'm too scared. Have you?

R: No, I ⁵_____ . I don't like heights.

S: Really?

R: ⁶_____ (Kate/ever/go) hang-gliding?

S: No, she ⁷_____ . And she ⁸_____ (never/ride) a camel either. I'm sure she'd love to come too.

R: Good idea!

5 Read GRAMMAR FOCUS 2. Then complete it with *Present Perfect* or *Past Simple*.

GRAMMAR FOCUS 2

Present Perfect and Past Simple

- You use the ¹_____ to talk about finished actions in time up to now. You never say when they happened.
- If you know when something happened, use the ²_____ .

Have you ever ridden a camel?
Yes, I rode a camel last year.

6 Write questions with *Have you ever ...?* and the phrases in the box. Then, in pairs, ask and answer the questions following the example.

> break a leg/an arm   go to a concert
> try a new sport   visit a foreign country
> win a competition   work for money

A: *Have you ever broken a leg?*
B: *Yes, I have.*
A: *When did you break your leg?*
B: *I broke it last year when I was on holiday.*

Grammar Focus page 117

86

7.3 Listening

Multiple choice

I can identify detail in short travel conversations.

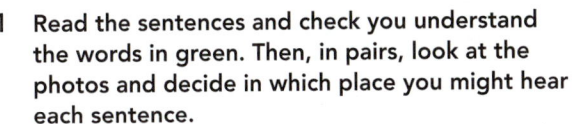

B — train station

A — travel agency

C — airport check-in desk

D — hotel reception desk

1 Read the sentences and check you understand the words in green. Then, in pairs, look at the photos and decide in which place you might hear each sentence.

1 Have you got any **luggage**?
2 Can I have a look at some **brochures**?
3 Which **platform** does the 8.45 train to London leave from?
4 Can I see your **passport**, please?
5 I'd like to **check in**, please.
6 Is the **flight** on time?
7 **Passengers** must wait in the waiting room.
8 I can't find my **ticket**.
9 Do you have a **booking**?

2 **CD·3.25 MP3·122** Listen to four recordings. Where does each of them take place? Match the recordings (1–4) with the photos (A–D).

1 ☐ 2 ☐ 3 ☐ 4 ☐

EXAM FOCUS | Multiple choice

3 **CD·3.25 MP3·122** Listen again and choose the correct answer, A, B, or C.

1 Where is the passenger travelling to?
   A Frankfurt
   B Rome
   C Madrid

2 Which platform is the train arriving on?
   A 3
   B 4
   C 11

3 Where does the woman want to go?
   A Barcelona
   B Basque Country
   C She is not sure.

4 How many nights has the man booked for?
   A one
   B two
   C three

4 In pairs, think about your dream holiday. Decide:
   • where to go and how to travel.
   • what bookings to make.
   • what information you need.
   • what to take.

PRONUNCIATION FOCUS

5 **CD·3.26 MP3·123** In English the letter o is pronounced in different ways. Listen and repeat.

/əʊ/	/ɒ/	/ʌ/	/ɔː/
hotel	off	come	or

6 **CD·3.27 MP3·124** Listen and put the words in the correct column in the table in Exercise 5.

brochure   clock   door   holiday   home   hostel
hot   Monday   money   month   morning   platform
photo   short   some

7 **CD·3.28 MP3·125** Listen, check and repeat.

WORD STORE 7D

8 **CD·3.29 MP3·126** Complete WORD STORE 7D with the words in green in Exercise 1. Then listen and check.

87

7.4 Reading

Multiple choice

I can understand a magazine article about a fundraising adventure.

1 In pairs, look at the photos and the title of the article. What do you think it is about?

2 Read the introduction and check your answer to Exercise 1. Then answer the questions.
   1 Why are Michiel and Joost taking this trip?
   2 How many kilometres is their journey?
   3 How long do they expect their trip to take?
   4 How many countries have they visited so far?

3 Read the article and match headings 1–5 with paragraphs A–E.
   1 Our bikes
   2 The most amazing things on the trip
   3 The lessons we have learnt
   4 Our reasons for the trip
   5 The worst things on the trip

EXAM FOCUS | Multiple choice

4 Read the text again and choose the correct answer, A, B or C.
   1 Michiel and Joost
     A have been to the Antarctic.
     B have been to the Arctic.
     C have reached Ushuaia.
   2 One of the reasons for their trip is
     A to cycle from the Arctic to the Antarctic.
     B to visit towns and villages in South America.
     C to tell the world about the problems of getting clean water.
   3 During the trip
     A they have stayed in people's homes.
     B they have visited many different water projects.
     C they appeared on television in Guatemala.
   4 Before the trip started,
     A Michiel had a problem with his bike.
     B they didn't practise at all.
     C they practised hard.
   5 Their bikes are good
     A because they are comfortable to ride.
     B but they feel all the bumps in the road.
     C because the frame is metal.
   6 They say that travelling by bike is
     A much slower than going by car.
     B not as interesting as going by coach.
     C a good way to meet people.

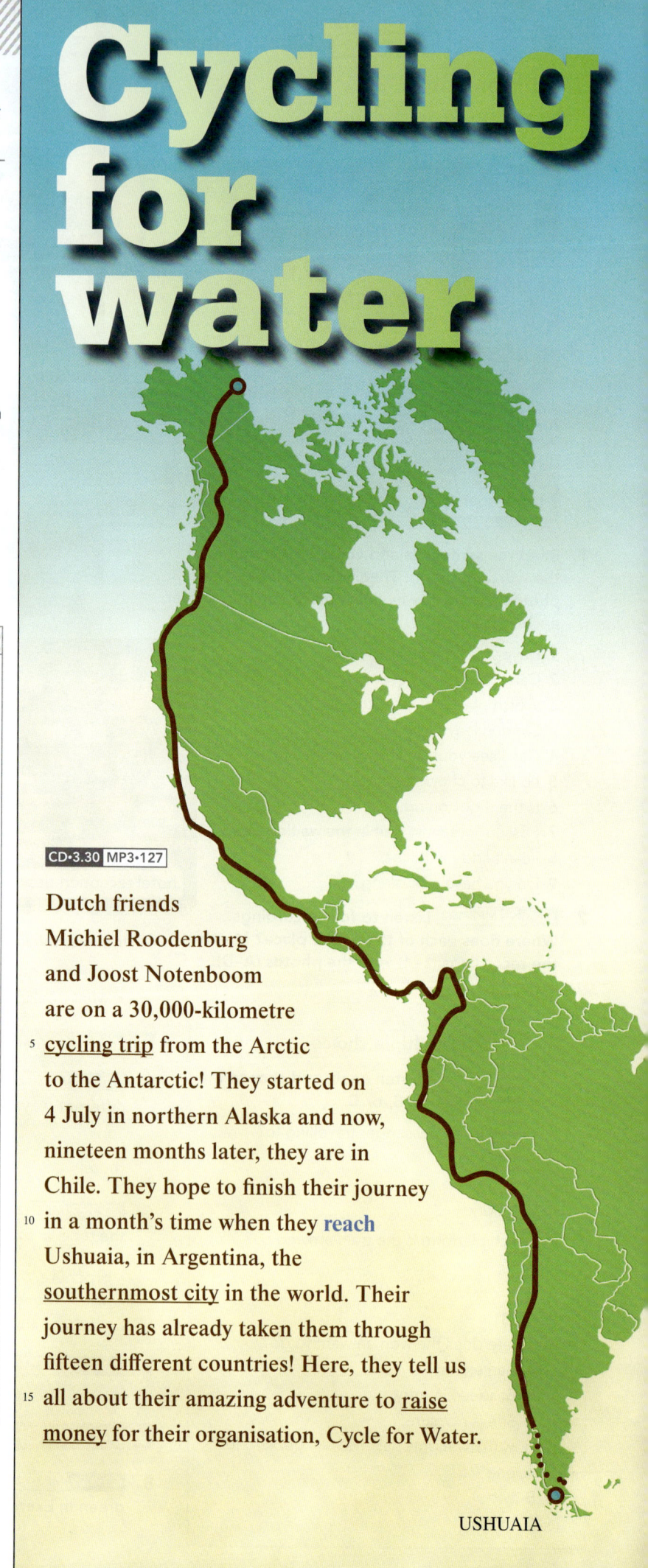

Cycling for water

CD·3.30 MP3·127

Dutch friends Michiel Roodenburg and Joost Notenboom are on a 30,000-kilometre cycling trip from the Arctic to the Antarctic! They started on 4 July in northern Alaska and now, nineteen months later, they are in Chile. They hope to finish their journey in a month's time when they reach Ushuaia, in Argentina, the southernmost city in the world. Their journey has already taken them through fifteen different countries! Here, they tell us all about their amazing adventure to raise money for their organisation, Cycle for Water.

USHUAIA

88

A [4]
There's a world water crisis and we want people to know about it. We also want to raise money for our organisation, Cycle for Water. It provides clean, safe water for towns and villages in Central and South America. We've carried a bottle of water from the Arctic all the way! At the end of the trip, we plan to pour it into the Antarctic.

B ☐
We've met so many wonderful people! People have invited us to stay in their homes, given us food, laughed with us and shared our story. When we were in San Francisco, CNN asked us to go on their news show – that was really cool too. We also went to visit one of our water projects in San Juan La Laguna in Guatemala. It was fantastic to see the difference it makes to people's lives.

C ☐
The beginning of the trip was really tough because we didn't train before we started and it was hard work pulling a heavy trailer behind our bikes. There were also millions of mosquitoes, dogs chased us and Michiel's bike broke. Luckily, after a few weeks things got much better!

D ☐
We've got bamboo bikes. The frame is bamboo, not metal. It's very strong and flexible so you don't feel the bumps in the road. They're really comfortable bikes to ride and they're environmentally friendly.

E ☐
When you travel by bike, you meet people more quickly than you do when you are in a car or a coach. It is the best way to experience a place and you don't harm the environment in any way. It's a great way to learn about how people live and to learn about the world.

---

5 Match the words in the box with the pictures.

[bumps   frame   mosquito   pour   trailer]

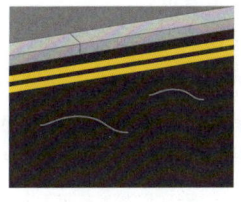

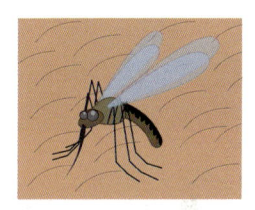

1 _____   2 _____
3 _____   4 _____
5 _____

6 Complete the sentences with the correct form of the words and phrases in blue in the article.

1 Modern cars have a very light *frame*, so they are more economical.
2 Please drive slowly because there are a lot of _____ in the road.
3 If you want to _____ London, take a bus, not the underground.
4 Our cycling trip was really _____ – we had to cycle for eight hours a day!
5 Most plastics are _____ and so they don't break easily.
6 We _____ the end of the journey after 605 days on the road.
7 Electric cars are the most _____ cars.
8 They stole our money, but they didn't _____ us.

7 Discuss the questions in pairs.

1 Would you like to go on a trip like Michiel and Joost's? Why?/Why not?
2 What kind of organisation would you like to raise money for? Why?

WORD STORE 7E

8 CD·3.31 MP3·128 Complete WORD STORE 7E. Look at the underlined phrases in the article and match 1–6 with a–f to make collocations. Then listen, check and repeat.

7.5 Grammar

Present Perfect with just/already/yet

I can use the Present Perfect with just, already and yet.

1 Discuss the questions in pairs.
1 How many countries have you visited?
2 Which countries would you like to visit? Why?

2 In pairs, look at the photo, read the text and match the questions with the answers. What did you find most surprising?

1 Who is Charles Veley? — e
2 When did he start travelling? Why?
3 How many countries has he visited?
4 Where is he now? When did he arrive there?
5 Has he been to Scott Island yet?

a He **has already been** to 805 countries and he's not stopping! The United Nations recognises only 193 countries. Charles visited all of these and then started travelling to islands, provinces and protectorates. He calls these countries too.

b No, he **hasn't been** there **yet**! Only six people have ever been there! He'd like to visit the tiny island near the Antarctic some time.

c He started travelling in 2000 – he decided to visit all the countries in the world.

d He **has just arrived** in Heligoland, small islands near Germany. He arrived there only a few hours ago.

e He is the world's most-travelled person – he's travelled to more countries than anyone else in the world!

3 Read the GRAMMAR FOCUS. Then complete the examples with the words in blue in the text.

GRAMMAR FOCUS

Present Perfect with just/already/yet

- You use **just** to talk about things that happened a very short time ago.
  He ¹<u>has</u> just <u>arrived</u> in Heligoland.
- You use **already** in affirmative sentences for things that happened earlier than expected.
  He ²_____ already _____ to 805 countries.
- You use (**not**) **yet** in questions and negative sentences for things that haven't happened but probably will happen. **Yet** goes at the end of the sentence.
  ³_____ he _____ to Scott Island **yet**?
  No, he ⁴_____ there **yet**.

4 Complete the text with the correct form of the verbs in brackets. Then choose the correct word, *just, already* or *yet*.

The Hotel in the Heavens

Would you like to go on a unique holiday? Some tourists ¹<u>have</u> yet / (already) <u>travelled</u> (travel) into space, but nobody ² _____ (stay) in a space hotel *just / yet*. That could all change soon! Russian engineers ³_____ already / yet _____ (start) to build the first space hotel. Work ⁴_____ only *just / already* _____ (begin), but a few people ⁵_____ already/yet _____ (try) to book a room! The Hotel in the Heavens has four rooms for up to seven guests. When does it open? The organisers ⁶_____ (not say) *just / yet*.

5 Use the prompts to write questions. Then read the text in Exercise 4 again and answer the questions.

1 any tourists / go / into space / yet?
Have any tourists been into space yet?
Yes, they have.
2 anybody / stay / in a space hotel / yet?
3 the Russian engineers / start / to build the hotel / yet?
4 anybody / try / to book a room / yet?
5 the organisers / say / when the hotel will open / yet?

6 Mike is getting ready for a trip. Look at his list and write questions. Then answer them.

To do:
- pack case ✗
- buy camera ✓
- book room ✗
- read guidebook ✓
- get new passport ✗

Has Mike packed his case yet?
No, he hasn't.

7 Complete the sentences to make them true for you.

1 I've just …
2 I've already …
3 I haven't … yet.

I've just finished reading an article about travelling.

Grammar Focus page 118

7.6 Speaking

Asking for and giving directions

I can ask for and give simple directions to a place.

1 In pairs, match sentences 1–6 with places A–F on the map.

1 Bookworms Bookshop is in Park Street, **between** the bank and Jolly Café. [B]
2 The Ritzy Theatre is **on the corner** of King's Road and High Street. [ ]
3 The town hall is in Shakespeare's Road, **opposite** the park. [ ]
4 The stadium is **in** the park. [ ]
5 The sports centre is in Park Street, **next to** the bank. [ ]
6 The chemist's is on the corner of Park Street and High Street, opposite the post office. [ ]

2 CD•3.32 MP3•129 Listen to the first part of a conversation between Chloe and Jeff. What's the problem?

a They've already seen the film.
b Chloe doesn't know about the new cinema.
c They don't know what's on.

3 CD•3.33 MP3•130 Read the SPEAKING FOCUS and listen to the second part of the conversation. Underline the phrases you hear.

SPEAKING FOCUS

Asking for directions

Excuse me, can you tell me the way to …?
How do I get to …?
Excuse me, where's the (post office)?

Giving directions

Go out of … and turn left/right.
Turn left/right into (High Street).
Walk along the (road) past the (post office) on your left/right.
Take/It's the first/second/third turning on the left/right.
Go straight on.
Go across the road.
The (museum) is opposite the (shop).
The (theatre) is on the left/right.
It's between the (station) and the (hotel).
It's next to/opposite the (station).
It's next door.
It's on the corner of (Shakespeare's Road) and (King's Road).

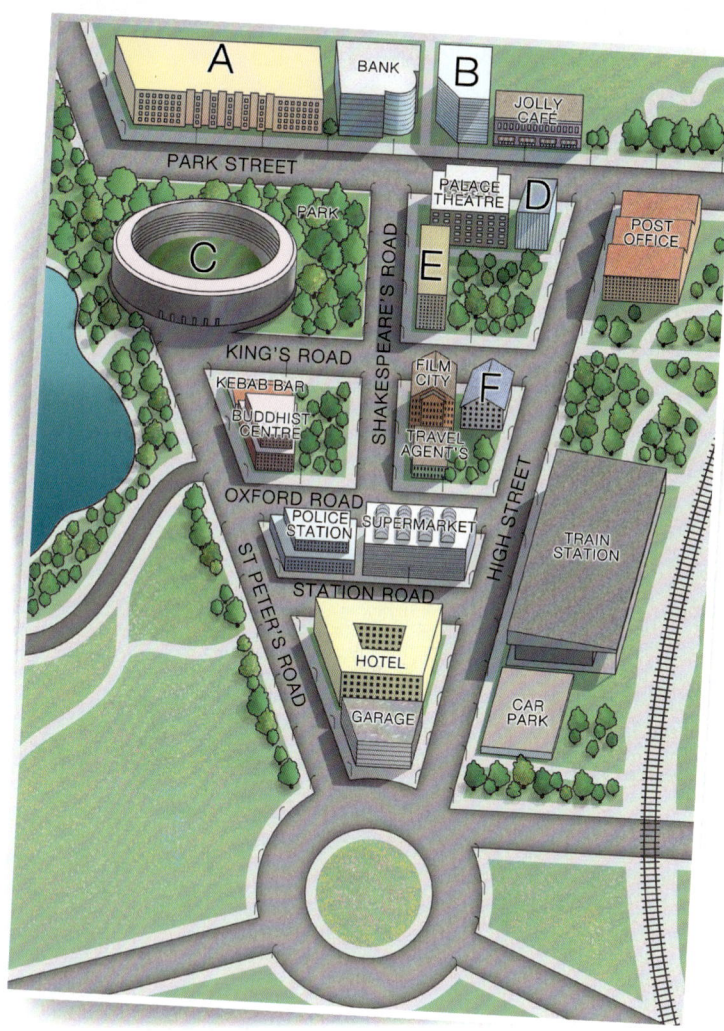

4 CD•3.34 MP3•131 Look at the map and complete the conversation with phrases from the SPEAKING FOCUS. Then listen and check.

Joanne: Excuse me, can you tell me the ¹*way* to the stadium?
Man: Sure. It's in the park – not far from here. Go out of the station and ²_____ right. Take the first ³_____ on the left into Oxford Road. Then turn ⁴_____ into Shakespeare's Road. Walk ⁵_____ the road ⁶_____ the travel agent's ⁷_____ your right. Go ⁸_____ King's Road and the park is on your ⁹_____ .

5 In pairs, look at the map. Decide where you are and where you want to go to. Take turns to ask for and give directions.

7.7 Writing

An email of enquiry
I can write a formal email of enquiry.

1 Read Laura's email and answer the questions.
   1 What did Laura leave in the hotel?
   2 What does she want the hotel to do?

2 Read the email again. Match the parts of the email (A–F) with the descriptions (1–6).
   1 saying what you want to happen — D
   2 conclusion
   3 greeting
   4 ending the email
   5 giving your contact details
   6 explaining why you are writing

To: Hotel reception
Subject: Lost watch

[A] Dear Sir or Madam,

[B] I was a guest at the hotel on 21 July in room 219 and I believe that I left my watch on the table next to the bed. I am writing to enquire if anyone has found it. It is a gold watch with a black leather strap.

[C] Please could you confirm by replying to this email or phoning me on my mobile number: 07841 223679. [D] I hope you are able to send the watch to me by courier when you find it. I would be happy to pay for the postage.

[E] I look forward to hearing from you. Thank you for your help with this matter.

[F] Yours faithfully,
Laura Dryden

---

3 Compete the WRITING FOCUS with the words in purple in the email.

WRITING FOCUS
A formal email

- **Starting a formal email**
  ¹ Dear Sir or Madam, /Dear (Mrs Jackson/Mr Smith),

- **Saying why you are writing**
  I am writing
  - to ² _____ if anyone has found …
  - to enquire about your special offers.
  - in response to your newspaper advert.

- **Saying what you want**
  Please ³ _____ you …?/I ⁴ _____ you are able to …
  Would it be possible to …?/I ⁵ _____ be happy to …

- **Giving contact details**
  Please reply to this email.
  Email me at …/My email is …
  My (mobile) phone number is …
  Please phone me ⁶ _____ my mobile.

- **Conclusion**
  I look forward to hearing from you.
  Thank you for your help with this matter.

- **Ending a formal email**
  ⁷ _____ , (if you began *Dear Sir or Madam,*)
  Yours sincerely, (if you began *Dear* + name)

4 Match the informal enquiries (1–5) with the more formal ones (a–e).
   1 Send me my iPod. — c
   2 Can I book a room?
   3 Ask all the staff.
   4 Can you send my mobile phone to me?
   5 Give me your website address.

   a Would it be possible to book a room?
   b I hope you are able to send my mobile phone to me.
   c Please could you send me my iPod?
   d Would it be possible to give me your website address?
   e Could you please ask all the staff?

5 Put the words in the correct order to make formal enquiries.

1 you / could / please / check?
   Please could you check?
2 possible / would / to send / it / be / some more information / me?
3 hope / able / I / are / you / email / to / me
4 you / could / to me / post / please / it?
5 to organise a guide / it / would / possible / be?

6 Choose the correct answer, A, B or C.

1 Thank you for ___ me.
   A help   B your helping   C your help
2 I am writing ___ about the concert tickets.
   A enquire   B for enquiring   C to enquire
3 Please phone me ___ 2099678425.
   A in   B on   C at
4 Would it ___ possible to contact me soon?
   A be   B to be   C for being
5 Thank you for your letter ___ to my request.
   A in response   B for responding   C respond
6 Please reply ___ this email.
   A at   B for   C to
7 I look forward ___ from you.
   A hearing   B for hear   C to hearing
8 I ___ be happy to help you.
   A am   B would   C have

7 You are writing to a travel agent. Write polite sentences about these things. Try to use different polite expressions for each sentence.

1 You are contacting this travel agent because a friend recommended him.
2 You want to enquire about holidays in Egypt.
3 You want to make a reservation at a five star hotel.
4 You want some information about excursions.
5 You want to pay extra for first class on the plane.
6 You want the travel agent to reply to your email.

8 You left your MP3 player in a restaurant. Write an email of enquiry of 80–130 words to the manager. Include the information below.

- Say when you were there and which table you sat at.
- Describe your MP3 player.
- Ask the manager if they have found it.
- Give your contact details.
- Ask the manager to send you the MP3 player.

9 Check.
✓ Have you written a polite, formal email?
✓ Have you included all the points in the question?
✓ Have you used phrases from the WRITING FOCUS?
✓ Have you organised your email well?
✓ Have you checked spelling and punctuation?

FOCUS REVIEW 7

VOCABULARY AND GRAMMAR

1 Complete the sentences with the words in the box. There are two extra words.

> arrive book drive fly go make ride stay

1 I want to _____ a booking.
2 I must remember to _____ my flight to Italy.
3 We can _____ climbing in the mountains.
4 What time does the train _____ at the station?
5 Why don't you _____ in a hotel?
6 Let's _____ from Paris to London in my car.

2 Complete the sentences with the correct form of the words in capitals.

1 I'd like to go on an _____ holiday and try some new sports. **ACTIVE**
2 Can you make a _____ at the hotel? **RESERVE**
3 I've never been _____ . Have you? **KAYAK**
4 The price doesn't include _____ . **ACCOMMODATE**
5 Who makes the holiday _____ in your family? **ARRANGE**
6 I'm going on a _____ holiday with my friends. **BACKPACK**

3 Use the prompts to write sentences.

1 Jane / never / ride / an elephant
2 you / ever / try / hang-gliding?
3 we / not be / up in a hot-air balloon
4 Kathy / already / visit / over twenty countries
5 they / not ride / a camel / yet
6 Sam / ever / break / his arm?

4 Complete the sentences with the Present Perfect or Past Simple form of the verbs in brackets.

1 a I _____ (never/be) so happy in my life.
  b We _____ (not be) happy when we heard the news.
2 a Sara _____ (visit) Madrid last week.
  b Steve _____ (already/visit) Madrid.
3 a John _____ (arrive) two hours ago.
  b Katie _____ (just/arrive).
4 a Mark _____ (not ride) an elephant yet.
  b Sam _____ (ride) an elephant for the first time yesterday.
5 a _____ (Sue/ever/break) her leg?
  b When _____ (Matt/break) his arm?

LANGUAGE IN USE

5 Choose the correct answer, A, B or C.

1 A: Excuse me, where's the post office?
   B: It's not far. ____ left into Cranmer Road and it's on the right.
   A Take   B Turn   C Get
2 A: How did you get from Britain to France?
   B: We went on a ____ . It took six hours.
   A ferry   B tram   C tube
3 A: We went to Germany ____ .
   B: Oh, did you enjoy it?
   A yet   B already   C last year
4 A: What was the best part of your holiday in Madrid?
   B: One day we went on ____ to visit Toledo. It's about seventy kilometres from Madrid.
   A an adventure   B an excursion   C foot
5 A: What's your favourite kind of holiday?
   B: ____ , because I love relaxing by the sea.
   A An adventure holiday   C A cycling trip
   B A beach holiday

6 Read the text and choose the correct answer, A, B or C.

Hi Chris!
I'm staying at a ¹____ in France with some friends. I've ²____ been on holiday with friends before and I'm really enjoying it.

We travelled ³____ plane and then got a bus and we arrived here yesterday. There was a problem checking in because I couldn't find my passport (you know me – I'm always losing things 😊). Finally, I found it at the bottom of my ⁴____ .

Last night we ate in a restaurant. We ⁵____ cooked any meals yet, but I'm cooking pasta tonight! Today we ⁶____ sailing at a local beach. It was fantastic!
Hope you are having a great holiday too. 😊 😊
Love,
Simon

1 A tent   B camping   C campsite
2 A ever   B never   C already
3 A in   B on   C by
4 A case   B platform   C ticket
5 A haven't   B hasn't   C didn't
6 A played   B went   C done

READING

7 Read the text and choose the correct answer, A, B or C.

HITCHBOT

Have you ever seen a hitchhiker standing by the side of a road? Hitchhiking is popular with young people because it doesn't cost anything – drivers stop and take you on all or part of your journey. Of course, it's not like a bus or train because it can take a long time, but hitchhikers say they meet some amazing people. Now drivers in Canada might see an unusual hitchhiker – Hitchbot, a hitchhiking robot. One of its inventors, David Harris Smith, has hitched across Canada three times and says he had some of the best experiences of his life. Smith and a colleague, Frauke Zeller, have built Hitchbot because they wanted to see if people would stop and give the robot a lift and talk to it. The robot can chat about things it has learnt, about its inventors and about its journey. It has access to Wikipedia and it runs on solar power. You might think it's a joke, but Smith and Zeller's experiment has a serious point – can robots and people get on together?

Hitchbot's journey started in Nova Scotia in July. It has already completed a third of its 6,000 mile journey to Victoria. It's now near Lake Superior. More than 57,000 people are following its journey on Facebook and Twitter and travellers have posted lots of photos on the website. Hitchbot has also done some shopping, eaten motor oil and had fun with travellers. Nobody knows when it will finish its journey – Zeller and Smith want Hitchbot to get as many rides as possible. It hasn't been in a self-driving car yet, but anything is possible!

1 Hitchhiking isn't like travelling by bus or train because it's
 A free.
 B quicker.
 C boring.
2 When Smith hitchhiked, he
 A didn't have a good time.
 B had some incredible experiences.
 C took a long time to travel across Canada.
3 Hitchbot
 A can't talk about many things.
 B can only describe its inventors.
 C can talk about many different things.
4 Hitchbot
 A has nearly completed its journey.
 B has completed about 2,000 miles.
 C has already travelled 57,000 miles.
5 Hitchbot hasn't
 A been to any shops.
 B posted photos on the website.
 C had fun.

LISTENING

8 CD•3.35 MP3•132 Listen to four conversations and choose the correct answer, A, B or C.

1 Where does the conversation take place? 
2 Where is the man sleeping tomorrow night? 
3 Which cases has the woman got? 
4 How much does the passenger's new ticket cost?
 A £15.00 B £15.50 C £50.00

SPEAKING

9 In pairs, look at the map. Student A, you want to go to the market. Student B, give directions to Student A.

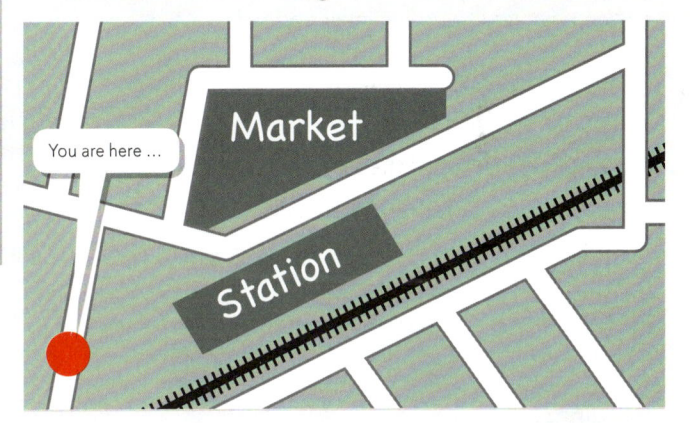

WRITING

10 Read the email and write a reply of about 100 words to Mr Soames.

From: Mr Soames, Southern Trains

Thank you for your email about your lost suitcase. Please send me some more information. When did you travel and what train were you on? Please describe your suitcase. What was in it? Send me your contact details, including your address and phone number.

8 NATURE

Colours are the smiles of nature.

LEIGH HUNT (1784–1859),
AN ENGLISH POET

UNIT LANGUAGE AND SKILLS

Vocabulary:
- Show what you know – animals and plants
- landscape
- wildlife
- environmental problems

Grammar:
- future with *will*
- *be going to*

Listening:
- a radio weather forecast
- matching

Reading:
- three short texts related to nature
- right/wrong/doesn't say

Speaking:
- agreeing and disagreeing

Writing:
- expressing an opinion and presenting arguments

FOCUS EXTRA

- Grammar Focus page 119
- WORD STORE booklet pages 16–17
- Workbook pages 92–103 or MyEnglishLab

8.1 Vocabulary

Landscape • Wildlife • Environmental problems

I can talk about wildlife and the countryside.

SHOW WHAT YOU KNOW

1 Put the words in the box under the appropriate heading.

[~~bush~~   crocodile   fish   flower
  grass   monkey   penguin   tree]

Animal	Plant
	bush

2 In pairs, add as many other words to the table as you can in sixty seconds.

4 WONDERS OF NATURE

ASIA
The Valley of Flowers

The Valley of Flowers lies about 4,000 metres above sea level in the Himalayas. You have to walk seventeen kilometres to get there. The **valley** is famous for its **mountain**
5 flowers. It changes colour almost every day, when different kinds of plants begin to flower. This lovely spot is home to many rare animals – bears, snow leopards and different
10 kinds of butterflies.

AFRICA
The Congo Rainforest

Not many places on Earth are as full of life as the Congo **rainforest**, the world's second largest tropical **forest**. It covers two million square kilometres in six
15 countries along the **river** Congo. About 10,000 kinds of tropical plants grow here. Many of them are unique to the Congo area. Rare animals such as forest elephants, chimpanzees and three kinds of gorillas live in the **jungle**.

96

3 In pairs, match photos A–D with the words in the box.

coral reef [c]   jungle/forest [ ], [ ]   mountain [ ]
river [ ], [ ]   sea [ ]   valley [ ]   waterfall [ ]

4 Read the article and answer the questions.
1 How can tourists travel to the Valley of Flowers?
2 How large is the Congo rainforest?
3 How many kinds of turtles are there in the world? How many live in the Coral Triangle?
4 Why are the sea snails in the Coral Triangle unusual?
5 Why are the plants in the Iguazu Falls unusual?

5 Which places from the article would you most like to see? Why?

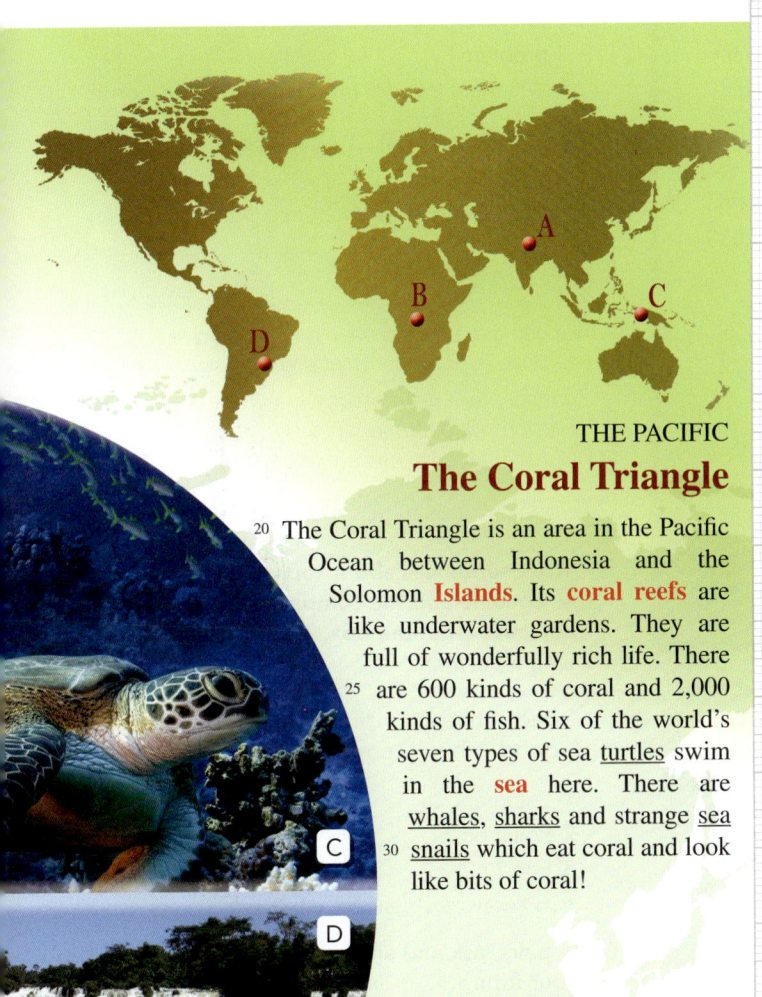

THE PACIFIC
The Coral Triangle

20 The Coral Triangle is an area in the Pacific Ocean between Indonesia and the Solomon **Islands**. Its **coral reefs** are like underwater gardens. They are full of wonderfully rich life. There 25 are 600 kinds of coral and 2,000 kinds of fish. Six of the world's seven types of sea turtles swim in the **sea** here. There are whales, sharks and strange sea 30 snails which eat coral and look like bits of coral!

SOUTH AMERICA
Iguazu Falls

You can hear it from miles away. On the border between Brazil and Argentina lies Iguazu, one of the 35 world's largest **waterfalls**, surrounded by subtropical rainforest. The curtain of water is nearly three kilometres wide and eighty-two metres in the highest place. Rare plants which can only live in running water grow 40 in the waterfall. In the 1986 film *The Mission*, you can see Robert de Niro climbing the Iguazu Falls.

Go to **WORD STORE 8** page 17.

WORD STORE 8A

6 CD•3.36 MP3•133 Complete WORD STORE 8A with the singular form of the words in red in the article. Then listen, check and repeat.

7 Complete the sentences with words from WORD STORE 8A.
1 Great Britain is an _island_.
2 The Baltic is a cold _____ with not very much salt.
3 Mont Blanc is the highest _____ in Europe.
4 The Amazon _____ is the largest forest in the world.
5 The Nile is the world's longest _____ .

WORD STORE 8B

8 CD•3.37 MP3•134 Label the pictures in WORD STORE 8B with the underlined words in the article. Then listen, check and repeat.

9 Which of the animals in WORD STORE 8B live in your country?

WORD STORE 8C

10 CD•3.38 MP3•135 Check you understand the words in red. In pairs, guess which groups of problems 1–4 exist in each of the four places in the article. Then listen and check.
1 illegal hunting, cutting down trees — B
2 illegal fishing, water pollution, global warming [ ]
3 noise and air pollution from helicopters [ ]
4 not many problems, because it's so high up [ ]

11 CD•3.39 MP3•136 Complete the sentences with the correct form of the words in the box. Then listen and check.

air   climate   cut   destroy   ~~noise~~   protect

1 The helicopters **made** a lot of _noise_ and **polluted** the _____ .
2 People also _____ **down trees**, and this _____ the natural environment of those animals.
3 _____ **change** can destroy coral reefs completely.
4 We really should do everything we can to _____ the environment.

12 CD•3.40 MP3•137 Complete WORD STORE 8C with the words in red in Exercises 10–11. Then listen, check and repeat.

13 Choose the correct options.
1 Cutting (down) / up trees destroys / protects the environment.
2 Modern cars make / do less noise than old ones.
3 Oil from ships can cause dangerous air / water pollution.
4 Illegal fishing / hunting is a danger to elephants.
5 Climate warming / change is perhaps the world's greatest problem today.

97

8.2 Grammar

Future with *will*

I can use will *to talk about the future and predict future events.*

1 What do you know about polar bears? Choose the correct options. Then read the text and check your answers.

   1 Polar bears live in *the Arctic / the Antarctic*.
   2 Polar bears spend a lot of time *on small islands / on sea ice*.
   3 Global warming *is / isn't* a danger to polar bears.

Will there still be polar bears in the world in 2100?

Polar bears need sea ice to hunt, rest and travel. But the ice in the Arctic is melting because of global warming. Scientists believe that some time between 2059 and 2078 there **will be** no sea ice in summer in the Arctic Sea. The polar bear's habitat will become smaller and smaller. Bears **won't get** enough food in the summer; they won't be able to feed their young and many bears will die in winter.

There are now between 20,000 and 25,000 polar bears in the world. Some scientists predict that sixty percent **will disappear** before 2050. **Will** they all **die** before the end of the century?

2 Read the GRAMMAR FOCUS. Then complete the examples with the words in blue in the text.

GRAMMAR FOCUS

will

We use **will** to predict future events.

+ There ¹ _will_ be no sea ice in summer.
  Sixty percent of polar bears ² _____ **disappear** before 2050.

– Bears ³ _____ get enough food in the summer.

? ⁴ _____ all polar bears **die** before the end of the century?
  Yes, they **will**./No, they **won't**.

Short forms:
I'll = I will, you'll = you will, etc.; won't = will not

REMEMBER THIS

The future form of *can* is **will be able to**. The negative form is **won't be able to**.
Female bears won't be able to feed their young.

3 What do you think will happen in the next fifty years? Complete the sentences with *will* or *won't*. Then compare with a partner.

   1 People _____ travel less.
   2 Summers _____ get hotter.
   3 Nuclear energy _____ become safer and more popular.
   4 Elephants _____ die out.
   5 There _____ be enough food in Europe.
   6 Pollution _____ become worse.

4 In pairs, ask and answer the questions.

   1 Will people still use cars in sixty years' time?
   2 Will Venice and Amsterdam disappear under the sea?
   3 Will there be enough food for everyone?
   4 Will scientists solve the world energy problem?
   5 Will there be a lot more people in the world?

   A: *Will people still use cars in sixty years' time?*
   B: *Yes, they will./No, they won't.*

REMEMBER THIS

You use **get** or **become** + a comparative adjective to say how things will change.
Summers will get hotter.
Pollution will become worse.
Will food become more expensive?

5 Write sentences about topics 1–5 with *get* or *become* and the comparative form of an adjective from the box. Then share your ideas with a partner.

| bad | cheap | difficult | easy | expensive |
| good | hot | popular | safe | |

   1 Summers …
   2 Pollution …
   3 Food …
   4 Finding a job …
   5 Travel …

   Summers will become hotter.

6 In pairs, ask and answer questions about your future.

Will you … in the next ten years?
• get married
• have children
• make many new friends
• have your own flat or house
• earn a lot of money

   A: *Will you get married in the next ten years?*
   B: *Yes, I will./No, I won't.*

Grammar Focus page 118

8.3 Listening

Matching

I can identify specific detail in a weather forecast.

1 **CD•3.41 MP3•138** Look at pictures 1–7 on the right. Listen and repeat.

2 **CD•3.42 MP3•139** Make adjectives from the nouns. Then listen and repeat.

1 north – northern
2 south – _____
3 east – _____
4 west – _____

3 Find these places on the map. Which place do you think will be the coldest? Why?
- Southern England (with Cornwall)
- the Midlands
- Northern England
- Northern Ireland
- Wales
- Scotland

EXAM FOCUS Matching

4 **CD•3.43 MP3•140** Listen to a weather forecast and match the pictures (A–F) with the places 1–4. There are two extra pictures.

A 11°C
B 13°C
C 18°C
D 14°C
E 20°C
F 10°C

1 Southern England — C
2 Wales and the Midlands — ___
3 Northern England — ___
4 Scotland — ___

5 **CD•3.43 MP3•140** Listen again. Are the statements true (T) or false (F)?

1 Cornwall will be the warmest place tomorrow. ___
2 In Northern England a wind from the sea will bring rain. ___
3 The day will be very rainy in the Highlands. ___
4 It will snow in all of Scotland. ___

Great Britain

1 sunshine
2 cloud
3 rain, shower
4 snow
5 thunder and lightning
6 wind
7 fog

6 **CD•3.44 MP3•141** Complete the sentences from the weather forecast with the words in the box. Then listen and check.

[~~cloudy~~   foggy   rainy   sunny   windy]

1 It will be cloudy with showers most of the day.
2 We can expect a _____ day with some cloud.
3 The morning will be _____ , but the fog should soon clear.
4 And that strong west wind will bring _____ weather from the Atlantic.
5 Saturday will be a _____ day.

PRONUNCIATION FOCUS

7 **CD•3.45 MP3•142** Listen and repeat.

[degrees   during   clear   expect
forecast   temperature   weather]

8 **CD•3.46 MP3•143** Listen and repeat.

1 We can expect a rainy day tomorrow.
2 The temperature will be ten degrees.
3 It will be sunny with clear skies.
4 There will be some showers during the day.
5 Scotland will have the wettest weather.

9 In pairs, ask and answer the questions.

1 What's the weather like today? (It is …)
2 What was the weather like yesterday? (It was …)
3 What's the weather forecast for the coming weekend? (It will be …)
4 What sort of weather do you like? (I like …)

WORD STORE 8D

10 **CD•3.47 MP3•144** Complete WORD STORE 8D with the correct nouns and adjectives. Then listen and check.

99

8.4 Reading

Right/Wrong/Doesn't say

I can find specific detail in short texts about national parks.

1 Discuss the questions in pairs.
  1 Have you ever been to a national park?
  2 Tell your partner:
    • where you went
    • when you went there
    • what you saw.

2 In pairs, look at the photos and the headings in the texts on page 101 and answer the questions. Then read the texts and check your answers.
  1 Where are these national parks?
  2 What do you think you will be able to see there?

EXAM FOCUS Right/Wrong/Doesn't say

3 Read the texts again. Are the statements right (R), wrong (W) or do the texts not say (DS)?
  1 In the Nature Reserve it is all right to give fish to the seabirds.
  2 It is quite normal for seabirds to be afraid of people.
  3 Ellen saw wolves while she was walking in the National Park.
  4 Ellen has visited this park once before.
  5 A mountain in North America has names in two languages.
  6 The pubs in the Yorkshire Dales are well-known all over the world.
  7 A famous sports event once took place in the Yorkshire Dales.

4 In pairs, take turns to tell your partner which of the places from the texts you would like to see and why.

  I would like to see … because …

5 Match the words in blue in the texts with the definitions.
  1 **birdwatching** (n) – observing wild birds as a hobby
  2 _____ (n) – someone or something that annoys you or causes problems
  3 _____ (adj) – which you don't see very often; unusual
  4 _____ (adj) – the one which existed first, at the beginning
  5 _____ (phrase) – have a holiday
  6 _____ (n) – an emotion when you are afraid of something
  7 _____ (n) – a very large area of ice that moves slowly down a mountain valley
  8 _____ (n) – agreement to do what someone wants you to do

6 Complete the sentences with prepositions from the texts.
  1 When I have to spend hours __on__ a bus, I (read a long book).
  2 I like (playing the piano) and I can do it _____ hours.
  3 On my way to school, I walk _____ (the zoo).
  4 (Pandas) have a natural diet _____ (bamboo).
  5 (Human food) is not good _____ wild animals.
  6 I love (travelling) and I'm very interested _____ (visiting new places).
  7 I'm fit, but I don't have the legs _____ (cycling up mountains).
  8 Let's go to (the beach) – we can relax _____ (the sea) and have a swim.

7 Look at Exercise 6 again. Change the words in brackets to make true sentences. Then tell the class.

  When I have to spend hours on a bus, I listen to music.

8 Complete the collocations with adjectives from text C.
  1 an **incredible** place
  2 b_____ landscapes
  3 l_____, peaceful countryside
  4 p_____ villages
  5 the a_____ Yorkshire Dales
  6 a very s_____ place

9 In pairs, make notes about a national park or nature reserve under the headings below.

  Place:
  (The Lake District) is in (North West England).

  Landscape:
  There is/There are …

  Wildlife:
  … live there.

  Activities:
  You can …

  Adjectives:
  It's a (really) … place.

10 In pairs, tell the class about the national park you chose. Use your notes from Exercise 9.

WORD STORE 8E

11 CD·3.49 MP3·146 Complete WORDS STORE 8E with adjectives from the texts. Then listen, check and repeat.

A

Farne Islands Nature Reserve

PLEASE DO NOT FEED SEA BIRDS

Water birds have a natural diet of fish and sea plants. Human food, especially bread, is not good for their health.
5 Wild birds need to know how to find their own food. If you feed them, they may lose this important skill. When you feed animals, they may lose their natural fear of humans. This is dangerous for the birds and may be a nuisance to people – if, for example,
10 a bird tries to take your sandwich! Thank you for your understanding and cooperation.

HELP US KEEP OUR WILDLIFE WILD AND SAFE!

B

To: Peggy
Subject: Denali National Park

Hi Peggy,

I'm in Denali National Park in Alaska. It's an incredible place: twenty-four square kilometres of wild land with just one road across it. Yesterday we were on the park bus (you can't drive
5 your own car here) when, suddenly, three WOLVES ran past us along the road! One of them looked right up at me and I could see what a truly wild, dangerous, beautiful animal it was. It was amazing, but I was happy to be inside the bus.

Tomorrow I'm going to take a helicopter ride to the Yanert
10 Glacier to see ice pools, ice bridges and ice falls! Doesn't that sound cool? Wish you were here!

Ellen XXX

PS 'Denali' is the original Indian name for Mount McKinley, the highest mountain in North America. You can see it
15 wherever you are over here!

C

YORKSHIRE DALES NATIONAL PARK
A very special place

The Yorkshire Dales have some of the most
5 breathtaking landscapes in Britain. You can walk, cycle or ride for hours through the lovely, peaceful countryside, over hills and fields with their characteristic stone walls. You can relax by a river or waterfall and have lunch in an old pub
10 in one of the picturesque villages.

The Yorkshire Dales, with their many rare birds, are ideal for anyone interested in birdwatching. This is your opportunity to see peregrine falcons.

15 Take a break in the amazing Yorkshire Dales this year! Follow the route of riders in the 2014 Tour de France or, if you don't think you have the legs for that, try an easier valley route.

You can find loads of ideas on our site to help
20 you plan your visit to this very special place.

101

8.5 Grammar

be going to
I can use be going to to talk about plans.

1 Read the posts and answer the questions.
1 What plans has Holly got for the summer holidays?
2 Who thinks it's a good idea?
3 Would you like to go on a holiday like this? Why?/Why not?

Bob: Thirty-three days, sixteen hours, forty-six minutes left till the holidays! What are you going to do this summer? Any plans?
Yesterday at 22.14

Holly: I'm going to work as a volunteer in the Scottish Highlands.
5 hours ago

Ben: ??
2 hours ago

Holly: I'm going to look after Highland ponies … and the people who want to ride them, but don't know how to ride!
1 hour ago

Ben: Are they going to pay you?
30 minutes ago

Holly: No, they aren't. But I'm going to ride for free in the mountains!
25 minutes ago

Carol: Can I go too?
3 minutes ago

2 Read the GRAMMAR FOCUS. Then complete the examples with the words in blue in the posts.

GRAMMAR FOCUS
be going to
You use **be + going to + infinitive** to talk about plans.

+ I ¹*'m going* to work as a volunteer.
  He's going to work as a trainer.
− They aren't going to pay me.
? What ²_____ you _____ to do this summer?
  ³_____ they _____ to pay you?
  Yes, they are./No, they aren't.

3 CD•3.50 MP3•147 Listen to Lucy and Luke talking about their weekend. Tick the correct speaker for each activity.

	Lucy	Luke
1 stay with his/her cousin in Wales	✓	
2 go walking in the mountains		
3 visit a castle		
4 study for a test		
5 play tennis		
6 see the new James Bond film		

4 Use the prompts to write sentences with be going to about Lucy and Luke.
1 Lucy / stay / with her cousin in Wales
2 Luke / go / walking in the mountains
3 Luke / study / for a Geography test
4 Lucy / play / tennis
5 Luke / visit / a Welsh castle
6 Lucy and Luke / see / the new James Bond film

5 Use the prompts to write questions with be going to. Then match the questions with the answers.
1 what / you / do / this evening? e
   What are you going to do this evening?
2 you / do / anything interesting / this weekend?
3 what / you / do / this summer?
4 you / go / to university / after you finish school?
5 where / you / live / when you're at university?

a Yes, I am. I'm going to study Biology at Leeds University.
b I'm going to travel around Europe with a friend.
c I don't know! Probably with my parents!
d Not really. I'm going to study.
e I think I'm going to go to bed early. I'm really tired.

6 In pairs, ask and answer the questions in Exercise 5.

7 Complete the sentences to make them true for you. Use be going to.
1 This weekend I'm going to visit …
2 My friend …
3 This year my parents …
4 In the next school holidays my family …
5 When we leave school, my friends and I …

Grammar Focus page 119

8.6 Speaking

Agreeing and disagreeing

I can agree and disagree in a discussion and express my opinion.

1 In pairs, match two sentence endings to each beginning.

1 You waste energy when you — a ☐ ☐
2 You save energy when you — ☐ ☐

a turn on all the lights in the house.
b turn off unnecessary lights.
c turn on a dishwasher that's half empty.
d leave the car at home and cycle to work.

2 Read about Earth Hour. Do you think it's a good idea? Why?/Why not?

EARTH HOUR

What is it?
It's a global 'green' event.

Who organises it?
The World Wildlife Fund.

What happens?
Thousands of people around the world turn off all the lights and electrical devices for one hour.

Why do they do it?
To remind us all about climate change and the need to save energy.

When is it?
On the last Saturday of March.

Where and when did it start?
In Sydney, Australia, in 2007.

How many people take part?
In 2012 about 7,000 cities and towns in 152 countries on all the continents took part in Earth Hour.

3 CD•3.51 MP3•148 Listen to Alice and Leo talking about Earth Hour. Who thinks it's a good idea? Who doesn't think it's a good idea?

4 CD•3.51 MP3•148 Read the SPEAKING FOCUS and complete the conversation. Then listen again and check.

Alice: Hi, Leo. I'm going to take part in Earth Hour and I'm looking for people to join me.
Leo: Earth Hour? I'm not ¹ _sure_ … To be ² _____ , I don't think it makes much ³ _____ .
Alice: Why not? It's a great way to show you care about climate change.
Leo: ⁴ _____ , but one hour doesn't change anything. People waste energy all the time. You can't save much in sixty minutes.
Alice: Yes, I ⁵ _____ . It's true we won't save much energy during Earth Hour. But the point is to make people think about the problem, not just to save energy.
Leo: I see what you ⁶ _____ , but what about all those candles? People burn hundreds of candles at Earth Hour events and they produce a lot of CO_2. It's all a waste of time.
Alice: Mmm, you have a ⁷ _____ . But I still think it's a great event. And you know, people and even whole cities make decisions to be more green because of Earth Hour.
Leo: Well, maybe you're right. Would you like some help?
Alice: ⁸ _____ . Thank you.

SPEAKING FOCUS

Agreeing
I think so (too).
(Yes,) I agree.
Exactly./Absolutely.
That's/You're right.

Disagreeing
I'm not sure.
I don't think so.
I disagree.
To be honest, I don't think it makes much sense.

Agreeing in part/Agreeing and disagreeing
Perhaps/Maybe, but …
Maybe you're right …
I see what you mean, but …
You have a point, but …

5 Choose the correct options.

1 A: I think air pollution in our city is awful. When are they going to do something about it?
   B: *Exactly.* / *I don't think so.* You can't breathe normally.
2 A: I think governments should stop air travel. It pollutes the air and causes global warming.
   B: *I disagree / You have a point*, but isn't that a bit extreme? No air travel at all?
3 A: I think nuclear energy is the future.
   B: *That's right. / I'm not sure.* I think it's very dangerous.
4 A: I think in the city everybody should use public transport only.
   B: *You're right. / I disagree.* But do you think people will agree?
5 A: I'd like to organise Earth Hour in our city. I think it's a great idea.
   B: *I'm not sure. / Absolutely.* Let's do it!

6 In pairs, read A's opinions in Exercise 5 aloud. Agree or disagree. Give your opinion.

103

8.7 Writing

Expressing an opinion; presenting arguments
I can express my opinion in writing with reasons and explanations.

1 Read the sentences and check you understand the words in purple. Then, in pairs, tick the things you do to protect the environment. Compare your ideas with other pairs.

To protect the environment we should:
- **sort** our **rubbish** for **recycling**.
- **turn off the light**, the computer and all other electronic equipment when we're not using it.
- **save water** – for example, **turn off the water tap** when we clean our teeth.
- walk and cycle more.
- buy **recycled** things.
- plant trees.
- buy less and **throw away** less.

2 Read the blog and answer the questions.
1 What does the writer think we should do to protect the environment?
2 What three arguments does he give for his opinion?
3 Do you agree with him? Why?/Why not?

GREENER
Environment blog

Go veg to save the planet
by SamHarvey

[A] **In my opinion**, the best thing we can do for our planet is to become vegetarians.
[B] **First of all**, there is a lot of waste when we produce meat. For example, you need about sixteen kilograms of cereal and nearly 20,000 litres of water to produce one kilogram of meat. We should stop producing meat and grow cereals for humans instead. It will be much easier to feed all the people in the world.
[C] **In addition**, you need a lot of land to keep large farm animals such as cows. In South America, farmers are destroying tropical forests to create space for cows which will become hamburgers in other countries.
[D] **Finally**, remember the animals themselves! Animals on large 'factory farms' have a terrible life and a terrible death.
[E] You don't even have to stop eating meat completely. Just eat less. You'll help save the Earth and feed everyone on it!

3 Read the blog again. Match the parts of the blog (A–E) with the descriptions (1–5).
1 Add another argument. ☐
2 Repeat your opinion and/or encourage the reader to do something. ☐
3 Add the final argument. ☐
4 State your opinion. [A]
5 Give the first explanation/argument. ☐

4 Complete the WRITING FOCUS with the words in purple in the blog.

WRITING FOCUS
Expressing an opinion; presenting arguments

- Stating your opinion
  I think/I believe …   It seems (to me) …
  In my ¹*opinion* , …   In my view, …
- First argument
  Firstly, …   First ² _____ , …
- Next argument(s)
  Secondly, …   Also,
  In ³ _____ , …
- Final argument
  ⁴ _____ , …   Lastly, …

5 Replace the words in purple in the blog with different phrases from the WRITING FOCUS.

6 Put the sentences in order to make an opinion text.

a Lastly, why choose nuclear when there are other options? Why not build a wind farm?
b Please join the protest against the power plant today!
c Firstly, it's not safe. A mistake can cause a terrible disaster, like the one in Japan in 2011.
d I believe the plan to build a nuclear power station next to our town is a very bad idea. **1**
e Secondly, we should not use nuclear energy if we don't know what to do with the dangerous radioactive waste.

7 Read the topics of three blog entries about the environment. Then match the topics (a–c) with the arguments (1–9).

a We need more wind farms.
b Plastic bags are bad for the environment.
c Many people don't recycle.

1 We throw away too much rubbish.
2 The view will be terrible.
3 Birds and sea animals eat them.
4 We can make new things from old things.
5 We need new energy.
6 It takes up to 1,000 years for them to disappear.
7 They produce clean energy.
8 There aren't many places left to throw away our rubbish.
9 We can use other bags.

8 Write one more point for each topic in Exercise 7. It can be for or against the idea.

a _____
b _____
c _____

9 Match these suggestions with the topics in Exercise 7.

1 Go online and join our group, More Clean Energy! You will help the environment.
2 Make sure you put your rubbish in the right bags or boxes. It will make a difference.
3 So don't buy plastic bags in supermarkets. Soon, they will stop selling them!

10 Choose one of the topics from Exercise 7 and write a blog of about 100 words about it.

In your blog, you should:
• express your opinion.
• give at least two arguments to support your opinion.
• encourage readers to take action.

Divide your blog into these paragraphs:
• Give your opinion. Do you agree or disagree with the idea in the title?
• Give your first argument. Why do you agree or disagree?
• Give your second reason for agreeing or disagreeing.
• Advise the reader what he/she can do.

11 Check.
✓ Have you included all the points in the task?
✓ Have you divided your blog into paragraphs?
✓ Have you used phrases from the WRITING FOCUS?
✓ Have you checked your grammar and spelling?

FOCUS REVIEW 8

VOCABULARY AND GRAMMAR

1 Read the descriptions and complete the landscape words.
1 You can take a boat along this. r_ _ _ _
2 You find this between mountains and hills. v_ _ _ _ _
3 People like walking through the trees in this. f_ _ _ _ _
4 You can climb this. m_ _ _ _ _ _ _
5 You can see this when water drops a long way very quickly. w_ _ _ _ _ _ _ _
6 This is completely surrounded by water. i_ _ _ _ _

2 Choose the correct options.
1 Animals die out when people *destroy / disappear* their habitats.
2 Electric cars *pollute / recycle* the air less than petrol or diesel cars.
3 We should *save / sort* all our rubbish so it's easier to recycle.
4 Remember to always turn off the water tap so you don't *waste / save* water.
5 We live near the airport and the aeroplanes *make / do* such a lot of noise.
6 Global warming is causing the ice in the Arctic to *melt / grow*.

3 Complete the sentences with *be going to* and the verbs in the box.

[feed   not work   plant   take   throw   visit]

1 We _____ a break in the Scottish Highlands this year.
2 I _____ my dog now and then I can go out.
3 Our class _____ Dartmoor National Park in May.
4 My dad _____ an apple tree in our garden.
5 Lily _____ on a farm this summer.
6 _____ you _____ away this plastic bag? We can use it again.

4 Complete the sentences with *will* and the verbs in brackets.
1 The weather forecast says _____ (it/snow) tomorrow.
2 _____ (people/live) on other planets in the future?
3 _____ (we/not/get) back home before 8 p.m.
4 I don't think _____ (there/be) any rain this week.
5 _____ (you/not/can) see the lions at this time of day.
6 _____ (mountain gorillas/disappear) from the Congo rainforest because of the search for oil?

LANGUAGE IN USE

5 Choose the correct answer, A, B, or C.
1 One of the causes of global warming is ____ .
   A planting trees
   B cutting down trees
   C saving trees
2 Tigers are in danger as a result of ____ .
   A illegal fishing
   B air pollution
   C illegal hunting
3 I think we ____ too many things and that's why there is so much rubbish.
   A throw away
   B recycle
   C consume
4 The old power plant ____ the air.
   A sorts
   B wastes
   C pollutes
5 Governments should do more to ____ .
   A destroy the habitat
   B protect the environment
   C climate change

6 Choose the option, A, B or C, which has a similiar meaning to the underlined words or phrases.
1 We <u>are planning to see</u> the Coral Triangle this winter.
   A are going to see
   B will see
   C have seen
2 <u>You have a point</u>, but my opinion's different.
   A I agree with you
   B I see what you mean
   C I'm not sure
3 We saw some very <u>rare</u> butterflies.
   A lovely
   B famous
   C unusual
4 <u>It's a good idea</u> to buy and consume less.
   A We can
   B We should
   C We'll be able to
5 <u>I don't think we can</u> save all the animals, but perhaps we can save some of them.
   A We won't be able to
   B We shouldn't
   C We mustn't

READING

7 Read the texts. Are the statements right (R), wrong (W) or do the texts not say (DS)?

1 Adelie penguins are not very big.
2 There aren't many of them now.
3 At Longleat Safari Park all animals live in special buildings.
4 The Safari bus is free.
5 You can see the park with a guide just for you.
6 There are more tigers as pets than in the wild.
7 It may soon be illegal to keep tigers as pets.

Adelie penguins are smaller than most other penguins. They are 45–75 centimetres tall. They have black heads with white rings around the eyes. On land they look funny, but they are amazing swimmers and they can dive down to 180 metres. At present there are a lot of them in the Antarctic, but global warming is a danger to these lovely birds. Penguins eat small sea creatures which live under the Antarctic ice. As the ice melts, there will be less and less food for them.

Visit Longleat Safari Park!

Open since 1966, Longleat is the oldest drive-through safari park outside Africa. On thirty-six square kilometres of countryside in sunny Wiltshire in England, you can see animals running free, like in their natural environment. There are lions, elephants, giraffes and monkeys; there are tigers, wild dogs, bears, wolves and more. There is a gorilla colony, a penguin island and a special pavilion with exotic butterflies. You can drive your own car through the park or travel on a safari bus. You can also book a VIP tour in a 4x4 car with a personal guide.

There are only about 3,200 tigers still living in the wild in the whole world. But there are many more – perhaps 10,000 – living as pets in private homes in the USA. Some people think it's cool to have a tiger, lion or leopard as a pet. I think it's cruel and selfish and should be illegal! Firstly, a big wild cat needs a lot of space to run free. Secondly, the owners often don't know how to look after such cats. Their pets don't have the right kind of food or can't give them the medical care they need, and many die. Finally, they can be dangerous to people – it's in their nature!

LISTENING

8 CD·3.52 MP3·149 Listen to Jack talking to a friend about tourist attractions in his area. Match the places (1–5) with the attractions (a–h).

1 Nature Reserve   4 Brown's Island
2 Kirkland Hills   5 Headland Beach
3 New Forest

a butterflies   e pigs
b wolves   f seabirds
c rare flowers   g wild ponies
d waterfall   h glacier

SPEAKING

9 In pairs, do the task.

A friend of yours is trying to decide where to go and what to do on holiday. Talk about the different things he could do and see and then decide which would be best. Look at the photos to help you.

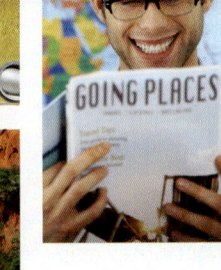

WRITING

10 Read the post about a new shopping centre and write your comment in about 100 words.

Have you heard? They're going to build a new shopping centre on Green Park! What do you think and why? Write your comment below.

Yesterday at 14.22

107

GRAMMAR FOCUS

0.1 Imperatives

We use the infinitive or *don't/do not* + infinitive to give instructions or orders:

Listen to the teacher.
Check the word in the dictionary.
Don't look at the text.
Don't run in the corridors.

We use *let's* + infinitive to make suggestions:
Let's talk about school.

1 Complete the sentences with the imperative form of the verbs in brackets.

1 _____ (not work) in pairs now. _____ (work) in groups of three. And _____ (speak) in English, please!
2 Please _____ (listen) to the conversation and _____ (choose) the correct answers.
3 _____ (do) the exercise together.
4 Please _____ (think) of a book, but _____ (not tell) anyone the title.

2 Choose the correct answer, A or B.

1 You want to go to the cinema with your friend. You say:
   A Let's go to the cinema!   B Go to the cinema!
2 You're in your English class. Your teacher says to you:
   A Let's speak in English.   B Don't speak in English.
3 Your teacher gives you homework. He/She says:
   A Let's do the homework.   B Do your homework.
4 You want to do your homework. You and your friend have free time now. You say:
   A Let's do our homework.   B Do our homework.

0.2 Subject pronouns, *to be*

Subject pronouns

Subject pronouns replace nouns:
He's seventeen.
Are **you** from London?
'Where are the dictionaries?' '**They**'re in the classroom.'

to be

Affirmative			Negative		
I	'm (am)		I	'm not (am not)	
You/We/They	're (are)	Spanish.	You/We/They	aren't/'re not (are not)	Spanish.
He/She/It	's (is)		He/She/It	isn't/'s not (is not)	

Yes/No questions			Short answers
Am	I		Yes, I **am**. No, I**'m not**.
Are	you/we/they	Spanish?	Yes, you/we/they **are**. No, you/we/they **aren't**.
Is	he/she/it		Yes, he/she/it **is**. No, he/she/it **isn't**.

Wh- questions			
Where	am	I	
	are	you/we/they	from?
	is	he/she/it	
How old	am	I	
	are	you/we/they	?
	is	he/she/it	
What nationality	am	I	
	are	you/we/they	?
	is	he/she/it	

1 Complete the sentences with the words in the box. There are two extra words.

| am   are   he   is   it   she   they |

1 Look at this boy. _____ he Portuguese?
2 Ruby and Ian _____ my best friends. _____ speak Russian.
3 This is Carol. _____'s from Australia.
4 Answer my question. _____ isn't difficult.

0.3 Demonstrative pronouns, plural nouns

Demonstrative pronouns

We use *this* (singular) and *these* (plural) to talk about people or objects close to us:
This is my new bicycle.   Are **these** your comics?

We use *that* (singular) and *those* (plural) to talk about people and things further away from us:
That book is really old.   Look at **those** T-shirts!

Plural nouns

	Singular	Plural
most nouns	table	tables
nouns ending in -sh, -ch, -s, -x, -z and some ending in -o	bus watch tomato	bus**es** watch**es** tomato**es**
nouns ending in a consonant and -y	family dictionary	famil**ies** dictionar**ies**
irregular nouns	man woman child	**men** **women** **children**

Some nouns are only plural (e.g. *sunglasses*, *headphones*):
Your **sunglasses** are cool.

108

1 Choose the correct options.
1 Look at *that / those* children! They're so happy!
2 I like *this / these* headphones. I take them everywhere.
3 *This is / They are* my favourite book. It's really funny.
4 Is *this / these* your beanbag?
5 *That / Those* are my T-shirts. They're old, but I like them.

0.4 Possessive adjectives, Possessive 's

Possessive adjectives

Personal pronouns	Possessive adjectives
I	my
you	your
he	his
she	her
it	its
we	our
you	your
they	their

How old are **your** sisters?
This is **their** school.

Possessive 's

We use the possessive 's to say that something belongs to someone:
Mark's photos
the students' headphones

We add:
- 's to singular nouns:
  My **mum's** favourite pop group is the Beatles
- ' to regular plural nouns:
  This is my **grandparents'** new house.
- 's to irregular plural nouns:
  The **children's** room is over there.

Be careful: 's can mean 'is' or show that something belongs to someone:
My brother**'s** a student. ('s = is)
My brother**'s** car is really old. ('s = possessive)

1 Complete the definitions with the words in the box and 's or '.

> aunt (x2)   father   grandparents
> mother   parents   uncle

1 Your mum is your _____ daughter.
2 Your cousin is your _____ and _____ daughter or son.
3 Your sister is your _____ daughter.
4 Your grandmother is your _____ mother or your _____ mother.
5 Your uncle is your _____ husband.

0.5 can/can't

We use *can/can't* to express ability:
Ella **can** sing, but she **can't** dance.   **Can** you paint?

Affirmative		Negative	
I/You/He/She/It/We/They	can cook.	I/You/He/She/It/We/They	can't (cannot) cook.

Yes/No questions		Short answers
Can	I/you/he/she/it/we/they cook?	Yes, I/you/he/she/it/we/they can. No, I/you/he/she/it/we/they can't.

Wh- questions		
What	can	I/you/he/she/it/we/they cook?

1 Complete the sentences with *can* or *can't*.
1 '_____ you cook?' 'Yes, I_____ !'
2 I don't want to go roller-skating! I _____ roller-skate!
3 My sister _____ sing and she _____ dance too.
4 My dad _____ run very fast, but he _____ swim, so we never go to the swimming pool.
5 '_____ Suzie draw comics?' 'No, she _____ .'

0.6 Prepositions, there is/there are

Prepositions

We use these prepositions to say where things are: *behind, between, in, in front of, next to, on, opposite, over, under*:
There's a supermarket **opposite** our school.

there is/there are

We use *there is/there are* to say where things are:
There are three books on the table.

Affirmative		
There is/There's	a sofa	in the living room.
There are	two posters	on the wall.

Yes/No questions			Short answers
Is there	a sofa	in the living room?	Yes, there is. No, there isn't.
Are there	posters	on the wall?	Yes, there are. No, there aren't.

Wh- questions		
How many posters	are there	on the wall?

GRAMMAR FOCUS

1 Complete the text with prepositions.

My bedroom is very small. There aren't many things ¹i_____ it. There's a window ²o_____ the door. My desk is ³u_____ the window. My bed is ⁴n_____ to the desk. My favourite posters are ⁵o_____ the bed ⁶o_____ the wall. ⁷B_____ my bed and the opposite wall there's a green carpet.

2 Choose the correct options.

1 There is / are a flower on my desk.
2 Is there / There is any milk in the fridge?
3 There isn't / aren't any chairs in the room.
4 There is / are two dogs outside.
5 There's / There isn't any water in this bottle. It's empty.
6 How many girls there is / are there in your class?

0.7 have got

We use *have got* to show possession:
I'**ve got** a smartphone, but I **haven't got** a watch.
Has James **got** a skateboard?

Affirmative		Negative	
I/You/We/They	've got (have got) a camera.	I/You/We/They	haven't got (have not got) a camera.
He/She/It	's got (has got)	He/She/It	hasn't got (has not got)

Yes/No questions		Short answers
Have	I/you/we/they got a camera?	Yes, I/you/we/they have. No, I/you/we/they haven't.
Has	he/she/it	Yes, he/she/it has. No, he/she/it hasn't.

Wh- questions		
How many cameras	have	I/you/we/they got?
	has	he/she/it

1 Complete the sentences with the words in the box.

> got   has   hasn't   have   haven't   've

1 I've _____ a laptop, but I haven't got a tablet.
2 A: Have you got a digital camera?
   B: Yes, I _____ !
3 A: She _____ got a mobile phone.
   B: Really? Why not?
4 I've got a DVD player, but I _____ got an MP3 player.
5 A: _____ Phil got a hobby?
   B: Yes, skateboarding!
6 I _____ got a piano, but I can't play it!

1.2 Present Simple: affirmatives and negatives

We use the Present Simple to talk about:
- regular activities:
  *In the afternoon I **watch** TV or **listen** to music.*
- states and permanent situations:
  *My grandparents **don't live** in Warsaw. They **live** in Sydney.*
- preferences, with verbs like *love, like, hate, prefer*:
  *My friends **hate** dancing, but I **love** it.*

Affirmative		Negative	
I/You/We/They	play.	I/You/We/They	don't (do not) play.
He/She/It	plays.	He/She/It	doesn't (does not)

SPELLING RULES – 3RD PERSON SINGULAR:
- general rule: infinitive + -s, e.g. *read – reads*
- verbs ending in a consonant and -y: -y + -ies, e.g. *carry – carries*
- verbs ending in -o, -ss, -x, -ch, -sh: + -es, e.g. *do – does, go – goes, relax – relaxes, watch – watches*
- *have: has*

In the Present Simple, we often use adverbs of frequency, such as *always, usually, often, sometimes* and *never*. These adverbs go:
- after the verb *to be*: *Walt **is usually** at home at the weekend.*
- before main verbs: *Walt **usually spends** his weekends at home.*

We also use other time phrases with the Present Simple, e.g. *every day, every Sunday, every weekend*. We usually put them at the end of the sentence.
*I visit my grandparents **every week**.*

1 Complete the sentences with the Present Simple form of the verbs in brackets.

1 I _____ (be) late for school every day.
2 My sister usually _____ (watch) films in the evenings.
3 My mum _____ (not read) the newspaper every day.
4 My parents _____ (not work) in the same office.
5 My brother often _____ (go) to the cinema.

2 Put the words in the correct order to make sentences.

1 sometimes / the piano / my sister / plays
2 don't / every day / I / sports / watch
3 studies / my brother / at the weekend / never
4 on weekdays / I / go out / sometimes
5 every day / Sam / play / computer games / doesn't
6 on Saturday nights / always / fun / he / has

110

1.5 Present Simple: yes/no and wh- questions

Yes/No questions	Short answers
Do I/you/we/they play?	Yes, I/you/we/they **do**. No, I/you/we/they **don't**.
Does he/she/it	Yes, he/she/it **does**. No, he/she/it **doesn't**.

Wh- questions

| What | do | I/you/we/they | play? |
| What | does | he/she/it | play? |

In *wh-* questions, we use question words:
- **What** do your friends usually post on Facebook?
- **What kind** of music does your father listen to?
- **What time** does your mother come back from work?
- **Where** do you live?
- **When** do you do your homework?
- **Which** musical instrument do you play?
- **Who** do you play chess with?
- **Whose** coat is this?
- **How** do you usually get to school?
- **How often** do you visit your cousin?
- **How many** eggs do we need?

1 Complete the conversations with *do*, *don't*, *does* or *doesn't*.

1 A: _____ you live with your parents?
   B: Yes, I _____ .
2 A: _____ he like parties?
   B: Yes, he _____ .
3 A: _____ your mother speak English?
   B: No, she _____ .
4 A: _____ they go to school with you?
   B: No, they _____ .

2 Complete the questions with the question words in the box. Then match the questions (1–6) with the answers (a–f).

> how many   what kind   what time
> when   where   which

1 _____ is your birthday?
2 _____ do you usually go on holiday?
3 _____ website is your favourite?
4 _____ of films do you usually watch?
5 _____ hours do you sleep every day?
6 _____ do you usually wake up?

a To the seaside.   d At 7.30.
b I like Twitter.   e It's in March.
c Seven or eight.   f Comedies.

2.2 Countable and uncountable nouns

Nouns can be countable or uncountable.

	Singular	Plural
Countable	banana	bananas
	egg	eggs
	bottle	bottles
Uncountable	bread	–
	cheese	–
	ham	–

Countable nouns
- name things we can count:
  There is an **orange** in the fridge.
- have singular and plural forms:
  This **hamburger** is delicious.
  These **hamburgers** are delicious.

Uncountable nouns:
- name things we cannot count:
  My little brother hates **milk**.
- do not have a plural form:
  Vegetarians don't eat **meat**.

We can use these words and phrases to refer to an amount or a number:

Plural countable nouns	Uncountable nouns
We've got **some** apples.	We've got **some** bread.
We haven't got **any** apples.	We haven't got **any** bread.
Have we got **any** apples?	Have we got **any** bread?
How many apples have we got?	**How much** bread have we got?
Not **many**. We haven't got **many** apples.	Not **much**. We haven't got **much** bread.
We've go **a lot of** apples.	We've got **a lot of** bread.

1 Match the sentence halves.

1 There isn't   a any eggs.
2 Is there   b some onions.
3 There is   c any ham in the fridge.
4 There aren't   d any mushrooms?
5 Are there   e any bread?
6 There are   f some cheese.

2 Choose the correct options.

1 There is *much / a lot of* mozzarella cheese on this pizza.
2 There isn't *any / some* tomato sauce on this pizza.
3 There is *an / some* onion in the fridge.
4 *How much / How many* bread have we got?
5 There isn't *some / much* milk in the fridge.
6 Don't worry, we've got *a lot of / much* eggs.
7 'How much / How many tomatoes do you eat a day?'
   'A lot. / Not much.'

111

GRAMMAR FOCUS

2.5 Articles

We use the indefinite article *a/an* with singular countable nouns when:
- the thing or person we are talking about is one of many similar people or things:
  The Oxo Tower is **a building** *in London.* (one of many)
- we mention a person or thing for the first time:
  There's **a restaurant** *on this street.*

We use the definite article *the* with singular and plural countable nouns and with uncountable nouns to talk about:
- something specific or unique:
  We often have a picnic in **the park**.
  Look at **the sky**.
- something we have mentioned before:
  There's a café and a restaurant on this street. **The restaurant** *is very expensive.*

We do not use an article:
- when we are talking about something in general:
  Juice *is very healthy.*
  I hate shopping in **supermarkets**.
- with months, days of the week, cities and most countries:
  every **August** *on* **Sundays** *near* **Valencia**
  from the south of **Italy**

1 Choose the correct options.

1 The Thames is *a / Ø* river in *the / Ø* England. *The / A* river is not very long.
2 I like *the / Ø* parties with *Ø / a* good food.
3 The Louvre is *an / Ø* art museum in *Ø / a* France. In *Ø / the* museum you can see *Ø / a* works of many artists.
4 I love *Ø / a* paella. It's *a / the* Spanish dish. It's delicious!
5 A: Try *a / the* grilled pork! It's very good.
   B: No, thank you. I don't eat *the / Ø* meat.
6 Ithaa is *an / Ø* undersea restaurant. When you're there, you can sometimes see *a / the* shark!
7 Thank you so much, *a / the* meal was delicious!
8 My mum usually cooks something special on *Ø / the* Sundays. It's usually *a / the* three-course meal.

2 Complete the sentences with *a/an*, *the* or *Ø* (no article).

1 _____ Cairo is _____ city in _____ Egypt. _____ city is very old.
2 We go to _____ Italy every year in _____ August.
3 A: What is the Tomatina?
   B: It's _____ festival in _____ Spain.
4 I meet my friends in _____ main square. We usually have _____ meal together.
5 For lunch I usually have _____ orange or _____ banana and some juice.
6 I don't really like _____ tuna.
7 I recommend this dish. _____ tuna salad is also fantastic.
8 _____ people from many countries come to _____ festival because it's lots of fun!

3.2 Present Continuous

We use the Present Continuous to talk about actions happening at the moment of speaking:
What **are** *you* **doing**?
The baby's **sleeping**.

SPELLING RULES – -ING FORM
- general rule: infinitive + *-ing*, e.g. *play – playing*
- verbs ending in a consonant + *-e*: -e + *-ing*, e.g. *come – coming*
- one-syllable verbs ending in a single vowel + a single consonant: double the consonant + *-ing*, e.g. *run – running*

Affirmative		Negative	
I	'm (am)	I	'm not (am not)
You/We/They	're (are) teaching.	You/We/They	aren't (are not) teaching.
He/She/It	's (is)	He/She/It	isn't (is not)

Yes/No questions		Short answers
Am	I	Yes, I am. No, I'm not.
Are	you/we/they teaching?	Yes, you/we/they are. No, you/we/they aren't.
Is	he/she/it	Yes, he/she/it is. No, he/she/it isn't.

Wh- questions			
Who	am	I	
	are	you/we/they	teaching?
	is	he/she/it	

1 Put the *-ing* form of the verbs in the box in the correct column.

build   chop   dig   fit   give   have   look   ride   sell

play – playing	come – coming	run – running

2 Complete the questions with the Present Continuous form of the verbs in brackets. Then match the questions (1–6) with the answers (a–f).

1 _____ (dog/run) round the garden? ☐
2 _____ (you/make) me a sandwich? ☐
3 _____ (they/sit) on the roof? ☐
4 _____ (he/fry) a fish? ☐
5 _____ (she/take) a shower? ☐
6 _____ (we/go) to the beach? ☐

a No, she isn't.   d Yes, it is.
b Yes, we are.   e No, I'm not.
c No, he isn't.   f Yes, they are.

3 Choose the correct options.

1 My wife *are / is* playing with the kids in the living room.
2 A: Are you working in the garden?
   B: Yes, *I am / I'm not*.
3 A: *The baby is / Is the baby* sleeping?
   B: No, *isn't / she isn't*. She's crying!
4 He *isn't / aren't* fishing right now; he's working.
5 *I'm not / aren't* watching TV at the moment.
6 A: What *are / is* the students doing?
   B: They*'re writing / write* an essay.
7 Why are you *wear / wearing* my coat?
8 We *is / are* planning our holiday in Greece. Do you want to come with us?

3.5 Present Simple and Present Continuous

We use the Present Simple to talk about:
- regular activities:
  I **have** breakfast at 7 o'clock.
- states and permanent situations:
  Do accountants **earn** a good salary?
- preferences, with verbs like *like, love, hate, prefer*:
  Children **love** water.

Common time expressions used with the Present Simple:
- *always*
- *often*
- *never*
- *sometimes*
- *usually*
- *every day/evening/week/winter*
- *on Sundays*

We use the Present Continuous to talk about:
- activities and events taking place at the moment of speaking:
  The manager **is talking** to the receptionist.
- temporary situations:
  I'm working at a holiday resort this summer.

Common time expressions used with the Present Continuous:
- *at the moment/right now*
- *now*
- *today*
- *this morning/evening*
- *this month*
- *this summer*

With some verbs (e.g. *believe, hate, know, like, love, mean, need, prefer, understand, want*) we don't use the Present Continuous even if they describe things happening at the moment of speaking:
I really **need** some help with this exercise!
I'm sorry, I **don't understand**.

1 Choose the correct options.

1 In some schools children often *learn / are learning* German. I like it, but *I'm preferring / prefer* English.
2 Today we *learn / are learning* about German culture.
3 This summer my sister *works / is working* in a local pub.
4 I'm a teacher. I *work / am working* with children.
5 The volunteers sometimes *teach / are teaching* local children agriculture.
6 This week we *teach / are teaching* them how to drive.

2 Complete the sentences with the words in the box.

| are | do | does | doesn't | is | isn't | 'm not |

1 I _____ not watching TV right now. I'm at school!
2 Why _____ you playing computer games? Do your homework first!
3 Which newspaper _____ you usually read?
4 She _____ understand you.
5 A: _____ she preparing food for us right now?
   B: No, she _____ .
6 A: What _____ he do?
   B: He's a lawyer.
7 I'm _____ gaining new experience in my job. It's really boring.

4.2 Comparative and superlative adjectives

- We use comparative adjectives and *than* to compare two people or things:
  My father is **younger than** my mother.
- We use superlative adjectives to say that someone or something has the highest degree of a certain quality (when compared with at least two other people or things):
  Sean is **the most intelligent** boy in our class.

Adjectives		Comparative	Superlative
one-syllable	kind	kinder	the kindest
	nice	nicer	the nicest
	fit	fitter	the fittest
one- and two-syllable ending in -y	funny	funnier	the funniest
	easy	easier	the easiest
two-syllable or longer	serious	more serious	the most serious
	difficult	more difficult	the most difficult
irregular	good	better	the best
	bad	worse	the worst
	far	further	the furthest

- We use *less* + comparative adjective to say that someone or something has a certain quality to a lesser degree:
  Daniel is **less sociable than** James.
- We use *the least* + adjective to say that someone or something has a certain quality to the least degree:
  This job is **the least demanding**.

GRAMMAR FOCUS

1 **Choose the correct ending for each sentence beginning.**
1 Julie is prettier
2 Megan is the prettiest
a girl in our school.   b than Emily.

3 You look more attractive
4 You look the most attractive
a in this skirt than in those jeans.   b in this dress.

5 This scarf is more stylish
6 This scarf is the most stylish
a thing I have.   b than that one.

7 She is funnier than
8 She is the funniest
a person in our family.   b most people.

2 **Complete the sentences with the words in the box.**

> better   kindest   less   more   most
> sociable   than   the   worst

1 My aunt is the most _____ person I know.
2 Is German more difficult _____ English?
3 A tracksuit is _____ formal than a suit.
4 These trainers are the _____ comfortable shoes I have.
5 Do you think Jason is _____-looking than Martin?
6 My grandma is the _____ person in the world. Everyone loves her.
7 This is the _____ restaurant in town. But it's also _____ cheapest one.
8 This jumper is _____ fashionable than that jacket.

4.5 have to/don't have to

We use *have to* to talk about rules, regulations and orders from other people:
I **have to** wear smart clothes at work.

We use *don't have to* to say that something is not necessary:
Celebrities **don't have to** get up early.

Affirmative		Negative		
I/You/We/They	have to	I/You/We/They	don't (do not) have to	work hard.
He/She/It	has to	He/She/It	doesn't (does not) have to	

Yes/No questions		Short answers
Do	I/you/we/they	Yes, I/you/we/they do.
	have to work hard?	No, I/you/we/they don't.
Does	he/she/it	Yes, he/she/it does.
		No, he/she/it doesn't.

Wh- questions				
Why	do	I/you/we/they	have to	work hard?
	does	he/she/it		

1 **Choose the correct answer, A, B or C for each group of sentences.**
1 I ____ or go to university. I don't know yet.
2 I ____ because my parents give me money.
3 I need money, so I ____ .
   A have to get a job
   B can get a job
   C don't have to get a job

4 What a mess! Your birthday party is tonight, so you ____ .
5 It's OK, you ____ tonight. You can do it later.
6 A: Mum, I'm bored!
   B: Well, you _____ and clean the kitchen!
   A don't have to tidy your room
   B can tidy your room
   C have to tidy your room

7 I'm sure it's the right size, but you ____ if you want to.
8 You look great in this shirt, but you ____ tonight. Wear something less formal.
9 I don't know if this is my size. I ____ and see.
   A have to try it on
   B can try it on
   C don't have to wear it

5.2 must/mustn't, should/shouldn't

- **Must** expresses obligation and necessity:
  You **must** be very careful with other people's things.
- **Mustn't** expresses prohibition:
  You **mustn't** cross that bridge. It isn't safe.
- To express lack of necessity or obligation, we use *don't have to*, not *mustn't*:
  You **don't have to** come with us. You can stay at home.
- Like all modal verbs, must and *mustn't* have the same form for every person:
  I/You/He/She/It/We/They **must** train a lot.
  I/You/He/She/It/We/They **mustn't** work so hard.
- We use *should/shouldn't* to give or ask for advice:
  You **should** study more.
  You **shouldn't** drink so much coffee.
  Should I ask for help?

Affirmative			Negative		
I/You/He/She/It/We/They	should	take risks.	I/You/He/She/It/We/They	shouldn't (should not)	take risks.

Yes/No questions			Short answers
Should	I/you/he/she/it/we/they	take risks?	Yes, I/you/he/she/it/we/they should. No, I/you/he/she/it/we/they shouldn't.

Wh- questions			
Why	should	I/you/he/she/it/we/they	take risks?

1 Complete the sentences with the words in the box.

> doesn't have to   don't have to   must (x2)
> mustn't (x2)   should   shouldn't

1 Do you think I _____ go to a film school? Is it a good idea?
2 We _____ cheat in exams at our school. It's the rule!
3 You _____ do your homework now. You can do it later.
4 I get up at six because I _____ be at school at eight.
5 My sister _____ wear a uniform at her school. She's so lucky! I hate my uniform.
6 You _____ leave school yet – it's not a good idea. Pass your exams first.
7 You _____ use your phones in class. Never do that!
8 To be a vet, you _____ like animals. It's important!

2 Complete the sentences with *must*, *mustn't*, *should*, *shouldn't* or *don't/doesn't have to*. The context is given in brackets.

1 _____ I go to that college? (Do you think it's a good idea?)
2 We _____ practise the violin every day. (It's necessary.)
3 You _____ miss so many classes. (It's not a good idea.)
4 We _____ be late for lessons. (It's the rule.)
5 You _____ do extra activities. (It's not necessary.)
6 You _____ train to become a teacher. (It's a good idea.)
7 My daughter _____ wear a school uniform. (It's not necessary.)
8 You _____ try to get good marks! (It's necessary.)

5.5 Past Simple: was/were, could

- We use the Past Simple to talk about events and situations that started and ended in the past:
John and I **were** at the same school.
We both **could** play basketball and football, but we **couldn't** play tennis.
- The Past Simple form of the verb *to be* is *was/were*:

Affirmative		Negative		
I/He/She/It	was	I/He/She/It	wasn't (was not)	at school.
You/We/They	were	You/We/They	weren't (were not)	

Yes/No questions		Short answers
Was	I/he/she/it	Yes, I/he/she/it was.
	at school?	No, I/he/she/it wasn't.
Were	you/we/they	Yes, you/we/they were.
		No, you/we/they weren't.

Wh- questions		
Where	was	I/he/she/it?
	were	you/we/they?

The Past Simple form of *can* is *could*.

Affirmative		Negative	
I/You/He/She/It/We/They	could sing.	I/You/He/She/It/We/They	couldn't (could not) sing.

Yes/No questions		Short answers
Could	I/you/he/she/it/we/they sing?	Yes, I/you/he/she/it/we/they could. No, I/you/he/she/it/we/they couldn't.

Wh- questions			
What	could	I/you/he/she/it/we/they	sing?

1 Choose the correct options.

1 School *wasn't / couldn't* always fun for me.
2 When I was younger, I *wasn't / weren't* very good at sports.
3 I *wasn't / couldn't* understand Maths.
4 A: *Could / Were* you play a musical instrument when you were a child?
  B: Yes, I *was / could*.
5 A: *Were / Was* high school a nice experience for you?
  B: Yes, it *was / were*.
6 All my children *was / were* bad at History when they were at school.
7 A: What *was / were* your favourite school subjects?
  B: History *was / could* great. I *couldn't / wasn't* speak French well, but that *was / could* interesting, too!
8 Your sister *could / was* Miss Teen London. *Could / Were* you jealous?

2 Complete the sentences with *was/wasn't*, *were/weren't* or *could/couldn't*.

1 Science _____ a compulsory subject at my school. I _____ study Geography instead.
2 When I _____ five, I _____ speak a little French.
3 A: _____ you a noisy child?
  B: No, I _____ .
4 The other kids my age _____ very friendly to me, so I often felt lonely.
5 At school I _____ understand science at all. I _____ very bad at it.
6 A: _____ Einstein good at Maths?
  B: Yes, he _____ .
7 A: What _____ you good at as a child?
  B: Well, I _____ run really fast.
8 When my children _____ at primary school, they _____ play any musical instruments yet.
9 Her secondary school _____ single-sex. There _____ boys and girls in her class.
10 Last week it _____ very cold in the classroom. We _____ think or write!

GRAMMAR FOCUS

6.2 Past Simple: affirmatives

We use the Past Simple to talk about activities and events that happened in the past. We often say when they happened:
My dad **climbed** in the Himalayas in 1988.
I **had** eggs for breakfast.

SPELLING RULES – PAST SIMPLE FORM

Regular verbs
- general rule: infinitive + -ed, e.g. *work – worked*
- verbs ending in -e: + -d, e.g. *like – liked*
- verbs ending in a vowel + a consonant: double the consonant + -ed, e.g. *stop – stopped*
- verbs ending in a consonant + -y: -y + -ied. e.g. *cry – cried*

Irregular verbs
There are many irregular verbs (e.g. *go, say, run*). There is a list of irregular verbs in Word Store, page 23.

1 Put the Past Simple form of the verbs in the box in the correct column.

arrive   cycle   fit   marry   plan   stay   try   walk

work – worked	like – liked	stop – stopped	cry – cried

2 Complete the sentences with the Past Simple form of the verbs in brackets.
  1 We _____ (play) tennis for two hours yesterday.
  2 Last weekend my son _____ (break) his arm and _____ (go) to hospital.
  3 She _____ (want) to go to the mountains for the holidays.
  4 We _____ (spend) the day at the seaside.
  5 I _____ (look) for yoga classes in my town, but I couldn't find anything.
  6 My mum _____ (help) me do my Maths homework.
  7 He _____ (shout) for help, but no one heard him.
  8 They _____ (say) they wanted to stay at home.

3 Complete the sentences with the Past Simple form of the verbs in the box.

bake   carry   cry   give   stop   study

  1 We _____ at the same university.
  2 The baby _____ for three hours!
  3 My mum _____ a cake for my birthday.
  4 My parents _____ me a puppy for my birthday.
  5 He _____ my suitcase. Such a gentleman!
  6 We _____ for a short break.

6.5 Past Simple: questions and negatives

Negative

I/You/He/She/It/We/They   didn't (did not)   win.

Yes/No questions	Short answers
Did I/you/he/she/it/we/they win?	Yes, I/you/he/she/it/we/they **did**. No, I/you/he/she/it/we/they **didn't**.

Wh- questions

What   did   I/you/he/she/it/we/they   win?

1 Complete the sentences with *did* or *didn't*.
  1 When _____ the first Olympic Games take place?
  2 A: _____ the winner get a gold medal?
    B: No, he _____ .
  3 A: _____ you take part in that competition?
    B: No. I _____ want to.
  4 A: What _____ you win?
    B: I _____ win anything. But it's not a problem for me.
  5 A: _____ you watch the 2012 Summer Olympics?
    B: Yes, I _____ .
  6 A: Where _____ you go skiing last winter?
    B: We _____ go skiing. We went to Egypt.
  7 _____ they promise to pay for your treatment?
  8 I _____ want to play football like my older brother. I preferred hockey.

2 Choose the correct answer, A, B or C, for each group of sentences.
  1 Mum is angry with you because _____ go to school today.
  2 Why _____ go to school today? You're not sick!
  3 Where _____ go after school? I want to know.
    A didn't you   B did you   C you didn't
  4 How many medals _____ win?
  5 She was a great gymnast, but _____ win any medals at the 2012 Olympics.
  6 A: Why _____ go sailing with us?
    B: She was ill.
    A she didn't   B didn't she   C did she

116

7.2 Present Perfect with ever/never

Present Perfect
- We use the Present Perfect to talk about actions and events which ended in the past but we don't know or it's not important when exactly they happened:
  Kate **has swum** in the ocean.
  Have you ever **travelled** by plane?
- We form the Present Perfect with the auxiliary verb *have/has* and the past participle form of the main verb.

Affirmative			Negative		
I/You/We/They	've (have)	visited Rome.	I/You/We/They	haven't (have not)	visited Rome.
He/She/It	's (has)		He/She/It	hasn't (has not)	

Yes/No questions			Short answers
Have	I/you/we/they	visited Rome?	Yes, I/you/we/they **have**. No, I/you/we/they **haven't**.
Has	he/she/it		Yes, he/she/it **has**. No, he/she/it **hasn't**.

Wh- questions			
What	have	I/you/we/they	visited?
	has	he/she/it	

SPELLING RULES – PAST PARTICIPLE:

Regular verbs
The spelling rules for the past participle form of regular verbs are the same as the Past Simple form; you can find them on page 116.

Irregular verbs
There are many irregular verbs (e.g. *go, say, run*). There is a list of irregular verbs in Word Store, page 23.

be and go
- The past participle form of *be* is *been*:
  Have you ever **been** really scared?
- *Go* has two past participle forms, *been* and *gone*, which have different meanings:
  My parents **have been** to Italy. (Some time ago. They are no longer there.)
  My parents **have gone to** Italy. (They are still in Italy).
- We often use *been* when talking about sports or other physical activities:
  I've been bungee jumping.

ever and never
We often use *ever* and *never* with the Present Perfect:
- We use *ever* in questions:
  Have you **ever** been camping?
- We use *never* in negatives. Remember that in sentences with *never*, we use the affirmative form of the verb:
  Our teacher has **never** taken us on a school trip.

Present Simple and Past Simple
- We use the Present Perfect to talk about actions and events that ended in the past. We do not say when exactly they happened:
  I'**ve seen** the Statue of Liberty.
- If we want to say or ask when something happened, we use the Past Simple.
  When **did** you **see** the Statue of Liberty?
  I **saw** the Statue of Liberty last year.

1 Complete the sentences with the words in the box.

[been   ever   gone   has   hasn't   have   haven't   never]

1 A: _____ he ever been on an adventure holiday?
   B: No, he hasn't.
2 I've _____ tried hang-gliding. Is it fun?
3 Pat isn't in town at the moment. She's _____ on holiday.
4 A: Have you _____ stayed in a luxury hotel?
   B: No, I _____ , but I'd love to do that!
5 A: Susan, _____ you ever been abroad?
   B: Yes, I've _____ to France. I went there last year.
6 A: Has she ever ridden a camel?
   B: No, she _____ . That's why she's so excited about the trip to Egypt!

2 Complete the sentences with *been* or *gone*.

1 I can't believe you've never _____ kayaking!
2 My parents have _____ to Spain for two weeks. There's nobody in the house, so we can have a picnic in our garden.
3 We've already _____ to Rome and Paris. We'd like to go again next year.
4 Has she ever _____ mountain biking?
5 Jack isn't in the office today. He's _____ to Berlin.

3 Choose the correct options.

A: ¹Have you ever booked / Did you ever book a flight online?
B: Yes, I ²have / did. In fact, I ³have booked / booked a flight to Greece yesterday.

A: Last summer we ⁴'ve gone / went to the mountains.
B: Oh, great! ⁵Have you gone / Did you go rock-climbing?
A: Yes, we ⁶did / have. It ⁷was / has been great!

A: Tom isn't here right now. He ⁸'s gone / went on holiday.
B: Really? When ⁹has he left / did he leave?
A: He ¹⁰'s taken / took a train to Hungary two days ago. I think he's in Croatia now.

117

GRAMMAR FOCUS

7.5 Present Perfect with just/already/yet

We often use these adverbs with the Present Perfect:
- *just* – in affirmative sentences, before the main verb:
  They have **just** reached the Antarctic.
- *already* – in affirmative sentences, before the main verb:
  The children have **already** been to the science centre.
- *(not) yet* – in questions or negatives, at the end of the sentence:
  Have you raised enough money **yet**?
  No, we haven't raised enough **yet**.

1 Complete the sentences with *just*, *already* or *yet*.

1. A: Have you booked a hotel for us _____ ?
   B: Yes, I've _____ done it, don't worry.
2. A: Has Charles been to Scott Island _____ ?
   B: No, he hasn't been there _____ .
3. A: Why are you so happy?
   B: I've _____ booked us a trip abroad!
4. A: Have they opened a space hotel _____ ?
   B: No, they haven't done it _____ .
5. A: You look very fit!
   B: Well, I've _____ come back from a cycling trip.
6. He's _____ been to over 500 countries, but he hasn't been to the English seaside _____ !

2 Put the words in the correct order to make sentences.

1. restaurant / eaten / yet / haven't / I / this / at
   _____
2. arrangements / I / the / made / have / already
   _____
3. New Zealand / he / reached / just / has
   _____
4. London / yet / have / to / moved / you?
   _____
5. ferry / I / already / this / taken / have
   _____
6. from / back / a / have / we / just / camping holiday / come
   _____
7. hasn't / yet / he / booking / changed / the
   _____
8. seen / sights / already / have / the / we
   _____

8.2 Future with *will*

We use *will/won't* to make predictions based on our opinions, feelings or experiences:
I think people **will travel** in time.
Will climate change **destroy** coral reefs?

Affirmative			Negative		
I/You/He/She/It/We/They	'll (will)	change.	I/You/He/She/It/We/They	won't (will not)	change.

Yes/No questions			Short answers
Will	I/you/he/she/it/we/they	change?	Yes, I/you/he/she/it/we/they will. No, I/you/he/she/it/we/they won't.

Wh- questions				
How	will	I/you/he/she/it/ we/they	change?	

The future form of *can/can't* is *will/won't be able to*:
Sixteen-year-olds **will be able to** vote in elections.
Cars **won't be able to** fly.
We use *will + get/become + comparative adjective* to say that a situation is going to change:
Rail travel **will become more popular**.
Things **won't get better**.

1 Complete the short answers.

1. A: Do you think air pollution will get worse in the future?
   B: Yes, _____ . I'm sure.
2. A: Will there be snowy winters in the future?
   B: Yes, _____ . Don't worry.
3. A: Will the climate become tropical all over the world?
   B: No, _____ .
4. A: Will people save water in the future?
   B: No, _____ . People are too lazy.

2 Complete the sentences with *will* and the verbs in the box.

| can   die   disappear   get   not be |

1. Scientists predict that the climate _____ warmer in the future.
2. Some islands _____ under the sea.
3. Some people fear that there _____ enough clean water for everyone.
4. I believe that we _____ solve the world energy problem.
5. Some animals _____ out before the end of the century.

8.5 be going to

We use *be going to* to talk about future intentions and plans:
I**'m going to** study Medicine.
Is Meg **going to** invite me to her birthday party?

Affirmative				Negative			
I	'm (am)			I	'm not (am not)		
You/We/They	're (are)	going to	travel.	You/We/They	aren't (are not)	going to	travel.
He/She/It	's (is)			He/She/It	isn't (is not)		

Yes/No questions				Short answers
Am	I			Yes, I **am**. No, I**'m not**.
Are	you/we/they	going to	travel?	Yes, you/we/they **are**. No, you/we/they **aren't**.
Is	he/she/it			Yes, he/she/it **is**. No, he/she/it **isn't**.

Wh- questions				
Where	am	I	going to	travel?
	is	he/she/it		
	are	you/we/they		

1 Complete the sentences with the words in the box. There are two extra words.

> are   aren't   going   is   isn't   'm   not   to

1. I'm going _____ travel to the Amazon this summer.
2. My friend _____ going to rescue sea turtles as a volunteer. It sounds exciting.
3. I'm _____ going to do any birdwatching. I'm sure it's really boring.
4. She _____ going to travel east. She's going to travel west!
5. I love the ocean, so I _____ going to travel to the Pacific next year.
6. A: _____ they going to go to university after school?
   B: No, they aren't.

2 Complete the sentences with *be going to* and the correct form of the verbs in brackets.

1. We _____ (not visit) Cornwall this weekend.
2. How many trees _____ (they/cut down)?
3. We _____ (not see) the Himalayas.
4. She _____ (travel) round Europe by car.
5. _____ (we/visit) any museums?
6. You _____ (swim) in the coral reef! That's amazing!

119

01 WORD LIST • FAMILY AND FRIENDS

Free time
coach a football team /ˌkəʊtʃ ə ˈfʊtbɔːl tiːm/
go for a swim/a walk /ˌgəʊ fər ə ˈswɪm/ə ˈwɔːk/
go on holiday /ˌgəʊ ɒn ˈhɒlədeɪ/
go on the Internet /ˌgəʊ ɒn ði ˈɪntənet/
go out (with friends) /ˌgəʊ ˌaʊt (wɪð ˈfrendz)/
go out for dinner /ˌgəʊ ˌaʊt fə ˈdɪnə/
go rollerblading/dancing /ˌgəʊ ˈrəʊləbleɪdɪŋ/ˈdɑːnsɪŋ/
go shopping/to the shops /ˌgəʊ ˈʃɒpɪŋ/tə ðə ˈʃɒps/
go to a party/concert /ˌgəʊ tə ə ˈpɑːti/ˈkɒnsət/
go to the park/cinema/gym/sports centre/youth club /ˌgəʊ tə ðə ˈpɑːk/ˈsɪnəmə/ˈdʒɪm/ˈspɔːts ˌsentə/ˈjuːθ klʌb/
have a picnic /ˌhæv ə ˈpɪknɪk/
have fun/a good time /ˌhæv ˈfʌn/ə ˌgʊd ˈtaɪm/
listen to music /ˌlɪsən tə ˈmjuːzɪk/
play a musical instrument/the guitar/the piano/the drums /ˌpleɪ ə ˌmjuːzɪkəl ˈɪnstrəmənt/ðə gɪˈtɑː/ðə piˈænəʊ/ðə ˈdrʌmz/
play ball/chess/snooker/football/tennis/computer games /ˌpleɪ ˈbɔːl/ˈtʃes/ˈsnuːkə/ˈfʊtbɔːl/ˈtenəs/kəmˈpjuːtə geɪmz/
play together /ˌpleɪ təˈgeðə/
post photos on Facebook /ˌpəʊst ˌfəʊtəʊz ɒn ˈfeɪsbʊk/
read books/magazines/news websites /ˌriːd ˈbʊks/ˌmægəˈziːnz/ˈnjuːz ˌwebsaɪts/
relax /rɪˈlæks/
spend a lot of time alone/together/with my friends/with my grandparents /ˌspend ə ˌlɒt əv ˌtaɪm əˈləʊn/təˈgeðə/wɪð maɪ ˈfrendz/wɪð maɪ ˈgrænd ˌpeərənts/
spend time at home/at school/at my grandparents'/in my room/in my bedroom /ˌspend taɪm ət ˈhəʊm/ət ˈskuːl/ət maɪ ˈgrænd ˌpeərənts/ɪn maɪ ˈruːm/ɪn maɪ ˈbedrʊm/
stay at home /ˌsteɪ ət ˈhəʊm/
take photographs/photos /ˌteɪk ˈfəʊtəgrɑːfs/ˈfəʊtəʊz/
talk about books/films /ˌtɔːk əˌbaʊt ˈbʊks/ˈfɪlmz/
visit friends/different places /ˌvɪzət ˈfrendz/ˌdɪfərənt ˈpleɪsɪz/
watch a film/a DVD/music videos on YouTube/TV/the telly/sports on TV /ˌwɒtʃ ə ˈfɪlm/ə ˌdiː viː ˈdiː/ˈmjuːzɪk ˌvɪdiəʊz ɒn ˈjuːtjuːb/ˌtiː ˈviː/ðə ˈteli/spɔːts ɒn ˌtiː ˈviː/
write a blog /ˌraɪt ə ˈblɒg/

Interests and preferences
be interested in /bi ˈɪntrəstəd ɪn/
hate/can't stand (Twitter/rollerblading) /ˌheɪt/ˌkɑːnt ˌstænd (ˈtwɪtə/ˈrəʊləbleɪdɪŋ)/
like (films/reading) /ˌlaɪk (ˈfɪlmz/ˈriːdɪŋ)/
love (weekends/cooking) /ˌlʌv (ˌwiːkˈendz/ˈkʊkɪŋ)/
prefer (rap/to relax at home) /prɪˌfɜː (ˈræp/tə rɪˌlæks ət ˈhəʊm)/

Adjectives
awesome /ˈɔːsəm/
awful /ˈɔːfəl/
brilliant /ˈbrɪljənt/
favourite /ˈfeɪvərət/
good /gʊd/
great /greɪt/
interesting /ˈɪntrəstɪŋ/
rubbish /ˈrʌbɪʃ/
terrible /ˈterəbəl/

Music
dance class /ˈdɑːns klɑːs/
fantastic voice /fænˌtæstɪk ˈvɔɪs/
guitar lesson /gɪˈtɑː ˌlesən/
practise/play (the guitar) /ˌpræktəs/ˌpleɪ (ðə gɪˈtɑː)/
rock star /ˈrɒk stɑː/
singer /ˈsɪŋə/
studio /ˈstjuːdiəʊ/
write songs /ˌraɪt ˈsɒŋz/

Kinds of music
classical /ˈklæsɪkəl/
jazz /dʒæz/
pop /pɒp/
rap /ræp/
reggae /ˈregeɪ/
rock /rɒk/

Musical instruments
drums /drʌmz/
guitar /gɪˈtɑː/
piano /piˈænəʊ/

Books and films
actor/actress /ˈæktə/ˈæktrəs/
author/writer /ˈɔːθə/ˈraɪtə/
fantasy /ˈfæntəsi/
film star /ˈfɪlm stɑː/
movie/film /ˈmuːvi/fɪlm/
read a lot /ˌriːd ə ˈlɒt/
true life films /ˌtruː ˈlaɪf fɪlmz/
science fiction /ˌsaɪəns ˈfɪkʃən/
vampire stories /ˈvæmpaɪə ˌstɔːriz/

Family and friends
aunt /ɑːnt/
baby /ˈbeɪbi/
best friend /ˌbest ˈfrend/
brother /ˈbrʌðə/
child/children /tʃaɪld/ˈtʃɪldrən/
father/dad /ˈfɑːðə/dæd/
grandmother /ˈgræn ˌmʌðə/
grandparents /ˈgrænd ˌpeərənts/
husband /ˈhʌzbənd/
mother/mum /ˈmʌðə/mʌm/
sister /ˈsɪstə/
son /sʌn/
uncle /ˈʌŋkəl/
wife /waɪf/

Everyday life
be busy (with sth) /ˌbi ˈbɪzi (wɪð ˌsʌmθɪŋ)/
be late for school /bi ˌleɪt fə ˈskuːl/
clean the house/flat /ˌkliːn ðə ˈhaʊs/ˈflæt/
come/go back home from work/school /ˌkʌm/ˌgəʊ bæk ˌhəʊm frəm ˈwɜːk/ˈskuːl/
do homework /ˌduː ˈhəʊmwɜːk/
do the shopping /ˌduː ðə ˈʃɒpɪŋ/
get ready for work /ˌget ˌredi fə ˈwɜːk/
go to bed (early) /ˌgəʊ tə ˌbed (ˈɜːli)/
have a bath/a shower /ˌhæv ə ˈbɑːθ/ə ˈʃaʊə/
have breakfast/lunch/dinner/supper /ˌhæv ˈbrekfəst/ˈlʌntʃ/ˈdɪnə/ˈsʌpə/
look after the children /ˌlʊk ˌɑːftə ðə ˈtʃɪldrən/
start /stɑːt/
study /ˈstʌdi/
take/drive the child to school/to the playgroup /ˌteɪk/ˌdraɪv ðə tʃaɪld tə ˈskuːl/tə ðə ˈpleɪgruːp/
wake up/get up (early) /ˌweɪk ˈʌp/ˌget ˌʌp (ˈɜːli)/
wash the car/the dishes /ˌwɒʃ ðə ˈkɑː/ðə ˈdɪʃɪz/
work in the garden /ˌwɜːk ɪn ðə ˈgɑːdn/

Time expressions
at night /ət ˈnaɪt/
at noon/at midnight/at one o'clock /ət ˈnuːn/ət ˈmɪdnaɪt/ət ˌwʌn əˈklɒk/
at the weekend /ət ðə ˌwiːkˈend/
every day/Saturday/weekend /ˌevri ˈdeɪ/ˈsætədi/wiːkˈend/
in the morning/afternoon/evening /ɪn ðə ˈmɔːnɪŋ/ˌɑːftəˈnuːn/ˈiːvnɪŋ/
on a typical weekend/school day /ɒn ə ˌtɪpɪkəl ˌwiːkˈend/ˈskuːl deɪ/
on Friday afternoon/Friday night /ɒn ˌfraɪdi ˌɑːftəˈnuːn/ˌfraɪdi ˈnaɪt/
on Friday/Saturday /ɒn ˈfraɪdi/ˈsætədi/
on Saturdays/Sundays /ɒn ˈsætədeɪz/ˈsʌndeɪz/
on Sunday mornings /ɒn ˌsʌndi ˈmɔːnɪŋz/
on weekdays /ɒn ˈwiːkdeɪz/
what time? /ˌwɒt ˈtaɪm/

Adverbs of frequency
always /ˈɔːlwəz/
never /ˈnevə/
often /ˈɒfən/
sometimes /ˈsʌmtaɪmz/
usually /ˈjuːʒuəli/

Work
earn (a lot of money) /ˌɜːn (ə ˌlɒt əv ˈmʌni)/
have a job (in one's family's business) /ˌhæv ə ˈdʒɒb (ɪn wʌnz ˌfæməliz ˈbɪznəs)/
make money /ˌmeɪk ˈmʌni/
weekend job /ˌwiːkend ˈdʒɒb/
work as (a programmer/a teacher) /ˌwɜːk əz (ə ˈprəʊgræmə/ə ˈtiːtʃə)/
work for (a construction company) /ˌwɜːk fər (ə kənˈstrʌkʃən ˌkʌmpəni)/
work in (a restaurant) /ˌwɜːk ɪn (ə ˈrestərɒnt)/
work with (children) /ˌwɜːk wɪð (ˈtʃɪldrən)/

Other
age /eɪdʒ/
exercise /ˈeksəsaɪz/
give advice /ˌgɪv ədˈvaɪs/
grow /grəʊ/
hour /aʊə/
invite /ɪnˈvaɪt/
miss /mɪs/
normal /ˈnɔːməl/

02 WORD LIST • FOOD

Fruit
apple /ˈæpəl/
banana /bəˈnɑːnə/
orange /ˈɒrəndʒ/
strawberry /ˈstrɔːbəri/

Vegetables
carrot /ˈkærət/
mushroom /ˈmʌʃruːm/
onion /ˈʌnjən/
potato /pəˈteɪtəʊ/
tomato /təˈmɑːtəʊ/

Dairy
milk /mɪlk/
(mozzarella) cheese /(ˌmɒtsəˌrelə) ˈtʃiːz/
ice cream /ˌaɪs ˈkriːm/

Meat and fish
chicken /ˈtʃɪkən/
ham /hæm/
pork /pɔːk/
tuna /ˈtjuːnə/

Drinks
cola /ˈkəʊlə/
juice /dʒuːs/
lemonade /ˌleməˈneɪd/
(mineral) water /(ˈmɪnərəl) ˌwɔːtə/
tea /tiː/

Other products
basil /ˈbæzəl/
bread /bred/
chocolate /ˈtʃɒklət/
cornflakes /ˈkɔːnfleɪks/
crisps /krɪsps/
egg /eg/
fat /fæt/
flour /flaʊə/
honey /ˈhʌni/
ketchup /ˈketʃəp/
mayonnaise /ˌmeɪəˈneɪz/
oil /ɔɪl/
olive oil /ˈɒlɪv ɔɪl/
rice /raɪs/
seafood /ˈsiːfuːd/
tomato sauce /təˈmɑːtəʊ sɔːs/

Dishes
hamburger/burger /ˈhæmbɜːɡə/ˈbɜːɡə/
hot dog /ˈhɒt dɒɡ/
Indian meal /ˌɪndiən ˈmiːl/
omelette /ˈɒmlət/
pancake /ˈpænkeɪk/
pasta /ˈpæstə/
pizza /ˈpiːtsə/
salad /ˈsæləd/
sandwich /ˈsænwɪdʒ/
sausage /ˈsɒsɪdʒ/
sauce /sɔːs/
soup /suːp/
spaghetti /spəˈɡeti/

Meals
breakfast /ˈbrekfəst/
dessert /dɪˈzɜːt/
for breakfast/for dessert /fə ˈbrekfəst/ fə dɪˈzɜːt/
lunch /lʌntʃ/
lunch time /ˈlʌntʃ taɪm/
(main) course /(ˌmeɪn) ˈkɔːs/
snack /snæk/
tea /tiː/

(two-/three-course) dinner /ˌtuː/ˌθriː kɔːs ˈdɪnə/

Containers
a bag of (potatoes) /ə ˌbæɡ əv (pəˈteɪtəʊz)/
a bar of (chocolate) /ə ˌbɑːr əv (ˈtʃɒklət)/
a bottle of (ketchup) /ə ˌbɒtl əv (ˈketʃəp)/
a can of (lemonade) /ə ˌkæn əv (ˌleməˈneɪd)/
a carton of (milk) /ə ˌkɑːtn əv (ˈmɪlk)/
a cup of (flour) /ə ˌkʌp əv (ˈflaʊə)/
a jar of (honey) /ə ˌdʒɑːr əv (ˈhʌni)/
a loaf of (bread) /ə ˌləʊf əv (ˈbred)/
a packet of (crisps) /ə ˌpækət əv (ˈkrɪsps)/
a tin of (tuna) (BrE)/a can of (tuna) (AmE) /ə ˌtɪn əv (ˈtjuːnə)/ə ˌkæn əv (ˈtjuːnə)/
a tub of (ice cream) /ə ˌtʌb əv (ˌaɪs ˈkriːm)/

Preparing food
boil /bɔɪl/
chop /tʃɒp/
fridge /frɪdʒ/
fry (on both sides) /fraɪ (ɒn ˌbəʊθ ˈsaɪdz)/
heat /hiːt/
(main) ingredient /(ˌmeɪn) ɪnˈɡriːdiənt/
make a snack /ˌmeɪk ə ˈsnæk/
mix /mɪks/
mixture /ˈmɪkstʃə/
pan /pæn/
prepare /prɪˈpeə/
put sth on top of sth /ˌpʊt ˌsʌmθɪŋ ɒn ˈtɒp əv ˌsʌmθɪŋ/
recipe /ˈresəpi/
slice /slaɪs/
take out /ˌteɪk ˈaʊt/
try /traɪ/

Food adjectives
delicious /dɪˈlɪʃəs/
fantastic /fænˈtæstɪk/
favourite /ˈfeɪvərət/
fresh /freʃ/
grilled /ɡrɪld/
healthy /ˈhelθi/
hot/spicy /hɒt/ˈspaɪsi/
local /ˈləʊkəl/
strong /strɒŋ/
sweet /swiːt/
traditional /trəˈdɪʃənəl/
typical /ˈtɪpɪkəl/
unhealthy /ʌnˈhelθi/
vegetarian /ˌvedʒəˈteəriən/
wild /waɪld/

Shopping
checkout /ˈtʃekaʊt/
go shopping /ˌɡəʊ ˈʃɒpɪŋ/
shelf/shelves /ʃelf/ʃelvz/
shopping basket /ˈʃɒpɪŋ ˌbɑːskət/
supermarket /ˈsuːpəˌmɑːkət/
trolley /ˈtrɒli/

Restaurants
burger bar /ˈbɜːɡə bɑː/
chef/cook /ʃef/kʊk/
choose /tʃuːz/
cost /kɒst/
Enjoy your meal! /ɪnˌdʒɔɪ jə ˈmiːl/
expensive /ɪkˈspensɪv/
fast food /ˌfɑːst ˈfuːd/
get a takeaway /ˌɡet ə ˈteɪkəweɪ/
go out for a meal /ˌɡəʊ ˌaʊt fər ə ˈmiːl/
kebab bar /kəˈbæb bɑː/
large/small /lɑːdʒ/smɔːl/
menu /ˈmenjuː/

order /ˈɔːdə/
oriental restaurant /ˌɔːriˌentl ˈrestərɒnt/
pizza place /ˈpiːtsə pleɪs/
price /praɪs/
serve /sɜːv/
waiter/server /ˈweɪtə/ˈsɜːvə/

Other
at least /ət ˈliːst/
below /bɪˈləʊ/
birthday party /ˈbɜːθdeɪ ˌpɑːti/
celebrate /ˈseləbreɪt/
countryside /ˈkʌntrisaɪd/
crocodile /ˈkrɒkədaɪl/
dangerous /ˈdeɪndʒərəs/
each /iːtʃ/
experience /ɪkˈspɪəriəns/
fancy-dress party /ˈfænsi ˈdres ˌpɑːti/
(food) festival /(ˈfuːd) ˈfestəvəl/
from above /frəm əˈbʌv/
happen /ˈhæpən/
have /hæv/
hungry /ˈhʌŋɡri/
hurt /hɜːt/
in front of the telly /ɪn ˌfrʌnt əv ðə ˈteli/
it doesn't matter /ɪt ˌdʌzənt ˈmætə/
(main) square /(ˌmeɪn) ˈskweə/
messy /ˈmesi/
need /niːd/
north /nɔːθ/
push /pʊʃ/
rate /reɪt/
recommend /ˌrekəˈmend/
shark /ʃɑːk/
south /saʊθ/
stairs /steəz/
taste /teɪst/
team /tiːm/
throw /θrəʊ/
touch screen /ˈtʌtʃ skriːn/
tracks /træks/
undersea /ˌʌndəˈsiː/
upstairs /ʌpˈsteəz/
worth /wɜːθ/

121

03 WORD LIST • WORK

Jobs
accountant /əˈkaʊntənt/
actor/actress /ˈæktə/ˈæktrəs/
architect /ˈɑːkətekt/
artist /ˈɑːtəst/
au pair /ˌəʊ ˈpeə/
author /ˈɔːθə/
builder /ˈbɪldə/
dentist /ˈdentəst/
doctor /ˈdɒktə/
engineer /ˌendʒəˈnɪə/
factory worker /ˈfæktəri ˌwɜːkə/
farmer /ˈfɑːmə/
gardener /ˈɡɑːdnə/
hairdresser /ˈheəˌdresə/
journalist /ˈdʒɜːnələst/
lawyer /ˈlɔːjə/
mechanic /mɪˈkænɪk/
nurse /nɜːs/
photographer /fəˈtɒɡrəfə/
plumber /ˈplʌmə/
programmer /ˈprəʊɡræmə/
receptionist /rɪˈsepʃənəst/
scientist /ˈsaɪəntəst/
secretary /ˈsekrətəri/
shop assistant /ˈʃɒp əˌsɪstənt/
soldier /ˈsəʊldʒə/
sports instructor /ˈspɔːts ɪnˌstrʌktə/
taxi driver /ˈtæksi ˌdraɪvə/
teacher /ˈtiːtʃə/
vet /vet/
waiter/waitress /ˈweɪtə/ˈweɪtrəs/

Workplaces
business /ˈbɪznəs/
café /ˈkæfeɪ/
factory /ˈfæktəri/
holiday resort /ˈhɒlədeɪ rɪˌzɔːt/
hospital /ˈhɒspɪtl/
hotel /həʊˈtel/
(international) company /(ˌɪntəˌnæʃənəl) ˈkʌmpəni/
office /ˈɒfəs/
school /skuːl/
supermarket /ˈsuːpəˌmɑːkət/
travel company /ˈtrævəl ˌkʌmpəni/

At work
finish work at (5 p.m.) /ˌfɪnɪʃ ˌwɜːk ət (faɪv ˌpiː ˈem)/
gain experience /ˌɡeɪn ɪkˈspɪəriəns/
have a job /ˌhæv ə ˈdʒɒb/
holiday job /ˈhɒlədeɪ dʒɒb/
learn sth/about sth/to do sth /ˈlɜːn ˌsʌmθɪŋ/ əˌbaʊt ˌsʌmθɪŋ/tə ˌduː ˌsʌmθɪŋ/
meet people /ˌmiːt ˈpiːpəl/
meeting /ˈmiːtɪŋ/
physical work /ˌfɪzɪkəl ˈwɜːk/
practical skills /ˌpræktɪkəl ˈskɪlz/
work (eight) hours a day /ˌwɜːk (eɪt) ˌaʊəz ə ˈdeɪ/
work abroad /ˌwɜːk əˈbrɔːd/
work alone/in a team /ˌwɜːk əˈləʊn/ɪn ə ˈtiːm/
work for (a company) /ˌwɜːk fər (ə ˈkʌmpəni)/
work from home /ˌwɜːk frəm ˈhəʊm/
work full-time/part-time /ˌwɜːk ˌfʊl ˈtaɪm/ˌpɑːt ˈtaɪm/
work hard /ˌwɜːk ˈhɑːd/
work in (a supermarket) /ˌwɜːk ɪn (ə ˈsuːpəˌmɑːkət)/
work long hours /ˌwɜːk lɒŋ ˈaʊəz/
work nine to five /ˌwɜːk naɪn tə ˈfaɪv/
work outside /ˌwɜːk aʊtˈsaɪd/

work with people/children/adults/numbers /ˌwɜːk wɪð ˈpiːpəl/ˈtʃɪldrən/ˈædʌlts/ˈnʌmbəz/
work with your hands /ˌwɜːk wɪð jə ˈhændz/
working day /ˌwɜːkɪŋ ˈdeɪ/

Job duties
ask people their opinion /ˌɑːsk ˌpiːpəl ðeər əˈpɪnjən/
be responsible for /bi rɪˈspɒnsəbəl fə/
build /bɪld/
dig /dɪɡ/
email sb/write/send an email to sb /ˈiːmeɪl ˌsʌmbɒdi/ˌraɪt/ˌsend ən ˈiːmeɪl tə ˌsʌmbɒdi/
fill in questionnaires /ˌfɪl ˌɪn ˌkwestʃəˈneəz/
fit /fɪt/
fly /flaɪ/
look after /ˌlʊk ˈɑːftə/
order /ˈɔːdə/
organise /ˈɔːɡənaɪz/
phone /fəʊn/
play with the kids /ˌpleɪ wɪð ðə ˈkɪdz/
prepare (for) /prɪˈpeə (fə)/
repair /rɪˈpeə/
ride a bike /ˌraɪd ə ˈbaɪk/
sell /sel/
send sth to sb /ˈsend ˌsʌmθɪŋ tə ˌsʌmbɒdi/
sign /saɪn/
teach (sb) sth/(sb) about sth/sb to do sth /ˈtiːtʃ (ˌsʌmbɒdi) ˌsʌmθɪŋ/(ˌsʌmbɒdi) əˌbaʊt ˌsʌmθɪŋ/ˌsʌmbɒdi tə duː ˌsʌmθɪŋ/
test (products/beds/water slides/safety) /ˌtest (ˈprɒdʌkts/ˈbedz/ˈwɔːtə slaɪdz/ˈseɪfti)/
travel round Europe /ˌtrævəl raʊnd ˈjʊərəp/
visit interesting places /ˌvɪzət ˌɪntrəstɪŋ ˈpleɪsɪz/
write a blog /ˌraɪt ə ˈblɒɡ/

People at work
boss /bɒs/
co-worker /ˌkəʊˈwɜːkə/
colleague /ˈkɒliːɡ/
customer /ˈkʌstəmə/
employer /ɪmˈplɔɪə/
guest /ɡest/
manager /ˈmænɪdʒə/
owner of a business /ˌəʊnər əv ə ˈbɪznəs/
patient /ˈpeɪʃənt/
shopper /ˈʃɒpə/
worker /ˈwɜːkə/

Money
earn a good/high/low salary /ˌɜːn ə ˌɡʊd/ˌhaɪ/ˌləʊ ˈsæləri/
earn a lot of money (as a waiter) /ˌɜːn ə lɒt əv ˌmʌni (əz ə ˈweɪtə)/
earn enough to pay for the rent /ˌɜːn ɪˌnʌf tə ˌpeɪ fə ðə ˈrent/
earn money (to pay for my studies) /ˌɜːn ˈmʌni (tə ˌpeɪ fə maɪ ˈstʌdiz)/
earn (thirty pounds) a day /ˌɜːn (ˌθɜːti ˌpaʊndz) ə ˈdeɪ/
pay (for) /ˈpeɪ (fə)/

Adjectives to describe work and jobs
badly-paid /ˌbædli ˈpeɪd/
boring /ˈbɔːrɪŋ/
demanding /dɪˈmɑːndɪŋ/
difficult /ˈdɪfɪkəlt/
easy /ˈiːzi/
exciting /ɪkˈsaɪtɪŋ/
full-time /ˌfʊl ˈtaɪm/
hard /hɑːd/
lazy /ˈleɪzi/

part-time /ˌpɑːt ˈtaɪm/
scary /ˈskeəri/
unpleasant /ʌnˈplezənt/
well-paid /ˌwel ˈpeɪd/

Voluntary work
agriculture /ˈæɡrɪˌkʌltʃə/
do voluntary work /ˌduː ˈvɒləntəri wɜːk/
education /ˌedjʊˈkeɪʃən/
government programme /ˈɡʌvəmənt ˌprəʊɡræm/
health /helθ/
Peace Corps /ˈpiːs kɔː/
produce vegetables /prəˌdjuːs ˈvedʒtəbəlz/
promote peace and friendship /prəˌməʊt ˌpiːs ənd ˈfrendʃɪp/
volunteer /ˌvɒlənˈtɪə/

Other
advertise /ˈædvətaɪz/
be scared of /ˌbi ˈskeəd əv/
do sb a favour /ˌduː ˌsʌmbɒdi ə ˈfeɪvə/
dream job /ˌdriːm ˈdʒɒb/
flowerbed /ˈflaʊəbed/
foreign /ˈfɒrən/
get exercise /ˌɡet ˈeksəsaɪz/
guidebook /ˈɡaɪdbʊk/
negative aspect /ˌneɡətɪv ˈæspekt/
shower /ˈʃaʊə/
roof /ruːf/
unusual /ʌnˈjuːʒʊəl/
work /wɜːk/

04 WORD LIST • PEOPLE

Parts of the head and face
ear /ɪə/
eye /aɪ/
eyebrows /ˈaɪbraʊz/
eyelashes /ˈaɪlæʃɪz/
forehead /ˈfɒrəd/
hair /heə/
lips /lɪps/
mouth /maʊθ/
neck /nek/
nose /nəʊz/
tongue /tʌŋ/

Age
middle-aged /ˌmɪdəl ˈeɪdʒd/
old /əʊld/
young /jʌŋ/

Appearance
Hair colour
black /blæk/
blond /blɒnd/
brown /braʊn/
dark /dɑːk/
fair /feə/
grey /ɡreɪ/
red /red/

Hair type
curly /ˈkɜːli/
straight /streɪt/
wavy /ˈweɪvi/

Hair length
bald /bɔːld/
long /lɒŋ/
medium-length /ˌmiːdiəm ˈleŋθ/
short /ʃɔːt/

Eye colour
blue /bluː/
brown /braʊn/
green /ɡriːn/
grey /ɡreɪ/

Height
short /ʃɔːt/
tall /tɔːl/

Build and looks
attractive/good-looking /əˈtræktɪv/ˌɡʊd ˈlʊkɪŋ/
fat /fæt/
fit /fɪt/
flexible /ˈfleksəbəl/
pretty /ˈprɪti/
slim /slɪm/
sporty /ˈspɔːti/
thin /θɪn/
ugly /ˈʌɡli/
well-built /ˌwel ˈbɪlt/

Personality and emotions
ambitious /æmˈbɪʃəs/
boring /ˈbɔːrɪŋ/
busy /ˈbɪzi/
calm /kɑːm/
clever/intelligent /ˈklevə/ɪnˈtelədʒənt/
confident /ˈkɒnfədənt/
creative /kriˈeɪtɪv/
energetic /ˌenəˈdʒetɪk/
fun /fʌn/
funny /ˈfʌni/
generous /ˈdʒenərəs/
interesting /ˈɪntrəstɪŋ/
kind /kaɪnd/
naive /naɪˈiːv/
negative /ˈneɡətɪv/
positive /ˈpɒzətɪv/
relaxed /rɪˈlækst/
sense of humour /ˌsens əv ˈhjuːmə/
serious /ˈsɪəriəs/
shy /ʃaɪ/
sociable /ˈsəʊʃəbəl/
stupid /ˈstjuːpəd/
successful /səkˈsesfəl/
talented /ˈtæləntəd/
tolerant /ˈtɒlərənt/
unkind /ʌnˈkaɪnd/
unsociable /ʌnˈsəʊʃəbəl/
untidy /ʌnˈtaɪdi/
worried /ˈwʌrid/

Clothes and accessories
beads /biːdz/
boots /buːts/
coat /kəʊt/
dress /dres/
feathers /ˈfeðəz/
hat /hæt/
jacket /ˈdʒækət/
jeans/pair of jeans /ˈdʒiːnz/ˌpeər əv ˈdʒiːnz/
jumper /ˈdʒʌmpə/
make-up /ˈmeɪkʌp/
scarf /skɑːf/
shirt /ʃɜːt/
shoes /ʃuːz/
skirt /skɜːt/
socks /sɒks/
suit /suːt/
T-shirt /ˈtiː ʃɜːt/
tattoo /təˈtuː/
tie /taɪ/
top /tɒp/
tracksuit /ˈtræksuːt/
trainers /ˈtreɪnəz/
trousers /ˈtraʊzəz/
wig /wɪɡ/

Adjectives describing clothes and style
casual /ˈkæʒuəl/
comfortable /ˈkʌmftəbəl/
crazy/mad /ˈkreɪzi/mæd/
fashionable /ˈfæʃənəbəl/
formal /ˈfɔːməl/
organic /ɔːˈɡænɪk/
original /əˈrɪdʒɪnəl/
outrageous /aʊtˈreɪdʒəs/
smart /smɑːt/
stylish /ˈstaɪlɪʃ/
typical /ˈtɪpɪkəl/
well-designed /ˌwel dɪˈzaɪnd/

Fashion
be the centre of attention /ˌbi ðə ˌsentər əv əˈtenʃən/
casual/original/smart dresser /ˌkæʒuəl/əˌrɪdʒɪnəl/ˌsmɑːt ˈdresə/
changing room /ˈtʃeɪndʒɪŋ ruːm/
design /dɪˈzaɪn/
eco-fashion label /ˈiːkəʊˌfæʃən ˌleɪbəl/
fit (well) /ˌfɪt (ˈwel)/
inspire /ɪnˈspaɪə/
look /lʊk/
material /məˈtɪəriəl/
model /ˈmɒdl/
outfit /ˈaʊtfɪt/
quality /ˈkwɒləti/
slim/loose fit /ˌslɪm/ˌluːs ˈfɪt/
(small/medium/large/extra large) size /(ˌsmɔːl/ˌmiːdiəm/lɑːdʒ/ˌekstrə ˌlɑːdʒ) ˈsaɪz/
style icon /ˈstaɪl ˌaɪkɒn/
try on /ˌtraɪ ˈɒn/
wear /weə/

Interests
go jogging /ˌɡəʊ ˈdʒɒɡɪŋ/
hang out with friends /ˌhæŋ ˌaʊt wɪð ˈfrendz/
have fun /ˌhæv ˈfʌn/
spend time in the gym /ˌspend ˌtaɪm ɪn ðə ˈdʒɪm/
watch films /ˌwɒtʃ ˈfɪlmz/

Life events
be in education /ˌbi ɪn ˌedjʊˈkeɪʃən/
buy your first flat/house/home /ˌbaɪ jə ˌfɜːst ˈflæt/ˈhaʊs/ˈhəʊm/
fall in love /ˌfɔːl ɪn ˈlʌv/
get married /ˌɡet ˈmærid/
get your first job /ˌɡet jə ˌfɜːst ˈdʒɒb/
go on your first date /ˌɡəʊ ɒn jə ˌfɜːst ˈdeɪt/
learn to drive /ˌlɜːn tə ˈdraɪv/
leave home /ˌliːv ˈhəʊm/
train for a job (as an apprentice) /ˌtreɪn fər ə ˈdʒɒb (əz ən əˈprentəs)/
vote in an election /ˌvəʊt ɪn ən ɪˈlekʃən/

Other
have sth in common /ˌhæv ˌsʌmθɪŋ ɪn ˈkɒmən/
identity card /aɪˈdentəti kɑːd/
laugh /lɑːf/
permission /pəˈmɪʃən/
person /ˈpɜːsən/
support /səˈpɔːt/
twins /twɪnz/

05 WORD LIST • EDUCATION

School subjects
Chemistry /ˈkeməstri/
Geography /dʒiˈɒɡrəfi/
History /ˈhɪstəri/
IT (Information Technology) /ˌaɪ ˈtiː (ˌɪnfəˌmeɪʃən tekˈnɒlədʒi)/
Marine Biology /məˌriːn baɪˈɒlədʒi/
Maths /mæθs/
PE (Physical Education) /ˌpiː ˈiː (ˌfɪzɪkəl ˌedjʊˈkeɪʃən)/
Physics /ˈfɪzɪks/
Science /ˈsaɪəns/

Classroom objects
blackboard /ˈblækbɔːd/
calculator /ˈkælkjəleɪtə/
coursebook /ˈkɔːsbʊk/
desk /desk/
IWB (interactive whiteboard) /ˌaɪ ˌdʌbəljuː ˈbiː (ˌɪntərˌæktɪv ˈwaɪtbɔːd)/
(special) equipment /(ˌspeʃəl) ɪˈkwɪpmənt/

People at school
form teacher /ˈfɔːm ˌtiːtʃə/
head teacher /ˌhed ˈtiːtʃə/
professor /prəˈfesə/
pupil /ˈpjuːpəl/
secondary school student /ˈsekəndəri skuːl ˌstjuːdənt/
university student /ˌjuːnəˈvɜːsəti ˌstjuːdənt/

Places at school
canteen /kænˈtiːn/
corridor /ˈkɒrədɔː/
gym /dʒɪm/
hall /hɔːl/
library /ˈlaɪbrəri/
playground /ˈpleɪɡraʊnd/
science lab /ˈsaɪəns læb/
sports field /ˈspɔːts fiːld/
staff room /ˈstɑːf ruːm/
(well-equipped/comfortable) classroom /(welɪˈkwɪpt/ˌkʌmftəbəl) ˈklɑːsrʊm/

Types of schools
boys' school /ˈbɔɪz skuːl/
girls' school /ˈɡɜːlz skuːl/
kindergarten /ˈkɪndəɡɑːtn/
middle school /ˈmɪdl skuːl/
mixed school /ˌmɪkst ˈskuːl/
nursery school /ˈnɜːsəri skuːl/
primary school /ˈpraɪməri skuːl/
private school /ˌpraɪvət ˈskuːl/
secondary school /ˈsekəndəri skuːl/
single-sex school /ˌsɪŋɡəl ˌseks ˈskuːl/
state school /ˈsteɪt skuːl/

Higher education
academy /əˈkædəmi/
technical college /ˈteknɪkəl ˌkɒlɪdʒ/
university /ˌjuːnəˈvɜːsəti/

School activities
acting /ˈæktɪŋ/
club meeting /ˈklʌb ˌmiːtɪŋ/
compulsory activities /kəmˌpʌlsəri ækˈtɪvətiz/
end-of-year sports competition /ˌend əv ˌjɪə ˈspɔːts kɒmpəˌtɪʃən/
extra activities /ˌekstrə ækˈtɪvətiz/
outdoor activities /ˌaʊtˌdɔːr ækˈtɪvətiz/
sports team /ˈspɔːts tiːm/
theatre group /ˈθɪətə ɡruːp/
trials /ˈtraɪəlz/

volunteer programme/project /ˌvɒlənˈtɪə ˌprəʊɡræm/ˌprɒdʒekt/
workshop /ˈwɜːkʃɒp/

School trips
attraction /əˈtrækʃən/
book online /ˌbʊk ˈɒnlaɪn/
camping trip /ˈkæmpɪŋ trɪp/
close /kləʊz/
cost /kɒst/
cultural event /ˌkʌltʃərəl ɪˈvent/
discount /ˈdɪskaʊnt/
download an app /ˌdaʊnˌləʊd ən ˈæp/
education centre /ˌedjʊˈkeɪʃən ˌsentə/
explore /ɪkˈsplɔː/
family ticket /ˈfæməli ˌtɪkət/
free /friː/
free time /ˌfriː ˈtaɪm/
guided tour /ˌɡaɪdɪd ˈtʊə/
home stay /ˈhəʊm steɪ/
museum tour /mjuːˈziːəm tʊə/
open /ˈəʊpən/
opening times /ˈəʊpənɪŋ taɪmz/
train station /ˈtreɪn ˌsteɪʃən/

Sports
badminton /ˈbædmɪntən/
football /ˈfʊtbɔːl/
hockey /ˈhɒki/
sailing /ˈseɪlɪŋ/
snorkelling /ˈsnɔːkəlɪŋ/
volleyball /ˈvɒlibɔːl/
water sports /ˈwɔːtə spɔːts/

Music
band /bænd/
musician /mjuːˈzɪʃən/
play the piano/the guitar/the violin /ˌpleɪ ðə piˈænəʊ/ðə ɡɪˈtɑː/ðə ˌvaɪəˈlɪn/
record deal /ˈrekɔːd diːl/
sing /sɪŋ/

Verbs and phrases about school
be afraid/scared of /bi əˈfreɪd/ˈskeəd ə/
be good at (foreign languages) /bi ˌɡʊd ət (ˌfɒrən ˈlæŋɡwɪdʒɪz)/
be late/early/on time for lessons /bi ˌleɪt/ˌɜːli/ɒn ˌtaɪm fə ˈlesənz/
be proud of /bi ˈpraʊd ə/
borrow a book from the library /ˌbɒrəʊ ə ˌbʊk frəm ðə ˈlaɪbrəri/
cheat in exams /ˌtʃiːt ɪn ɪɡˈzæmz/
design a study programme /dɪˌzaɪn ə ˈstʌdi ˌprəʊɡræm/
do a course /ˌduː ə ˈkɔːs/
do/play sport /ˌduː/ˌpleɪ ˈspɔːt/
do experiments /ˌduː ɪkˈsperɪmənts/
do extra activities /ˌduː ˌekstrə ækˈtɪvətiz/
do your best /ˌduː jə ˈbest/
do your homework /ˌduː jə ˈhəʊmwɜːk/
do well/badly in an exam/a test /ˌduː ˌwel/ˌbædli ɪn ən ɪɡˈzæm/ə ˈtest/
fail an exam /ˌfeɪl ən ɪɡˈzæm/
get an education /ˌɡet ən ˌedjʊˈkeɪʃən/
get fit /ˌɡet ˈfɪt/
get a good/bad mark (for sth) /ˌɡet ə ˌɡʊd/ˌbæd ˈmɑːk (fə ˌsʌmθɪŋ)/
get lost /ˌɡet ˈlɒst/
get on OK /ˌɡet ˌɒn ˌəʊ ˈkeɪ/
get the most from sth /ˌɡet ðə ˈməʊst frəm ˌsʌmθɪŋ/
give a speech /ˌɡɪv ə ˈspiːtʃ/

go to university /ˌɡəʊ tə ˌjuːnəˈvɜːsəti/
have a meeting /ˌhæv ə ˈmiːtɪŋ/
have fun /ˌhæv ˈfʌn/
improve /ɪmˈpruːv/
learn a skill /ˌlɜːn ə ˈskɪl/
leave school /ˌliːv ˈskuːl/
meet friends /ˌmiːt ˈfrendz/
miss school/classes /ˌmɪs ˈskuːl/ˈklɑːsɪz/
participate in /pɑːˈtɪsəpeɪt ɪn/
pass an exam /ˌpɑːs ən ɪɡˈzæm/
practise /ˈpræktəs/
relax /rɪˈlæks/
rest /rest/
start school /ˌstɑːt ˈskuːl/
study a subject /ˌstʌdi ə ˈsʌbdʒɪkt/
train to become (a vet) /ˌtreɪn tə bɪˌkʌm (ə ˈvet)/
use a computer/tablet/mobile phone (in class/during lessons) /ˌjuːz ə kəmˈpjuːtə/ˈtæblət/ˌməʊbaɪl ˈfəʊn (ɪn ˈklɑːs/ˈdjʊərɪŋ ˈlesənz)/
wear a school uniform/an overall /ˌweər ə ˌskuːl ˈjuːnəfɔːm/ən ˌəʊvərˈɔːl/

Other
brain /breɪn/
danger /ˈdeɪndʒə/
exactly /ɪɡˈzæktli/
gap year programme /ˌɡæp ˈjɪə ˌprəʊɡræm/
genius /ˈdʒiːniəs/
litter/rubbish /ˈlɪtə/ˈrʌbɪʃ/
matter /ˈmætə/
solve a problem /ˌsɒlv ə ˈprɒbləm/
students' rights /ˌstjuːdənts ˈraɪts/
take risks /ˌteɪk ˈrɪsks/

06 WORD LIST • SPORT AND HEALTH

Sports
badminton /ˈbædmɪntən/
basketball /ˈbɑːskətbɔːl/
bungee jumping /ˈbʌndʒi ˌdʒʌmpɪŋ/
cycling /ˈsaɪklɪŋ/
football /ˈfʊtbɔːl/
golf /gɒlf/
hockey /ˈhɒki/
ice skating /ˈaɪs ˌskeɪtɪŋ/
jogging /ˈdʒɒgɪŋ/
karate /kəˈrɑːti/
kayaking /ˈkaɪækɪŋ/
kung fu /ˌkʌŋ ˈfuː/
rugby /ˈrʌgbi/
running /ˈrʌnɪŋ/
sailing /ˈseɪlɪŋ/
skateboarding /ˈskeɪtbɔːdɪŋ/
skiing /ˈskiːɪŋ/
swimming /ˈswɪmɪŋ/
table tennis/Ping-Pong /ˈteɪbəl ˌtenəs/ ˈpɪŋ pɒŋ/
tennis /ˈtenəs/
triathlon /traɪˈæθlən/
volleyball /ˈvɒlibɔːl/
yoga /ˈjəʊgə/
Zumba /ˈzʊmbə/

Types of sport
individual sports /ˌɪndəˈvɪdʒuəl spɔːts/
martial arts /ˌmɑːʃəl ˈɑːts/
Olympic sports /əˈlɪmpɪk spɔːts/
summer sports /ˈsʌmə spɔːts/
team sports/games /ˈtiːm spɔːts/geɪmz/
water sports /ˈwɔːtə spɔːts/
winter sports /ˈwɪntə spɔːts/

Sports competitions
career /kəˈrɪə/
challenge /ˈtʃæləndʒ/
climb /klaɪm/
competition /ˌkɒmpəˈtɪʃən/
complete /kəmˈpliːt/
cycle /ˈsaɪkəl/
do (yoga/karate) /ˌduː (ˈjəʊgə/kəˈrɑːti)/
equipment /ɪˈkwɪpmənt/
final /ˈfaɪnəl/
finish line /ˈfɪnɪʃ laɪn/
first/second half /ˌfɜːst/ˌsekənd ˈhɑːf/
football club /ˈfʊtbɔːl klʌb/
goal line /ˈgəʊl laɪn/
go cycling/sailing /ˌgəʊ ˈsaɪklɪŋ/ˈseɪlɪŋ/
marathon /ˈmærəθən/
Olympics/Olympic Games /əˈlɪmpɪks/əˌlɪmpɪk ˈgeɪmz/
Paralympics /ˌpærəˈlɪmpɪks/
play (football/volleyball) /ˌpleɪ (ˈfʊtbɔːl/ ˈvɒlibɔːl)/
play for a team /ˌpleɪ fər ə ˈtiːm/
practise /ˈpræktəs/
prize /praɪz/
result /rɪˈzʌlt/
run fast /ˌrʌn ˈfɑːst/
score (ten points) /ˌskɔː (ten ˈpɔɪnts)/
speed /spiːd/
sponsor /ˈspɒnsə/
sports event /ˈspɔːts ɪˌvent/
stadium /ˈsteɪdiəm/
take part in (kung fu) competitions /teɪk ˌpɑːt ɪn (ˌkʌŋ ˈfuː) ˌkɒmpəˈtɪʃənz/
take place /ˌteɪk ˈpleɪs/
(tennis) match /(ˈtenəs) mætʃ/
tournament /ˈtʊənəmənt/
train /treɪn/
win /wɪn/

win a gold/silver/bronze medal /ˌwɪn ə ˌgəʊld/ ˌsɪlvə/ˌbrɒnz ˈmedl/
win gold/bronze /ˌwɪn ˈgəʊld/ˈbrɒnz/
World Cup /ˌwɜːld ˈkʌp/

People in sport
athlete /ˈæθliːt/
basketball player /ˈbɑːskətbɔːl ˌpleɪə/
champion /ˈtʃæmpiən/
climber /ˈklaɪmə/
coach /kəʊtʃ/
competitor /kəmˈpetətə/
cyclist /ˈsaɪkləst/
footballer/football player /ˈfʊtbɔːlə/ˈfʊtbɔːl ˌpleɪə/
gymnast /ˈdʒɪmnæst/
hockey player /ˈhɒki ˌpleɪə/
instructor /ɪnˈstrʌktə/
jogger /ˈdʒɒgə/
professional sportsperson /prəˌfeʃənəl ˈspɔːtsˌpɜːsən/
runner /ˈrʌnə/
sailor /ˈseɪlə/
skier /ˈskiːə/
swimmer /ˈswɪmə/
tennis player /ˈtenəs ˌpleɪə/

Healthy lifestyle
do (stretching) exercises /ˌduː (ˈstretʃɪŋ) ˌeksəsaɪzɪz/
get enough sleep /ˌget ɪˌnʌf ˈsliːp/
give energy /ˌgɪv ˈenədʒi/
go to the gym /ˌgəʊ tə ðə ˈdʒɪm/
have a healthy breakfast/meal /ˌhæv ə ˌhelθi ˈbrekfəst/ˈmiːl/
have a healthy diet/eat well /ˌhæv ə ˌhelθi ˈdaɪət/ˈiːt wel/
have a healthy lifestyle /ˌhæv ə ˌhelθi ˈlaɪfstaɪl/
keep fit /ˌkiːp ˈfɪt/
relax /rɪˈlæks/
rest /rest/
spend time outdoors /ˌspend taɪm ˌaʊtˈdɔːz/
take regular breaks /ˌteɪk ˌregjələ ˈbreɪks/
walk /wɔːk/

Health
die /daɪ/
disabled /dɪsˈeɪbəld/
examine /ɪgˈzæmən/
feel (terrible/better) /ˌfiːl (ˈterəbəl/ˈbetə)/
feel dizzy /ˌfiːl ˈdɪzi/
grow /grəʊ/
headache /ˈhedeɪk/
health problem /ˈhelθ ˌprɒbləm/
hormone /ˈhɔːməʊn/
medical help /ˌmedɪkəl ˈhelp/
rescue /ˈreskjuː/
save sb's life /ˌseɪv ˌsʌmbɒdiz ˈlaɪf/
(serious) illness /(ˌsɪəriəs) ˈɪlnəs/
sore /sɔː/
treatment /ˈtriːtmənt/

Likes and dislikes
be interested in /ˌbi ˈɪntrəstəd ɪn/
be into /ˌbi ˈɪntə/
can't stand /ˌkɑːnt ˈstænd/
care about /ˈkeər əˌbaʊt/
enjoy sth/have fun in sth /ɪnˈdʒɔɪ ˌsʌmθɪŋ/ˌhæv ˈfʌn ɪn ˌsʌmθɪŋ/
hate /heɪt/
like /laɪk/
love /lʌv/
prefer /prɪˈfɜː/

Other
aim /eɪm/
at the age of (ten) /ət ði ˌeɪdʒ əv (ˈten)/
at the same time /ət ðə ˌseɪm ˈtaɪm/
believe in /bəˈliːv ɪn/
charity /ˈtʃærəti/
hang /hæŋ/
jump off /ˌdʒʌmp ˈɒf/
move (to) /ˈmuːv (tə)/
raise money /ˌreɪz ˈmʌni/
stay up late/all night /ˌsteɪ ʌp ˈleɪt/ˌɔːl ˈnaɪt/
support /səˈpɔːt/
top/bottom of the mountain /ˌtɒp/ˌbɒtəm əv ðə ˈmaʊntɪn/

07 WORD LIST • TRAVEL

Forms of transport
bike /baɪk/
boat /bəʊt/
bus /bʌs/
car /kɑː/
coach /kəʊtʃ/
ferry /ˈferi/
motorbike /ˈməʊtəbaɪk/
plane /pleɪn/
ship /ʃɪp/
taxi /ˈtæksi/
train /treɪn/
tram /træm/
underground/tube /ˈʌndəɡraʊnd/tjuːb/

Types of trips
activity holiday /ækˈtɪvəti ˌhɒlədeɪ/
adventure holiday /ədˈventʃə ˌhɒlədeɪ/
backpacking holiday /ˈbækˌpækɪŋ ˌhɒlədeɪ/
beach holiday /ˈbiːtʃ ˌhɒlədeɪ/
camping holiday /ˈkæmpɪŋ ˌhɒlədeɪ/
cycling trip /ˈsaɪklɪŋ trɪp/
excursion /ɪkˈskɜːʃən/
skiing holiday /ˈskiːɪŋ ˌhɒlədeɪ/
tour /tʊə/
trip abroad /ˌtrɪp əˈbrɔːd/
working holiday /ˈwɜːkɪŋ ˌhɒlədeɪ/

Before a holiday
book: /bʊk/
  a car /ə ˈkɑː/
  a flight /ə ˈflaɪt/
  a holiday /ə ˈhɒlədeɪ/
  a hotel /ə həʊˈtel/
  a room /ə ˈruːm/
  a seat on the train/bus /ə ˌsiːt ɒn ðə ˈtreɪn/ˈbʌs/
  a train/bus ticket /ə ˈtreɪn/ˈbʌs ˌtɪkət/
  an excursion /ən ɪkˈskɜːʃən/
  the accommodation /ði əˌkɒməˈdeɪʃən/
  the transport /ðə ˈtrænspɔːt/
brochure /ˈbrəʊʃə/
have a booking /ˌhæv ə ˈbʊkɪŋ/
make the arrangements /ˌmeɪk ði əˈreɪndʒmənts/
make/change a reservation/a booking /ˌmeɪk/ˌtʃeɪndʒ ə ˌrezəˈveɪʃən/ə ˈbʊkɪŋ/
special/top offer /ˌspeʃəl/ˌtɒp ˈɒfə/
travel agency/travel agent's /ˈtrævəl ˌeɪdʒənsi/ˈtrævəl ˌeɪdʒənts/

Accommodation
bed and breakfast (B & B) /ˌbed ənd ˈbrekfəst (ˌbiː ənd ˈbiː)/
campsite /ˈkæmpsaɪt/
check in /ˌtʃek ˈɪn/
guest /ɡest/
guesthouse /ˈɡesthaʊs/
(luxury/three-star) hotel /(ˌlʌkʃəri/ˌθriː ˌstɑː) həʊˈtel/
reception desk /rɪˈsepʃən desk/
staff /stɑːf/
stay in (a hotel)/at (a campsite) /ˌsteɪ ɪn (ə həʊˈtel)/ət (ə ˈkæmpsaɪt)/
youth hostel /ˈjuːθ ˌhɒstl/

On the journey
airport check-in desk /ˌeəpɔːt ˈtʃek ɪn desk/
arrive /əˈraɪv/
check in /ˌtʃek ˈɪn/
cycle /ˈsaɪkəl/
drive /draɪv/
flight /flaɪt/
fly /flaɪ/
get on/off (a train) /ˌɡet ˌɒn/ˌɒf (ə ˈtreɪn)/
go on foot /ˌɡəʊ ɒn ˈfʊt/
make an announcement /ˌmeɪk ən əˈnaʊnsmənt/
on time /ˌɒn ˈtaɪm/
passenger /ˈpæsɪndʒə/
platform /ˈplætfɔːm/
reach (a place) /ˌriːtʃ (ə ˈpleɪs)/
ride (a bike) /ˌraɪd (ə ˈbaɪk)/
road /rəʊd/
sail /seɪl/
street /striːt/
train station /ˈtreɪn ˌsteɪʃən/
travel/go by (train/plane) /ˌtrævəl/ˌɡəʊ baɪ (ˈtreɪn/ˈpleɪn)/
waiting room /ˈweɪt ɪŋ ruːm/

Holiday activities
be active /ˌbi ˈæktɪv/
eat at a restaurant /ˌiːt ət ə ˈrestərɒnt/
eat local food /ˌiːt ˌləʊkəl ˈfuːd/
escape to the countryside /ɪˌskeɪp tə ðə ˈkʌntrisaɪd/
experience (a place/white sand/clear water) /ɪkˈspɪəriəns (ə ˈpleɪs/ˌwaɪt ˈsænd/ˌklɪə ˈwɔːtə)/
go hang-gliding /ˌɡəʊ ˈhæŋ ˌɡlaɪdɪŋ/
go hiking /ˌɡəʊ ˈhaɪkɪŋ/
go kayaking /ˌɡəʊ ˈkaɪækɪŋ/
go mountain biking /ˌɡəʊ ˈmaʊntən ˌbaɪkɪŋ/
go to/visit museums /ˌɡəʊ tə/ˌvɪzət mjuˈziːəmz/
relax (by the sea) /rɪˌlæks (baɪ ðə ˈsiː)/
ride a camel/an elephant /ˌraɪd ə ˈkæməl/ən ˈeləfənt/
rock climb/go climbing /ˈrɒk klaɪm/ˌɡəʊ ˈklaɪmɪŋ/
see the sights /ˌsiː ðə ˈsaɪts/
travel round by (car) /ˌtrævəl raʊnd baɪ (ˈkɑː)/
try different kinds of activities /ˌtraɪ ˌdɪfərənt ˌkaɪndz əv ækˈtɪvətiz/
visit the sights /ˌvɪzət ðə ˈsaɪts/

Places to visit
beach /biːtʃ/
desert /ˈdezət/
island /ˈaɪlənd/
local market /ˌləʊkəl ˈmɑːkət/
local towns /ˌləʊkəl ˈtaʊnz/
mountains /ˈmaʊntɪnz/
museum /mjuːˈziəm/
rainforest /ˈreɪnfɒrɪst/
theatre /ˈθɪətə/
(top) tourist sites /(ˌtɒp) ˈtʊərəst saɪts/

Things to take on holiday
camera /ˈkæmərə/
case /keɪs/
cooking equipment /ˈkʊkɪŋ ɪˌkwɪpmənt/
guidebook /ˈɡaɪdbʊk/
luggage /ˈlʌɡɪdʒ/
passport /ˈpɑːspɔːt/
sleeping bag /ˈsliːpɪŋ bæɡ/
tent /tent/
trailer /ˈtreɪlə/
visa /ˈviːzə/
warm clothes /ˌwɔːm ˈkləʊðz/

Giving directions
along /əˈlɒŋ/
between /bɪˈtwiːn/
get to … /ˈɡet tə …/
go across the road /ˌɡəʊ əˌkrɒs ðə ˈrəʊd/
next door /ˌnekst ˈdɔː/
next to sth /ˈnekst tə ˌsʌmθɪŋ/
on the corner /ˌɒn ðə ˈkɔːnə/
on your right/left /ˌɒn jə ˈraɪt/ˈleft/
opposite /ˈɒpəzət/
straight on /ˌstreɪt ˈɒn/
take the (second) turning on the (left) /ˌteɪk ðə (ˌsekənd) ˈtɜːnɪŋ ɒn ðə (ˈleft)/
tell sb the way to … /ˌtel ˌsʌmbɒdi ðə ˈweɪ tə …/
turn left/right into (High Street) /ˌtɜːn ˌleft/ˌraɪt ˌɪntə (ˌhaɪ striːt)/
walk past sth /ˈwɔːk pɑːst ˌsʌmθɪŋ/

Other
bookshop /ˈbʊkʃɒp/
budget /ˈbʌdʒət/
bumps /bʌmps/
environmentally friendly /ɪnˌvaɪərənˌmentəli ˈfrendli/
flexible /ˈfleksəbəl/
frame /freɪm/
get better /ˌɡet ˈbetə/
guide /ɡaɪd/
harm the environment /ˌhɑːm ði ɪnˈvaɪərənmənt/
hiker /ˈhaɪkə/
mosquito /məˈskiːtəʊ/
news show /ˈnjuːz ʃəʊ/
provide /prəˈvaɪd/
safe /seɪf/
southernmost /ˈsʌðənməʊst/
tourist /ˈtʊərəst/
town hall /ˌtaʊn ˈhɔːl/
world (water) crisis /ˌwɜːld (ˈwɔːtə) ˌkraɪsəs/

WORD STORE 0

Intro Unit

WORD STORE 0.2

Argentinian   Australian   Brazilian
Canadian   Chinese   Czech   French
German   Greek   Hungarian   Irish   Italian
Japanese   Mexican   Polish   Portuguese
~~Russian~~   Scottish   Spanish   Swedish
Swiss   Turkish   Vietnamese

Country	Nationality
-an; -ian; -n	
Russia	Russian
Germany	
Australia	
Canada	
Italy	
Hungary	
Brazil	
Argentina	
Mexico	

Country	Nationality
-ish	
Scotland	
Poland	
Spain	
Sweden	
Turkey	
Ireland	
-ese	
China	
Japan	
Vietnam	
Portugal	
other	
France	
Greece	
the Czech Republic	
Switzerland	

WORD STORE 0.6

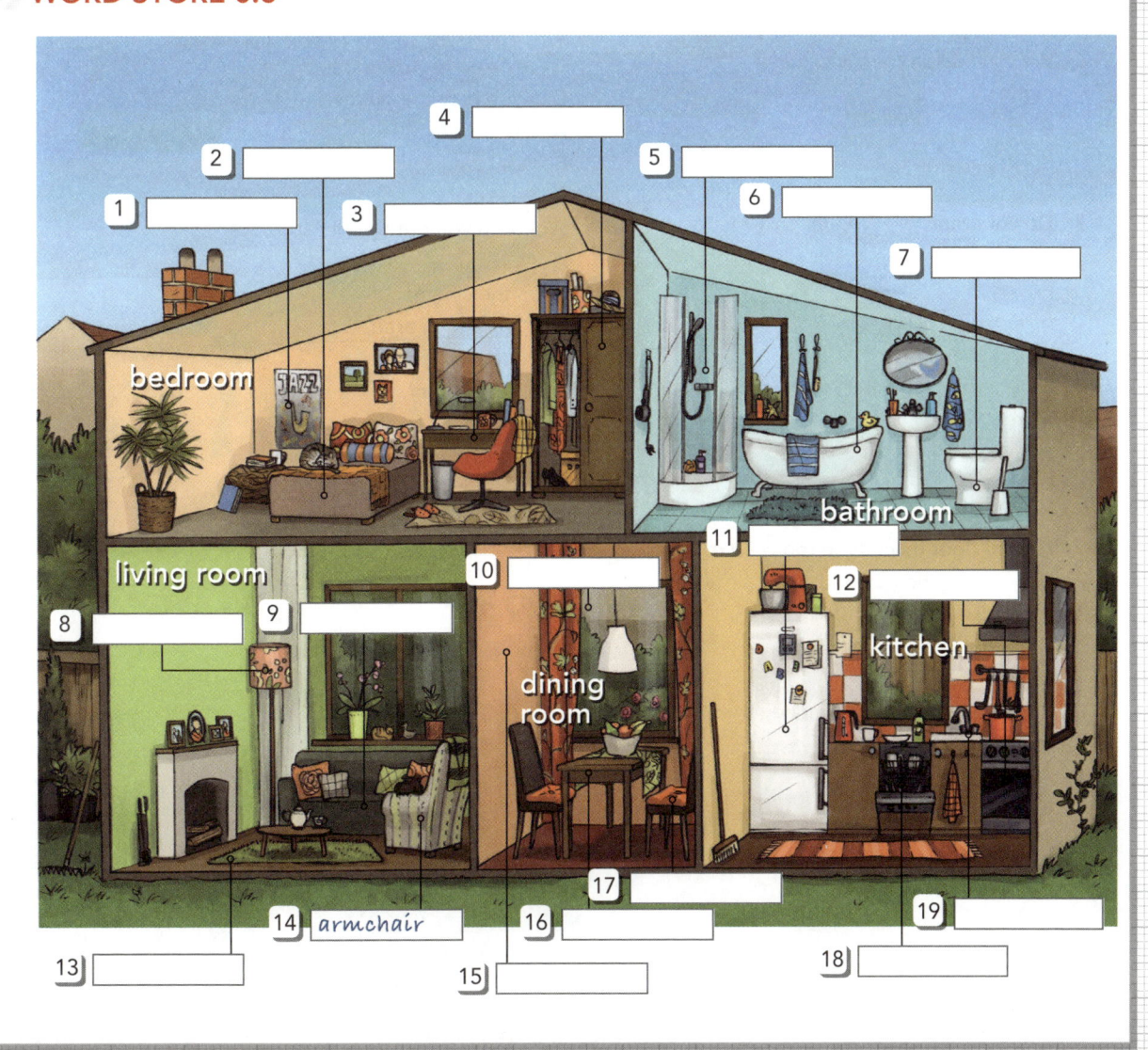

bedroom
bathroom
living room
dining room
kitchen

14 armchair

WORD PRACTICE 1

1 **Choose the correct answer, A, B or C.**
   1 Are you interested ___ dance classes?
      A in
      B on
      C at
   2 I can't stand this music – it's ___ .
      A rubbish
      B brilliant
      C awesome
   3 My dad coaches a local ___ in his free time.
      A restaurant
      B youth club
      C football team
   4 Italy is my favourite country. I love ___ different places there.
      A driving
      B coming
      C visiting
   5 On a ___ school day I wake up at seven o'clock.
      A typical
      B favourite
      C classical
   6 We can't listen to music loudly ___ night.
      A in
      B at
      C on
   7 Do you want to ___ a film on TV with me?
      A watch
      B look
      C get
   8 Jane's got a fantastic voice – she's a great ___ .
      A film star
      B singer
      C writer
   9 I haven't got much time today – I'm busy ___ my homework.
      A at
      B on
      C with
   10 Most singers don't ___ money from their music.
      A do
      B take
      C make

2 **Complete the words in the sentences. The first letter of each word is given.**
   1 C_ _ _ _ is a game that two people play with black and white pieces.
   2 The time when you don't work or go to school on Saturday and Sunday is called the w_ _ _ _ _ _ .
   3 A d_ _ _ is a musical instrument. You hit it to make sounds.
   4 Someone who writes books is an a_ _ _ _ _ .
   5 Something g_ _ _ _ is very big or very good.
   6 Musicians record songs in a s_ _ _ _ _ .
   7 When you have a p_ _ _ _ _ , you eat some food in a park or in the countryside.
   8 F_ _ _ _ _ _ books like *The Hobbit* are not true to life.
   9 When it's m_ _ _ _ _ _ _ , it's twelve o'clock at night.
   10 Your a_ _ _ is your mother's or your father's sister.

3 **Choose the best response, A, B or C.**
   1 Do you like going to the cinema?
      A Yes, I love.
      B Yes, I can't stand it.
      C Yes, I enjoy it.
   2 Do you often go swimming?
      A Yes, I go every Monday.
      B Yes, I always go.
      C Yes, I go in November.
   3 Can you play the guitar?
      A Yes, I do.
      B Yes, I am.
      C Yes, I can.
   4 When do you get up on Saturdays?
      A At 10.30.
      B To the cinema.
      C Because I'm tired.
   5 I love real life films.
      A It's awesome!
      B I prefer science fiction.
      C My brother prefers rap.

WORD STORE 1 — Family and friends

WORD STORE 1A
Collocations – have, go and play

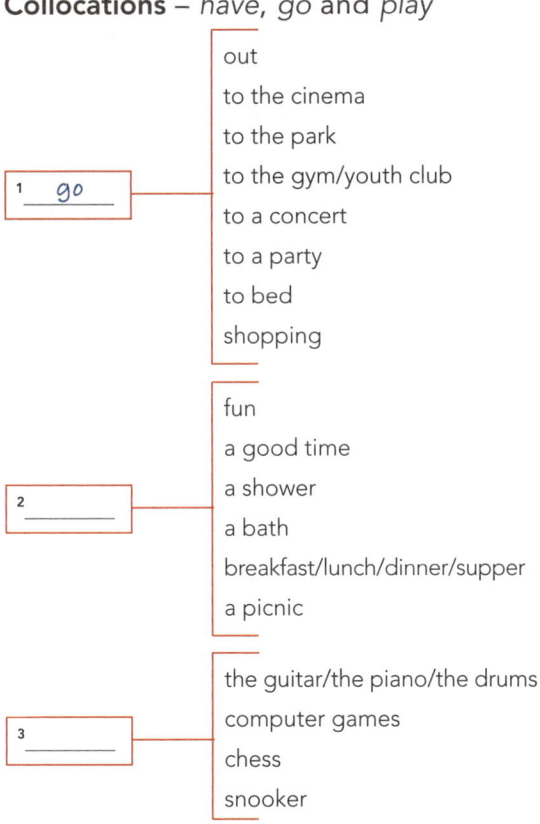

1 **go**
- out
- to the cinema
- to the park
- to the gym/youth club
- to a concert
- to a party
- to bed
- shopping

2 _____
- fun
- a good time
- a shower
- a bath
- breakfast/lunch/dinner/supper
- a picnic

3 _____
- the guitar/the piano/the drums
- computer games
- chess
- snooker

WORD STORE 1B
Verb + noun collocations

1 **read** books/magazines
2 s_____ time
3 v_____ friends
4 w_____ a film/a DVD/the TV/the telly
5 w_____ a blog

WORD STORE 1C
Verb + preposition collocations

1 go _____ a walk
2 go out _____ friends
3 listen **to** music
4 spend time _____ my friends/grandparents
5 spend time _____ home/school/my grandparents' house
6 spend time _____ my room/bedroom
7 stay _____ home
8 talk _____ books/films

REMEMBER THIS
go home   stay **at** home
come home   be **at** home

WORD STORE 1D
Prepositions

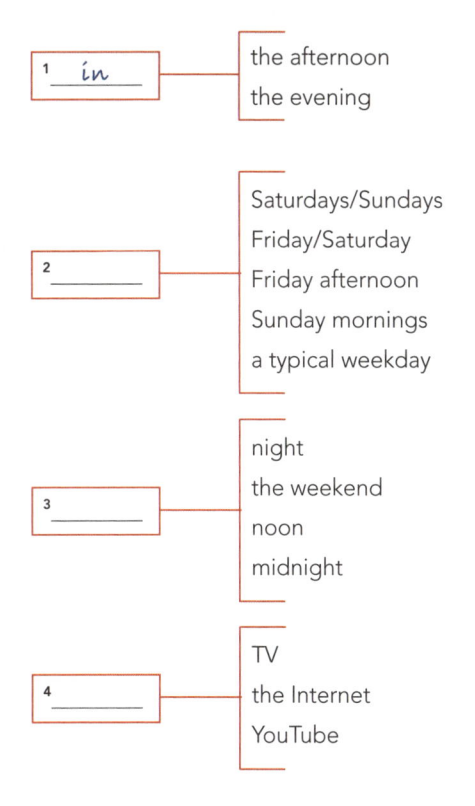

1 **in**
- the afternoon
- the evening

2 _____
- Saturdays/Sundays
- Friday/Saturday
- Friday afternoon
- Sunday mornings
- a typical weekday

3 _____
- night
- the weekend
- noon
- midnight

4 _____
- TV
- the Internet
- YouTube

WORD STORE 1E
Verb collocations

1 get **up** in the morning
2 look _____ my baby sister
3 work _____ a construction company
4 go _____ home
5 take a person _____ the park/school/the doctor
6 come home _____ work/school
7 go _____ bed/the shops

3

WORD PRACTICE 2

1 Choose the correct answer, A, B or C.

1. Can you buy a ___ of bread in the supermarket?
   A jar
   B can
   C loaf
2. First, ___ two litres of water with some salt.
   A fry
   B boil
   C chop
3. At the checkout, ___ .
   A you cook some food.
   B you try new food.
   C you pay for your food.
4. Put the cheese ___ to keep it cold.
   A in the fridge
   B on the shelf
   C in the trolley
5. I don't want to cook tonight. Let's ___ a pizza from a takeaway restaurant.
   A order
   B serve
   C prepare
6. It takes ___ least twenty minutes to make pancakes for a large family.
   A in
   B at
   C on
7. A recipe ___ .
   A tells you the price
   B gives you instructions
   C recommends a restaurant
8. Students often go to kebab bars because they are ___ .
   A messy
   B cheap
   C dangerous
9. My favourite restaurant is ___ , next to the cathedral.
   A upstairs
   B in the countryside
   C in the main square
10. Do you want to go ___ for a meal or do you want to eat at home?
    A out
    B away
    C down

2 Complete the words in the sentences. The first letter of each word is given.

1. A man who brings food to your table in a restaurant is a w_ _ _ _ _ .
2. S_ _ _ _ _ _ _ _ is long, thin pasta that people often eat with tomato sauce.
3. You eat something when you are h_ _ _ _ _ .
4. When you s_ _ _ _ bread, you cut it into thin pieces.
5. A list of things you can eat in a restaurant is a m_ _ _ .
6. T_ _ _ is a very popular type of fish. You usually buy it in tins.
7. A d_ _ _ _ _ _ is usually sweet. You eat it after the main course.
8. You can put and carry your shopping in a b_ _ _ _ _ in a supermarket.
9. An o_ _ _ _ _ is a round fruit. It's also the name of a colour.
10. You can use the word *hot* to describe food which is s_ _ _ _ , like an Indian curry.

3 Complete the conversation with sentences a–h. There are three extra sentences.

Lara: Hi, Jan. It's your birthday today, isn't it?
Jan: ¹_____
Lara: It's in my diary! Are you having a party?
Jan: ²_____
Lara: I'd love to, thanks. Do you want me to bring anything?
Jan: ³_____
Lara: Thanks. Everyone likes them! What time does the party start?
Jan: ⁴_____
Lara: Fine. And here's your present. It's a small birthday cake!
Jan: ⁵_____ .
Lara: That's OK. Enjoy it!

a I'd like a chicken salad.
b Some sandwiches, perhaps? You make fantastic sausage sandwiches.
c It's next month.
d Oh! That's awesome! I love chocolate. Thank you very much.
e Yes! How do you know?
f Yes, it's on Friday. Would you like to come?
g I don't eat a lot of cake.
h Come round at about 8.30.

4

WORD STORE 2 — Food

WORD STORE 2A
Food containers

1 a	_tin_	of	soup/tuna
2 a	_____	of	cola/lemonade
3 a	_____	of	cornflakes/crisps/flour/mushrooms/rice/spaghetti
4 a	_____	of	honey/mayonnaise/tomato sauce
5 a	_____	of	onions/potatoes/salad
6 a	_____	of	eggs/milk/orange juice
7 a	_____	of	chocolate
8 a	_____	of	ketchup/oil/water
9 a	_____	of	bread
10 a	_____	of	ice cream

REMEMBER THIS
Tin or can?

British English	American English
a **tin** of tuna	a **can** of tuna
a **can** of cola	a **can** of cola

WORD STORE 2B
Phrases related to food

1 _get a takeaway_ = buy cooked food from a shop or restaurant to eat at home
2 _____ = make something small to eat between meals, e.g. a sandwich
3 _____ = (eat) when you watch TV
4 _____ = as something sweet to eat at the end of a meal

WORD STORE 2C
In a supermarket

1 _basket_ 2 _____ 3 _____ 4 _____ 5 _____

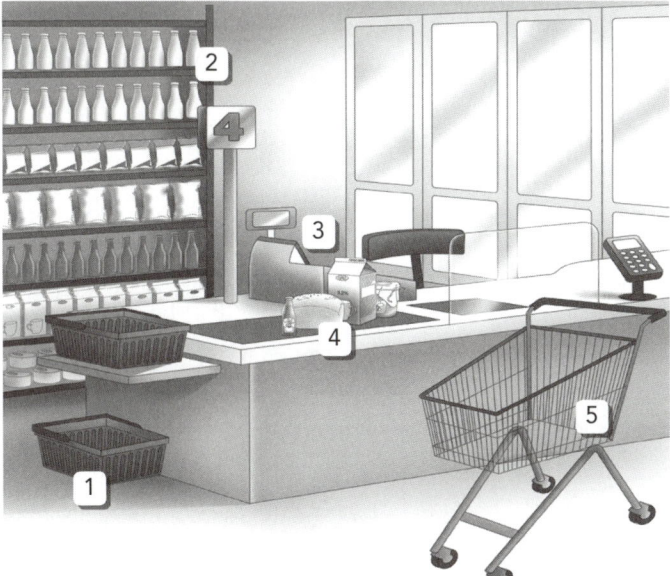

WORD STORE 2D
Cooking verbs

1 _Chop_ some fruit.
2 _____ four potatoes. 
3 _____ the potatoes. 
4 _____ some eggs. 
5 _____ the omelette. 

WORD STORE 2E
Food adjectives

1 _vegetarian_ food hasn't got any meat or fish in it.
2 _____ food tastes very good.
3 _____ food has a strong hot taste.
4 _____ food is food the cook buys and prepares just before you eat it.
5 _____ food is from a place near your home.
6 _____ food is the special recipes from a country.

5

WORD PRACTICE 3

1 Choose the correct answer, A, B or C.

1 George is really good with ___ . He wants to be an accountant.
 A children
 B numbers
 C his hands
2 It's a good idea to ___ voluntary work to gain experience.
 A do
 B have
 C make
3 I normally finish at five, but this week we're very busy, so I'm working ___ hours.
 A long
 B foreign
 C outside
4 Jane's on holiday this week, so I'm responsible ___ sending documents to our clients.
 A to
 B with
 C for
5 I'd like to be a famous pop star and ___ round Europe.
 A visit
 B travel
 C organise
6 I work for my uncle's company, so he's my ___ .
 A worker
 B customer
 C employer
7 I don't think you can earn a ___ salary as a waiter.
 A high
 B well-paid
 C demanding
8 My sister works at that café – she's ___ there.
 A an au pair
 B a waitress
 C a hairdresser
9 That shop ___ the best birthday cakes.
 A digs
 B sells
 C tests
10 Brighton is a popular ___ resort in the south of England.
 A hotel
 B travel
 C holiday

2 Complete the words in the sentences. The first letter of each word is given.

1 You need a good i_ _ _ _ _ _ _ _ to teach you how to do a new sport.
2 Doctors and nurses work at a h_ _ _ _ _ _ _ .
3 A t_ _ _ is a group of people who work together.
4 A j_ _ _ _ _ _ _ _ writes articles for a newspaper or a magazine.
5 A secretary works in an o_ _ _ _ _ .
6 A f_ _ _ _ _ grows vegetables and fruit in the countryside.
7 You can rent a room at a h_ _ _ _ to stay for a few days.
8 A m_ _ _ _ _ _ _ can repair your car.
9 C_ _ _ _ _ _ _ _ is another word for a co-worker.
10 A p_ _ _ _ _ _ can repair your toilet or your shower.

3 Choose the best response, A, B or C.

1 Why aren't you working today?
 A I do some work at home.
 B I'm on holiday.
 C I'm not working.
2 Could you do me a favour?
 A Yes, of course.
 B Yes, I like to.
 C Sorry to bother you.
3 What do you do?
 A I'm not studying.
 B I work as a mechanic.
 C I'm sorry, I can't help you.
4 How much milk is there?
 A Not many.
 B It's a lot.
 C There isn't much.
5 I can't do this homework.
 A Yes, it's very difficult!
 B Here you are.
 C I need your help.

WORD STORE 3   Work

WORD STORE 3A
Jobs with suffixes

1 -er   builder , _____ , _____ , _____ ,
         _____ , _____ , _____ , _____ ,
         _____ , _____ , _____ , _____
2 -or   _____ , _____
3 -ist   _____ , _____ , _____ , _____ ,
         _____
4 -ant   _____ , _____
5 Other _____ , _____ , _____ , _____

REMEMBER THIS
The pronunciation of *-or* (*actor, instructor*) and *-er* (*cleaner, builder*) is the same.
A man is a **waiter**. A woman is a **waitress**.
A man is an **actor**. A woman is an **actress**.

WORD STORE 3B
Collocations – *job* and *work*

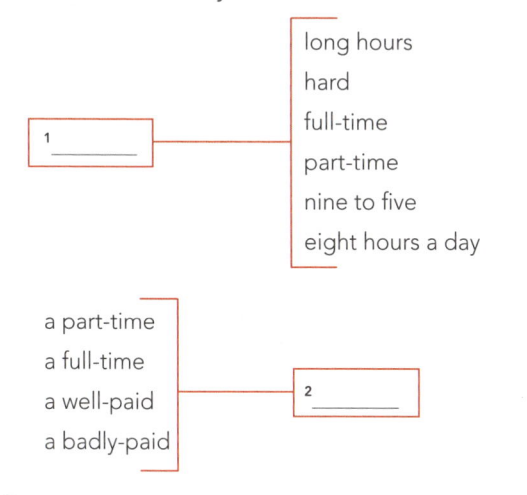

1 _____
- long hours
- hard
- full-time
- part-time
- nine to five
- eight hours a day

- a part-time
- a full-time
- a well-paid
- a badly-paid

2 _____

WORD STORE 3C
***work* + preposition**

1 work *for* a company
2 work _____ a supermarket/a café/a school/ a hospital
3 work _____ people/children/numbers/ your hands
4 work _____ home
5 work _____ a team

WORD STORE 3D
Collocations – *learn* and *teach*

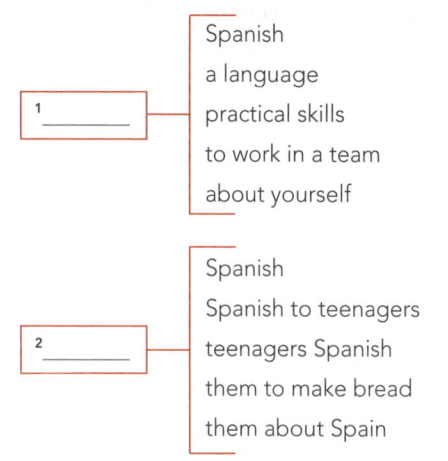

1 _____
- Spanish
- a language
- practical skills
- to work in a team
- about yourself

2 _____
- Spanish
- Spanish to teenagers
- teenagers Spanish
- them to make bread
- them about Spain

WORD STORE 3E
Collocations – money

_____
- thirty pounds a day
- a good/high/low salary
- money to pay for my studies
- a lot of money as a waiter
- enough to pay the rent

7

WORD PRACTICE 4

1 Choose the correct answer, A, B or C.

1 Can you see that girl with the ___ hair?
   A tall
   B curly
   C young
2 I'm sure Gary spends a lot of time in the gym. He's very ___ .
   A ugly
   B pretty
   C sporty
3 My brother is a bit ___ – he believes everything that people tell him.
   A shy
   B calm
   C naive
4 Doris is a lot of fun. She's got a great ___ of humour.
   A sense
   B model
   C election
5 This ___ is big, but it looks good on my head.
   A tie
   B hat
   C jacket
6 Most people wear a ___ to do sport.
   A coat
   B skirt
   C tracksuit
7 What ___ are you, medium or large?
   A fit
   B size
   C label
8 We don't have to wear ___ clothes on Fridays. We can come to the office in jeans and a T-shirt.
   A smart
   B untidy
   C organic
9 Excuse me, can I try these trousers ___ ?
   A on
   B in
   C up
10 I'd like to ___ in love and get married before I finish university.
   A fall
   B drop
   C break

2 Complete the words in the sentences. The first letter of each word is given.

1 You need a t_ _ _ _ _ to speak and taste food. It's inside your mouth.
2 A person who hasn't got any hair is b_ _ _ .
3 A person who has a lot of things to do is very b_ _ _ .
4 A d_ _ _ is a situation when you go out with your boyfriend or girlfriend.
5 A w_ _ is hair to wear on your head that is not your own.
6 An e_ _ _ _ _ _ _ is the situation when people vote for a new government etc.
7 A m_ _ idea is completely crazy.
8 An u_ _ _ _ _ _ _ _ _ person doesn't like being with other people or going to parties.
9 Blond and light brown hair is f_ _ _ .
10 You wear s_ _ _ _ on your feet under your shoes or boots.

3 Complete the conversation with sentences a–h. There are three extra sentences.

Ellie: Would you like to come shopping with me this afternoon?
Grace: [1]_____
Ellie: OK. We can go to the new sports shop in the mall.
Grace: [2]_____
Ellie: I'm looking for some new boots for the winter.
Grace: [3]_____
Ellie: Yeah, they're OK. But they're quite old now. I wear them all the time!
Grace: [4]_____
Ellie: But the shoes and boots there are quite expensive.
Grace: [5]_____
Ellie: You're right. And they sell trainers as well.

a When do you want to go?
b I really like your black ones.
c OK. The shop in the High Street is cheaper.
d I like the shops there.
e What do you want to buy?
f I like wearing trainers.
g We can look in Jumping Jacks Shoe Shop.
h That's a good idea. I have to get some new trainers.

8

WORD STORE 4 — People

WORD STORE 4A
Appearance

be

Age	¹_young_ → middle-aged → old
Height	short ≠ ² _____
Looks	pretty/³_____ ≠ ugly
Build	fit, ⁴s_____ , ⁵w_____ , slim/thin ≠ fat
Hair	bald (= no hair)

have got

Hair colour	brown, ⁶_____ , grey, red, fair/⁷_____ ≠ dark
Hair type	⁸_____ , straight, wavy
Hair length	long → medium-length → ⁹_____
Eye colour	blue, ¹⁰_____ , green, grey

> **REMEMBER THIS**
> - To ask about a person's appearance, you say, What **does** he **look like**? → He's tall with short red hair.
> - **'s** can be short for **is** or **has**.
> He's tall. = He is tall.
> She's got black hair. = She has got black hair.

WORD STORE 4B
Adjective order

Opinion	Length/Size	Type	Colour	Noun
beautiful	long	straight	brown	hair
nice	big	–	green	eyes

WORD STORE 4C
Personality adjectives

1 _confident_ ≠ shy
2 funny ≠ _serious_
3 _____ ≠ stupid
4 _____ ≠ unkind
5 _____ ≠ unsociable
6 _____ ≠ negative
7 _____ ≠ boring

> **REMEMBER THIS**
> To ask about a person's personality, you say, What **is** he **like**? → He's funny and kind.

WORD STORE 4D
Collocations – life events

1 _leave_ home
2 _____ on your first date
3 _____ married/your first job
4 _____ to drive
5 _____ in love
6 _____ your first flat/house/home

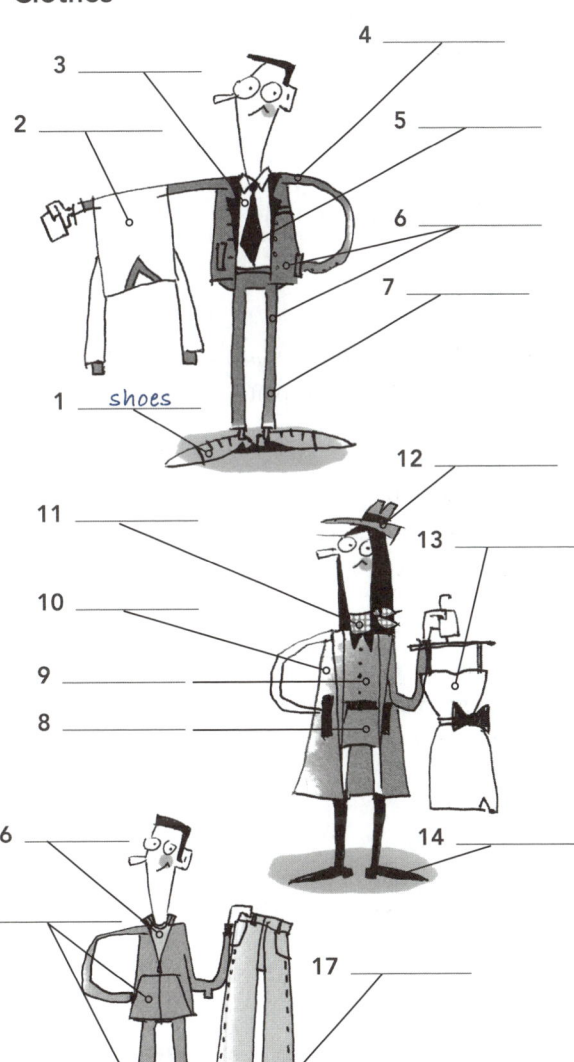

WORD STORE 4E
Clothes

1 _shoes_
2 _____
3 _____
4 _____
5 _____
6 _____
7 _____
8 _____
9 _____
10 _____
11 _____
12 _____
13 _____
14 _____
15 _____
16 _____
17 _____
18 _____
19 _____

WORD PRACTICE 5

1 Choose the correct answer, A, B or C.

1 There's a new canteen at my school. Everyone loves ___ there.
   A having lunch
   B playing sports
   C doing experiments

2 My parents get angry if I wake up late and ___ a class in the morning.
   A improve
   B leave
   C miss

3 I ___ my best in the exam, but I couldn't answer a lot of questions.
   A did
   B made
   C tested

4 The guided ___ of the museum starts in five minutes.
   A trip
   B tour
   C ticket

5 All the classes for first year students are ___ . They have to attend them.
   A gap year
   B volunteer
   C compulsory

6 Do you want to participate ___ the workshop on Saturday?
   A on
   B at
   C in

7 Sometimes it is a good idea to take a ___ even if you are not sure.
   A risk
   B trial
   C danger

8 Who is going to give a ___ on the last day of school this year?
   A course
   B speech
   C meeting

9 You should be proud ___ your exam results. Your grades are really good!
   A of
   B in
   C with

10 You can ___ a great new app from this website.
   A book
   B cheat
   C download

2 Complete the words in the sentences. The first letter of each word is given.

1 You learn about countries and continents in G_ _ _ _ _ _ _ _ .
2 A c_ _ _ _ _ _ _ _ _ helps you solve Maths problems faster.
3 You can borrow books from a l_ _ _ _ _ _ .
4 K_ _ _ _ _ _ _ _ _ _ is a type of school for very young children.
5 A m_ _ _ _ _ _ is a person who plays an instrument or writes songs.
6 Pupils sit at a d_ _ _ to do their homework.
7 Special clothes that you have to wear to school or work are called a u_ _ _ _ _ _ .
8 You need your b_ _ _ _ to think and take decisions.
9 A g_ _ _ _ _ is someone very, very intelligent or good at something.
10 When you get a d_ _ _ _ _ _ _ , you pay less for things.

3 Choose the best response, A, B or C.

1 Where's the museum?
   A It opens at 10.30
   B It's in Park Street.
   C It's an excellent museum.

2 Should we book a table?
   A Yes, it's very popular.
   B You mustn't book a table there.
   C No, it doesn't need to.

3 Thanks for your help.
   A I'm fine.
   B You're welcome.
   C You shouldn't bother.

4 How much is it to visit the Palace?
   A The ticket doesn't cost.
   B There aren't any tickets.
   C It's free for children.

5 Can I leave my bicycle there?
   A No, you mustn't put it in front of the door.
   B Yes, you could.
   C No, you don't leave it.

WORD STORE 5 — Education

WORD STORE 5A
Schools

2–18 years old

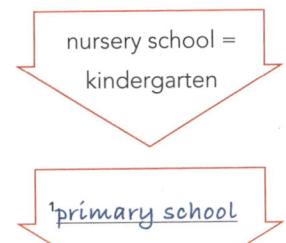

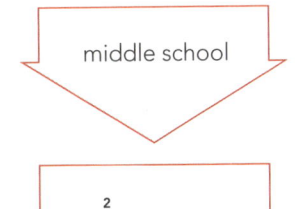

nursery school = kindergarten
↓
¹ _primary school_
↓
middle school
↓
2 _____

Higher education

- technical college
- 3 _____

Type of school

- 4 _____ ≠ private school
- boys' school ≠ girls' school
- single-sex school ≠ 5 _____

WORD STORE 5B
Phrases about school

1 do badly ≠ _do well_
2 get bad marks ≠ _____
3 fail an exam ≠ _____ an exam
4 be late for lessons ≠ be _____ for lessons
5 start school ≠ _____
6 come to class ≠ _____

> **REMEMBER THIS**
> You say a + subject + exam.
> a Maths exam NOT ~~an exam from Maths~~

WORD STORE 5C
Collocations – do, get and be

1 _do_ — my/your/their, etc. homework / badly in the exam / well in the test / my/your/their best

2 _____ — proud of a person/thing / early/late for dinner / early/late for the concert / on time for the doctor

3 _____ — an education / bad marks/a bad mark for the homework / good marks/a good mark for your project

WORD STORE 5D
Places in a school

1 co_rridor_
2 ca_____
3 cl_____
4 s_____ r_____
5 l_____
6 pl_____
7 g_____
8 h_____
9 s_____ l_____
10 s_____ f_____

WORD STORE 5E
Compound nouns

1 camping — c — a tours
2 home — — b time
3 museum — — c trips
4 free — — d stays
5 cultural — — e sports
6 water — — f events

11

WORD PRACTICE 6

1 Choose the correct answer, A, B or C.

1. Is Gabriel playing ___ the same team as last year?
   A at
   B for
   C on
2. I don't like running, but I ___ yoga twice a week.
   A do
   B play
   C make
3. Frank wasn't the fastest runner. He was third in the race and won a ___ medal.
   A gold
   B silver
   C bronze
4. Skiing is a ___ sport.
   A team
   B winter
   C water
5. The Olympic Games take ___ every four years.
   A place
   B time
   C part
6. In the 1990s my uncle John was a successful sportsman. One day he ___ ten points in one match.
   A scored
   B trained
   C completed
7. What time does the first ___ of the match finish?
   A career
   B line
   C half
8. I don't believe ___ anything this sports magazine says.
   A at
   B on
   C in
9. After the fifteen-kilometre race, Joanna's legs were completely ___ .
   A sore
   B dizzy
   C disabled
10. A professional sportsman should get enough ___ at night to feel well before an important event.
    A gym
    B sleep
    C challenge

2 Complete the words in the sentences. The first letter of each word is given.

1. Kung fu and karate are examples of **m**_ _ _ _ _ _ **a**_ _ _ .
2. You get a **p**_ _ _ _ when you win something.
3. You do **i**_ _ _ _ _ _ _ _ sports when you are on your own.
4. You need a bike to go **c**_ _ _ _ _ _ .
5. A person who gives you instructions on how to do something correctly is a **c**_ _ _ _ .
6. When you go up a mountain, you **c**_ _ _ _ it.
7. A **c**_ _ _ _ _ _ _ is a person who wins an important competition.
8. When a doctor looks at your body to check if you're OK, he/she **e**_ _ _ _ _ _ your body.
9. A person or company who gives money to help organise a sports event is a **s**_ _ _ _ _ _ .
10. A **j**_ _ _ _ _ is a person who goes running to keep fit and doesn't run very fast.

3 Complete the conversation with sentences a–h. There are three extra sentences.

Tom: Hi, Harry! How are you? You weren't at school yesterday.
Harry: ¹_____
Tom: How fantastic! I once went skiing in Scotland. Did you have fun?
Harry: ²_____
Tom: When I went, it was really cold, especially at night.
Harry: ³_____
Tom: Yes, your face is very brown! Come round now and tell me all about it.
Harry: ⁴_____
Tom: Well, come round later.
Harry: ⁵_____
Tom: Great! See you later.

a Did you go with your family?
b We had a warm hotel room! The sun was really hot during the day.
c I only got back half an hour ago. I need to unpack.
d Lots! It was awesome. I was with my best mates.
e Yes, that's a good idea. I've got a lot of photographs to show you.
f I didn't take warm clothes.
g We can chat at school tomorrow.
h I know. I went skiing in Austria at the weekend and our plane back was late.

WORD STORE 6 — Sport and health

WORD STORE 6A
Types of sport

Ending with -ing
1 cycling
2 i_ _ s_ _ _ _ _ _
3 j_ _ _ _ _ _
4 ka_ _ _ _ _ _
5 sa_ _ _ _ _
6 s_ _ _ _ _
7 s_ _ _ _ _ _ _
8 s_ _ _ _ _ _ _ _ _ _ _

Ending with -ball
9 b_ _ _ _ _ _ _ _ _
10 f_ _ _ _ _ _
11 v_ _ _ _ _ _ _ _ _

Other
12 b_ _ _ _ _ _ _ _
13 h_ _ _ _ _
14 k_ _ _ _ _
15 k_ _ _ f_
16 t_ _ _ _ t_ _ _ _ _
17 t_ _ _ _ _
18 y_ _ _
19 Z_ _ _ _

WORD STORE 6B
Collocations – do, go and play

1 _____ : badminton, basketball, football, hockey, volleyball, table tennis, tennis

2 _____ : cycling, ice skating, jogging, kayaking, sailing, skiing, swimming, running

3 do : exercises, karate, kung fu, yoga, Zumba

WORD STORE 6C
Collocations – sport and health

1 have a healthy breakfast/meal/diet/lifestyle
2 _____ for a team
3 _____ to the gym
4 _____ fit
5 _____ part in a competition

WORD STORE 6D
Likes and dislikes

+	−
I ¹like	I don't like
I ² _____	I don't enjoy
I love	I ³h_____
	I ⁴ _____ stand
I'm ⁵ _____	I'm not into
I prefer	I ⁶ _____ care about

WORD STORE 6E
Sportspeople

+ player	hockey player, ¹t_____ , ²b_____
+ -er	skier, ³f_____
+ double consonant + -er	jogger, ⁴swimmer
+ -or	sailor
+ -ist	cyclist

REMEMBER THIS
footballer = football player

WORD PRACTICE 7

1 Choose the correct answer, A, B or C.

1. I'm afraid of flying, so I never travel by ___ .
   A ship
   B train
   C plane
2. Is it necessary to book ___ on the bus to Cambridge?
   A a seat
   B accommodation
   C a reservation
3. When we arrived at the hotel, there was nobody at the ___ .
   A platform
   B waiting room
   C reception desk
4. A lot of people travel in the morning. Sometimes it's difficult to get ___ this train.
   A in
   B on
   C at
5. My parents like to ___ in the summer, so they always go on a beach holiday.
   A go climbing
   B see the sights
   C relax by the sea
6. Have you got a lot of ___ in your passport?
   A visas
   B trailers
   C guidebooks
7. Excuse me, could you tell me the ___ to the train station?
   A road
   B way
   C street
8. I'm an experienced hiker. I ___ to the countryside as often as I can.
   A reach
   B escape
   C stay
9. ___ left and then go straight on.
   A Take
   B Make
   C Turn
10. Stop and look around now! The theatre is ___ your right. You can't miss it.
    A at
    B on
    C from

2 Complete the words in the sentences. The first letter of each word is given.

1. A f_ _ _ _ is a type of ship that can carry people and cars across a river or sea.
2. An e_ _ _ _ _ _ _ _ is a short trip when people travel to visit a place.
3. A t_ _ _ _ _ a_ _ _ _ _ is a company that helps you find hotel rooms and buy tickets.
4. You can sleep in a tent at a c_ _ _ _ _ _ _ .
5. A piece of land surrounded by water is an i_ _ _ _ _ .
6. A m_ _ _ _ _ is a special building where you can see objects important for cultural or historical reasons.
7. The money that you can spend on something is called your b_ _ _ _ _ _ .
8. When something is s_ _ _ , it is not dangerous.
9. A t_ _ _ is a special car with a driver that you can stop in the street to go somewhere.
10. Passengers go to an a_ _ _ _ _ _ to catch a plane.

3 Choose the best response, A, B or C.

1. We can send you some brochures on Friday.
   A I would be happy to receive them before then.
   B Would it be possible to send them before?
   C I look forward to hearing from you.
2. Do you need some help?
   A Please! How do I get to the park from here?
   B Thank you for your help.
   C I should walk to the park.
3. Don't forget to do your homework!
   A I could forget it.
   B I didn't do it.
   C I've already done it.
4. I'd love to go to Norway on holiday.
   A I've gone there.
   B I've been there once.
   C How long did you go?
5. When did you go camping in Wales?
   A I've been there a long time.
   B When I was fourteen.
   C Next year, I think.

WORD STORE 7 — Travel

WORD STORE 7A
Types of holiday and transport

go on + type of holiday

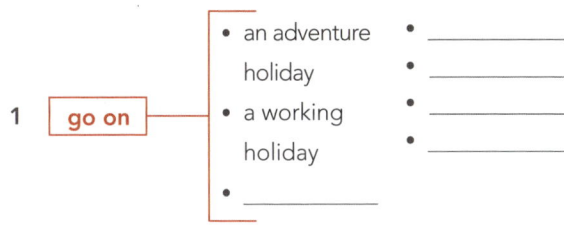

1 **go on**
- an adventure holiday
- a working holiday
- _____
- _____
- _____
- _____

go/travel by + type of transport

2 **go/travel by**
- boat
- ferry
- ship
- *plane*
- _____
- _____
- _____
- _____

REMEMBER THIS
go on a tour
travel by car, go by bike, go by bus
go on foot

WORD STORE 7B
Collocations – journeys and holidays

1 **book**
- a train/bus ticket
- a seat on the train/bus
- a hotel
- your a*ccommodation*
- a f_____
- an e_____
- a h_____
- your t_____

2 **make**
- a reservation
- the a_____

3 **visit**
- the m*useums*
- the s_____
- l_____ m_____

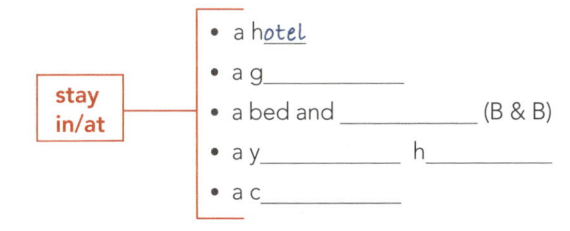

WORD STORE 7C
Accommodation

stay in/at
- a h*otel*
- a g_____
- a bed and _____ (B & B)
- a y_____ h_____
- a c_____

REMEMBER THIS
You say: **a three-star hotel**, etc., NOT a hotel with three stars.
Other examples: *a four-person tent, a three-month trip, a two-day excursion, a two-week holiday*

WORD STORE 7D
Travel

At a hotel
1 The hotel keeps your room for you if you have a *booking*.
2 You must _____ when you arrive at the hotel.

At the airport
3 Show your _____ and your _____ at the check-in desk.
4 At the check-in desk, they take your _____ and put it in a special place on the plane.
5 They make an announcement when your _____ is ready to leave.

At the train station
6 When the train arrives at the _____, you can get on or off the train.
7 _____ can buy their tickets before or during the train journey.

At a travel agency
8 You can get _____ about holidays in different countries.

WORD STORE 7E
Collocations

1 cycling — [f]
2 southernmost — [ ]
3 world — [ ]
4 news — [ ]
5 get — [ ]
6 raise — [ ]

a show
b money
c city
d better
e crisis
f trip

15

WORD PRACTICE 8

1 Choose the correct answer, A, B or C.

1 Most scientists agree that the problem of global ___ will get worse in the near future.
   A change
   B warming
   C pollution

2 These islands are famous ___ their population of penguins.
   A in
   B for
   C with

3 Take showers instead of baths. You will ___ a lot of water.
   A use
   B save
   C waste

4 The storm suddenly stopped and there was a ___ sky.
   A warm
   B foggy
   C clear

5 The park is ___ the border between Spain and Portugal.
   A on
   B at
   C in

6 Glaciers in Europe will ___ when the temperature rises.
   A melt
   B cover
   C die out

7 This is a very ___ species. You can only find it in the south of the island.
   A picturesque
   B rare
   C dangerous

8 The jungle is disappearing because too many companies are cutting down ___ .
   A cereal
   B fields
   C trees

9 It's a good idea to ___ rubbish to protect the environment.
   A sort
   B throw away
   C grow

10 Why don't we ___ some tomatoes in the garden next year?
   A plant
   B feed
   C hunt

2 Complete the words in the sentences. The first letter of each word is given.

1 A b_ _ _ _ _ _ _ _ is an insect with large wings. It is usually colourful.
2 A text describing what the weather will be like is a f_ _ _ _ _ _ _ .
3 C_ _ _ _ _ _ _ _ _ _ is a situation when two people work together.
4 A s_ _ _ _ _ is a short, light rain.
5 A h_ _ _ is smaller than a mountain.
6 Australia and Asia are c_ _ _ _ _ _ _ _ _ .
7 A place that produces energy is a p_ _ _ _ p_ _ _ _ .
8 A c_ _ is a large animal that people keep for its milk or meat.
9 A s_ _ _ _ is a fish that has sharp teeth and eats smaller fish.
10 An animal's natural environment is its h_ _ _ _ _ _ .

3 Complete the conversation with sentences a–h There are three extra sentences.

Jack: The Environmental Club has got a meeting after school today.
Sal: 1_____
Jack: They've changed it because there are extra Maths lessons in Room 15 this Thursday.
Sal: 2_____
Jack: Yes. I'm going to take some of my *Wild Life* magazines to show the others.
Sal: 3_____
Jack: I don't know. Why?
Sal: 4_____
Jack: I'll give them to him, no worries.
Sal: 5_____
Jack: Oh, he'll really love these! See you soon.

a Don't worry. I'm sure I'll see him tomorrow.
b OK. Are you going? To the club meeting, not the Maths, I mean!
c I can't come today, but I want to give him some animal photos for his project.
d I don't often go to the meetings.
e Really? It's usually on Thursdays.
f You don't need extra Maths! You're really good.
g Thanks a lot, Jack. Here they are.
h That will be interesting. Do you think Brad will be there?

16

WORD STORE 8 — Nature

WORD STORE 8A
Landscape

Land
1 forest
2 i_____
3 j_____
4 m_____
5 r_____
6 v_____

Water
7 c_____ r_____
8 r_____
9 s_____
10 w_____

WORD STORE 8B
Wildlife

1 _____
2 bear
3 _____
4 _____
5 _____
6 _____
7 _____
8 _____
9 _____
10 _____

WORD STORE 8C
Environmental problems

Noun phrases
1 air/water pollution
2 illegal _____/_____
3 global _____
4 _____ change

Verb + noun collocations
5 d_____/p_____ the (natural) environment
6 c_____ _____ trees
7 p_____ the air/water
8 make (a lot of) n_____

WORD STORE 8D
Weather nouns and adjectives

	NOUN	ADJECTIVE
1	cloud	cloudy
2	_____	sunny
3	rain	_____
4	_____	foggy
5	wind	_____

WORD STORE 8E
Nouns and adjectives

	NOUN	ADJECTIVE
1	nature	natural
2	danger	_____
3	peace	_____
4	character	_____
5	beauty	_____
6	picture	_____
7	importance	_____

17

PREPOSITIONS

PREPOSITIONS IN PHRASES

ABOVE
above sea level: *The valley lies about 4,000 metres above sea level.*

ALONG
along the river/road: *We took a walk along the river.*

AT
at (eight) (o'clock/a.m./p.m.): *The film starts at eight.*
at (sixteen) (years old): *At sixteen you can start learning to ride a moped.*
at a campsite: *You can stay at fantastic campsites for great prices.*
at a desk/table: *We are sitting at the table by the window and waiting for you.*
at a hotel/restaurant: *Let's stay at this hotel.*
at all: *They didn't practise at all.*
at first: *At first he seemed strict, but now I really like him.*
at home/school: *I stayed at home and watched television.*
at least: *Will you at least say you're sorry?*
at lunchtime: *Some people eat their main meal at lunchtime.*
at midnight/night/noon: *Peter often works at night.*
at platform (six): *The Edinburgh train standing at platform six will depart in two minutes.*
at sb's house: *We'll meet at Harry's house.*
at school/university: *My sister's at Leeds University.*
at the age of: *Jamie won his first tournament at the age of fifteen.*
at the beginning: *At the beginning of each lesson there is usually a revision exercise.*
at the end: *What did they do at the end of their journey?*
at the moment: *Julia's on holiday in Spain at the moment.*
at the Olympics/Paralympics: *She won a silver medal at the Paralympics in Athens.*
at the same speed: *They moved at the same speed.*
at the same time: *How can you write and speak at the same time?*
at the weekend (BrE)/on the weekend (AmE): *I like to play golf at the weekend.*
at a meeting: *She's at a meeting right now.*
at a supermarket: *My brother has a weekend job at the supermarket.*

BY
by bus/car/coach/plane/ship/train: *I usually go to school by bus.*
by courier: *I hope you are able to send the watch to me by courier.*
by the river/sea: *We've bought a small summer house by the sea.*

DURING
during the day/week: *Animals hide in the forest during the day.*

FOR
for an hour/(ten) minutes: *Fry the eggs for ten minutes.*
for dessert/dinner: *What are we having for dessert?*
for free: *Kylie's fixing my car for free.*
for hours: *We waited for the results for hours.*

FROM
from … to …: *The morning class is from 9.00 to 11.00.*
from above: *This is our house from above.*
from an early age: *She learnt English from an early age.*
from home: *She works from home twice a week.*
from the start: *They had problems from the start.*

IN
in (2014): *She was born in 1998.*
in a band: *My brother plays in a rock band.*
in a canteen/gym/hall/library: *We always meet up in the canteen after the first lesson.*
in a city/continent/country/place/village: *I live in New York.*
in a company: *Bill's parents work in an international company.*
in a cupboard/desk: *There are some pens in my desk.*
in a desert: *I rode a camel in the Sinai Desert.*
in a different/the same colour: *He bought these flowers in a different colour.*
in a different/the same way: *Make this drink the same way you make tea.*
in a hotel/house/pub/shop/supermarket: *Let's meet in the pub.*
in a lesson/meeting: *Tim fell asleep in the Maths lesson.*
in a size (12): *Do you have these trousers in a size 12?*
in a team: *I like working in a team.*
in (a/the) small/medium/large: *Have you got this T-shirt in a medium?*
in an exam/a test: *How did you do in your exams?*
in an hour/(sixty) years' time: *Gerry should be home in an hour.*
in an office: *Sorry, Amy's not in her office today.*
in any way: *You don't harm the environment in any way.*
in English: *Write this email in English.*
in front of (the telly): *They always eat breakfast in front of the telly.*
in groups of (three): *Do this exercise in groups of three.*
in January/February/March, etc.: *She started working there in January.*
in many ways: *Working at home makes sense in many ways.*
in my opinion: *In my opinion, he made the right decision.*
in pairs: *Work in pairs.*
in port: *The ship is in port for six days.*
in response to: *I am writing in response to your newspaper advert.*
in summer/autumn/winter/spring: *Miriam likes to relax in her garden in summer.*
in the (holiday) season: *Hotels are often full in the holiday season.*
in the afternoon/evening/morning: *Classes start in the morning.*
in the background: *In the background you can see the school.*
in the bathroom/living room: *The children are playing in the living room.*
in the correct order: *Put the events in the correct order.*
in the countryside: *My father spent his childhood in the countryside.*
in the crowd: *I saw Mary in the crowd.*
in the east/north/south/west: *They lived in a small town in the south.*
in the future: *In the future, people will be able to travel to other planets.*
in the last minute/second half (of the match): *They scored a goal in the second half.*
in the mountains: *I'm going to ride ponies for free in the mountains.*
in the ocean/sea: *I like swimming in the ocean.*
in the park: *Let's go for a walk in the park.*
in the photo/text: *In the photo, you can see a group of teenagers.*
in the world: *You're the best dad in the world.*
in town: *I buy my clothes at the local shops in town.*
in your free time: *He writes emails in his free time.*

PREPOSITIONS

ON
on (a day): They started on 7 July in northern Alaska.
on a boat/ship: He's on a boat in the middle of the lake.
on a bus/train: I always read newspapers on the train.
on a desk/table: I left my laptop on my desk.
on a farm: Animals on large 'factory farms' have a terrible life.
on a trip: What was the most amazing thing on the trip?
on a/your computer/laptop/tablet: I've got all my photos on my laptop.
on a/your phone: I've got all my music on my phone.
on an island: You can't drive a car on this island.
on both sides: Fry the pancake on both sides.
on earth: What is the longest river on earth?
on Facebook/Twitter: In the evening I post the best photos on Facebook.
on holiday: I saw lions when I was on holiday in Africa.
on Monday (etc.) afternoon/evening/morning: Let's go out for a meal on Monday afternoon.
on Monday/Tuesday/Wednesday, etc.: It rained on Monday.
on television/TV: They appeared on television in Guatemala.
on the beach: In summer, we play volleyball on the beach.
on the board: Write the correct answer on the board.
on the border: The river lies on the US-Mexican border.
on the corner (of sth and sth): The theatre is on the corner of Park Street and Green Road.
on the Internet: I read books, magazines or things on the Internet.
on the map: I can't find this place on the map.
on the road: We reached the end of the journey after 605 days on the road.
on the roof: He found the cat up on the roof.
on the same day: They were born on the same day.
on the sports field: When it rains, we don't have PE classes on the sports field.
on the/your (web)site: You can find loads of ideas on our site.
on the/your left/right: It's the first door on your left.
on time (for): In Japan the trains are always on time.
on top (of): The cake was burnt on top.
on weekdays: I always get up at six on weekdays.

PREPOSITIONS AFTER ADJECTIVES
afraid of: Small children are afraid of the dark.
bad for: Sweets are bad for your teeth.
busy with: My weekends are busy with football.
close to: The house is close to the beach.
early/late for: Peggy was late for school.
famous for: France is famous for its wine.
generous with (money/time): Jim is very generous with his time.
good at: Andrea is good at languages.
good for: Green vegetables are good for you.
interested in: Lisa is interested in law.
proud of: Her parents are very proud of her.
ready for: I don't think Joey is ready for school yet.
responsible for: The airline is responsible for the safety of its passengers.
rubbish at: I'm rubbish at Maths.
scared of: She's scared of flying.
sorry for: I'm sorry for his wife.
unique to: These animals are unique to Australia.
wrong with: What's wrong with this phone?

PREPOSITIONS AFTER NOUNS
advice about: She gave me advice about what to see in New York.
danger to: Illegal hunting is a danger to wildlife.
diet of: Water birds have a natural diet of fish.
excursion to: You can also book excursions to nearby towns.
fear of: He has a fear of flying.
feedback on: The teacher gave us feedback on our homework.
feelings about: What are your feelings about this place?
help with a matter/problem: Thank you for your help with this matter.
information about/on: I'd like some information about the ticket prices.
plans for: What plans have you got for your summer holidays?
reason for: He didn't give a reason for his decision.
right to: Everyone should have the right to free education.

PREPOSITIONS AFTER VERBS
arrive at/in (a place): What time does the train arrive in New York?
ask about: Visitors usually ask about the history of the castle.
ask for: Some people don't like to ask for help.
be into: I'm really into folk music.
borrow from: You can borrow six books a month from the library.
call at (a town/city): This train calls at all stations.
choose from: You can choose from three different cars.
compare to/with: They compare him to John F. Kennedy.
enquire about: I am writing to enquire about your special offers.
get off (a bus/plane/train): Let's get off the bus at the next stop.
get on (a bus/plane/train): She got on the bus at Clark Street.
go across (a road/street): Go across the road.
go for (a swim/walk): In good weather, we just go for a walk.
go on (a date/excursion/holiday/ride): We went on a trip to the mountains.
go on a (news) show: CNN asked us to go on their show.
go on a holiday: Are you going on a camping holiday again this year?
go on the Internet: In my free time, I usually go on the Internet.
go out of (a café/car): Go out of the café and turn left.
go to (the cinema/gym/park): When the weather's bad we go to the gym or the cinema.
invite to: He invited me to the meeting.
jump off: Boys jump off the bridge.
know about: He knows a lot about cars.
learn about: We only learnt about the accident later.
listen to: Have you listened to those CDs yet?
match to/with: Match the words on the left with the meanings on the right.
move to (a place): They moved to Birmingham last May.
pay for: How much did you pay for this watch?
phone sb on (a number/their mobile): Please confirm by phoning me on my mobile.
play for: Garcia plays for the Hornets.
pour into: We plan to pour the water into the Atlantic.
prepare for: I haven't even begun to prepare for tomorrow's test.
reply to: Please reply to this email.
speak in (English): In class, we usually speak in English.

KEY TO PHONETIC SYMBOLS

Consonants

p	**p**en, co**p**y, ha**pp**en
b	**b**ack, **b**u**bb**le, jo**b**
t	**t**ea, ci**t**y, bu**tt**on
d	**d**ay, la**dd**er, o**dd**
k	**k**ey, s**ch**ool, du**ck**, **c**ool
g	**g**et, **g**i**gg**le, **gh**ost
tʃ	**ch**urch, ma**tch**, na**t**ure
dʒ	**j**udge, a**ge**, sol**d**ier
f	**f**at, co**ff**ee, tou**gh**, **ph**ysics
v	**v**iew, hea**v**y, mo**v**e
θ	**th**ing, au**th**or, pa**th**
ð	**th**is, o**th**er, smoo**th**
s	**s**oon, **c**ease, **s**i**s**ter
z	**z**ero, **z**one, ro**s**es, bu**zz**
ʃ	**sh**ip, **s**ure, sta**t**ion
ʒ	plea**s**ure, vi**s**ion
h	**h**ot, **wh**ole, be**h**ind
m	**m**ore, ha**mm**er, su**m**
n	**n**ice, **kn**ow, fu**nn**y, su**n**
ŋ	ri**ng**, lo**ng**, tha**n**ks, su**ng**
l	**l**ight, va**ll**ey feel
r	**r**ight, so**rr**y, a**rr**ange
j	**y**et, **u**se, b**eau**ty
w	**w**et, **o**ne, **wh**en, q**u**een

Vowels

ɪ	k**i**t, b**i**d, h**y**mn
e	dr**e**ss, b**e**d
æ	b**a**d, c**a**t, tr**a**p
ɒ	l**o**t, **o**dd, w**a**sh
ʌ	l**o**ve, b**u**t, d**u**ck
ʊ	f**oo**t, g**oo**d, p**u**t
iː	s**ea**, f**ee**l, mach**i**ne
eɪ	f**a**ce, d**ay**, st**ea**k
aɪ	pr**i**ce, h**igh**, tr**y**
ɔɪ	b**oy**, ch**oi**ce
uː	tw**o**, bl**ue**, g**oo**se
əʊ	g**oa**t, sh**ow**, n**o**
aʊ	m**ou**th, n**ow**
ɪə	n**ear**, h**ere**, s**e**rious
eə	f**air**, v**ar**ious, sq**uare**
ɑː	st**ar**t, f**a**ther
ɔː	th**ough**t, l**aw**, n**or**th
ʊə	c**ure**, p**oor**
ɜː	n**ur**se, st**ir**
i	happ**y**, rad**i**ation, glor**i**ous
ə	**a**bout, comm**o**n
u	sit**u**ation, ann**u**al, infl**u**ence

08 WORD LIST • NATURE

Animals
butterfly /ˈbʌtəflaɪ/
chimpanzee /ˌtʃɪmpænˈziː/
coral /ˈkɒrəl/
cow /kaʊ/
crocodile /ˈkrɒkədaɪl/
fish /fɪʃ/
(forest) elephant /(ˈfɒrəst) ˌeləfənt/
gorilla /gəˈrɪlə/
Highland pony /ˌhaɪlənd ˈpəʊni/
monkey /ˈmʌŋki/
panda /ˈpændə/
penguin /ˈpeŋgwən/
peregrine falcon /ˌperəgrən ˈfɔːlkən/
(polar) bear /(ˌpəʊlə) ˈbeə/
(sea) bird /(ˈsiː) bɜːd/
(sea) snail /(ˈsiː) sneɪl/
(sea) turtle /(ˈsiː) ˌtɜːtl/
shark /ʃɑːk/
(snow) leopard /(ˈsnəʊ) ˌlepəd/
whale /weɪl/
wolf /wʊlf/

Plants
bamboo /ˌbæmˈbuː/
bush /bʊʃ/
cereal /ˈsɪəriəl/
flower /ˈflaʊə/
grass /grɑːs/
tree /triː/

Landscape
continent /ˈkɒntənənt/
coral reef /ˈkɒrəl riːf/
countryside /ˈkʌntrisaɪd/
field /fiːld/
glacier /ˈglæsiə/
hill /hɪl/
ice falls /ˈaɪs fɔːlz/
ice pools/bridges /ˈaɪs puːlz/ˌbrɪdʒɪz/
island /ˈaɪlənd/
jungle /ˈdʒʌŋgəl/
mountain /ˈmaʊntən/
ocean /ˈəʊʃən/
river /ˈrɪvə/
sea /siː/
(subtropical) rainforest /(sʌbˌtrɒpɪkəl) ˈreɪnfɒrɪst/
(tropical) forest /(ˌtrɒpɪkəl) ˈfɒrəst/
valley /ˈvæli/
waterfall/falls /ˈwɔːtəfɔːl/fɔːlz/

Location
above sea level /əˌbʌv ˈsiː ˌlevəl/
area /ˈeəriə/
cover /ˈkʌvə/
high up /ˌhaɪ ˈʌp/
lie /laɪ/
on the border (between) /ɒn ðə ˈbɔːdə (bɪˌtwiːn)/
south/north/east/west /saʊθ/nɔːθ/iːst/west/
southern/northern/eastern/western /ˈsʌðən/ˈnɔːðən/ˈiːstən/ˈwestən/
(square) kilometre /(ˌskweə) ˈkɪləˌmiːtə/
surrounded by sth /səˈraʊndɪd baɪ ˌsʌmθɪŋ/
(three kilometres) wide /(θriː ˌkɪləmiːtəz) ˈwaɪd/
underwater /ˌʌndəˈwɔːtə/

Environmental problems
air/water pollution /ˈeə/ˈwɔːtə pəˌluːʃən/
climate change /ˈklaɪmət tʃeɪndʒ/
cut down trees /ˌkʌt daʊn ˈtriːz/
danger /ˈdeɪndʒə/
dangerous /ˈdeɪndʒərəs/
destroy /dɪˈstrɔɪ/
die out /ˌdaɪ ˈaʊt/
disappear /ˌdɪsəˈpɪə/
disaster /dɪˈzɑːstə/
global warming /ˌgləʊbəl ˈwɔːmɪŋ/
green /griːn/
grow /grəʊ/
habitat /ˈhæbətæt/
hunt /hʌnt/
illegal fishing/hunting /ɪˌliːgəl ˈfɪʃɪŋ/ˈhʌntɪŋ/
make noise /ˌmeɪk ˈnɔɪz/
melt /melt/
(nuclear) energy /(ˌnjuːkliə) ˈenədʒi/
oil /ɔɪl/
plant trees /ˌplɑːnt ˈtriːz/
pollute the air/water /pəˌluːt ði ˈeə/ˈwɔːtə/
power station/power plant /ˈpaʊə ˌsteɪʃən/ˈpaʊə plɑːnt/
produce CO₂ /prəˌdjuːs ˌsiː əʊ ˈtuː/
protect the (natural) environment /prəˌtekt ðə (ˌnætʃərəl) ɪnˈvaɪrənmənt/
(radioactive) waste /(ˌreɪdiəʊˌæktɪv) ˈweɪst/
recycled /ˌriːˈsaɪkəld/
recycling /ˌriːˈsaɪklɪŋ/
safe /seɪf/
sea ice /ˈsiː aɪs/
sort rubbish /ˌsɔːt ˈrʌbɪʃ/
throw away /ˌθrəʊ əˈweɪ/
turn off the water tap /ˌtɜːn ɒf ðə ˈwɔːtə tæp/
turn on/off the light/electrical devices /ˌtɜːn ˌɒn/ˌɒf ðə ˈlaɪt/ɪˈlektrɪkəl dɪˌvaɪsɪz/
use public transport /ˌjuːz ˌpʌblɪk ˈtrænspɔːt/
waste/save energy/water /ˌweɪst/ˌseɪv ˈenədʒi/ˈwɔːtə/
wind farm /ˈwɪnd fɑːm/

National parks
birdwatching /ˈbɜːdwɒtʃɪŋ/
fear of /ˈfɪər əv/
feed /fiːd/
follow the route /ˌfɒləʊ ðə ˈruːt/
nature reserve /ˈneɪtʃə rɪˌzɜːv/
rule /ruːl/
spot /spɒt/
take a break /ˌteɪk ə ˈbreɪk/
visitor /ˈvɪzətə/
wildlife /ˈwaɪldlaɪf/

Adjectives describing wonders of nature
amazing/incredible /əˈmeɪzɪŋ/ɪnˈkredəbəl/
breathtaking /ˈbreθˌteɪkɪŋ/
characteristic /ˌkærəktəˈrɪstɪk/
famous (for sth) /ˈfeɪməs (fə ˌsʌmθɪŋ)/
full of life /ˌfʊl əv ˈlaɪf/
lovely /ˈlʌvli/
peaceful /ˈpiːsfəl/
picturesque /ˌpɪktʃəˈresk/
rare /reə/
special /ˈspeʃəl/
unique (to an area) /juːˈniːk (tə ən ˌeəriə)/
unusual /ʌnˈjuːʒuəl/
wild /waɪld/

Weather
clear /klɪə/
clear sky /ˌklɪə ˈskaɪ/
cloud /klaʊd/
cloudy /ˈklaʊdi/
cold /kəʊld/
degree /dɪˈgriː/
fog /fɒg/
foggy /ˈfɒgi/
hot /hɒt/
rain /reɪn/
rainy /ˈreɪni/
shower /ˈʃaʊə/
snow /snəʊ/
sun /sʌn/
sunny /ˈsʌni/
sunshine /ˈsʌnʃaɪn/
temperature /ˈtemprətʃə/
thunder and lightning /ˌθʌndər ənd ˈlaɪtnɪŋ/
warm /wɔːm/
weather forecast /ˈweðə ˌfɔːkɑːst/
wet /wet/
wind /wɪnd/
windy /ˈwɪndi/

Other
beauty /ˈbjuːti/
character /ˈkærəktə/
cooperation /kəʊˌɒpəˈreɪʃən/
importance /ɪmˈpɔːtəns/
important /ɪmˈpɔːtənt/
nuisance /ˈnjuːsəns/
original /əˈrɪdʒɪnəl/
peace /piːs/
picture /ˈpɪktʃə/

Pearson Education Limited,
Edinburgh Gate, Harlow
Essex, CM20 2JE, England
and Associated Companies throughout the world

www.pearsonelt.com/focus

© Pearson Education Limited 2016

The right of Patricia Reilly, Marta Umińska, Bartosz Michałowski and Lynda Edwards to be identified as authors of this work has been asserted by them in accordance with the Copyright, Designs and Patents Act, 1988.

All rights reserved. No part of this publication may be reproduced, stored in a retrieval system, or transmitted in any form or by any means, electronic, mechanical, photocopying, recording or otherwise without the prior written permission of the copyright holders.

First published 2016
Fourth impression 2017
ISBN: 9781447997672

Set in Avenir
Printed in Slovakia by Neografia

Patricia Reilly's acknowledgements

I would like to thank the team at Pearson for all their hard work. I would like to thank my family, especially Alexander, Tom and Amaya, who make everything worthwhile.

Acknowledgements

The publishers and authors would like to thank the following people for their feedback and comments during the development of the material:
Humberto Santos Duran, Anna Maria Grochowska, Inga Lande, Magdalena Loska, Rosa Maria Maldonado, Juliana Queiroz Pereira, Tomasz Siuta, Renata Tomaka-Pasternak

We are grateful to the following for permission to reproduce copyright material:

Photo acknowledgements

The publisher would like to thank the following for their kind permission to reproduce their photographs:
(Key: b-bottom; c-centre; l-left; r-right; t-top)

123RF.com: Brian Chase 15tr, mihitiander 107tc (left), pavalena 74r, yanlev 42t, Hongqi Zhang 36tl; **Alamy Images:** age fotostock Spain, S.L. 15b, Bubbles Photolibrary 86, Viktor Cap 55r, Charles O. Cecil 39b, Peter Crome 107cl, Denkou Images 18, Design Pics Inc. 17, Doug Blane 81tr, Jeff Greenberg 39c, Phil Hynds 80tl, i people 63br, Image Source 19, Peter Lane 104-105, Motoring Picture Library 57b, Jon Parker Lee 63tc, Eduardo Ripoll 30tl, Marc Tielemans 6 (comics), vario images GmbH & Co.KG 29r, Westend61 GmbH 87cr, ZUMA Press, Inc 62l; **Class Afloat - West Island College International:** 64-65, 65r; **Corbis:** Jens Buettner 9, 9r, epa / Harish Tyagi 96t, Hemis / Sylvain Cordier 102bc, J Wheeler and V Laws 16; **Cycle For Water:** 89t, 89c, 89b; **Fotolia.com:** Galyna Andrushko 107c (left), Antonioguillem 48t, apops 36b, 37cr, ArnIle 67l, Artens 25 (background), autofocus67 85t, Tanja Bagusat 88, bahram7 101tr, Chlorophylle 25t, contrastwerkstatt 87b, Coprid 10bl, Dangubic 91l, daw666 72-73 (icons), destina 6 (headphones), DragonImages 8/6, Erni 101bc, Liv Friis-larsen 6tl (photos), Alexey Fursov 8/7, Astrid Gast 8/5, Glamy 5tl, Antonio Gravante 6br (photos), grieze 36tr, Chris Hill 101br, huxflux 101tl, inurbanspace 85b, isuaneye 27b, JackF 8/3, Wojciech Jaskowski 13t, jkphoto69 6 (sunglasses), jolopes 12b, Kadmy 36cl, 36cr, 37t, Kalypso0 107tc (right), Karin & Uwe Annas 43t, khomich 5c, Khorzhevska 102 (Holly), kjekol 5bl, Robert Kneschke 43c, Arkadiusz Komski 56, kontur-vid 10 (camera), ksumano 107tl, Kzenon 8/2, ldprod 104, Ignat Lednev 7, Izf 5br, Maridav 84b, 85c, Martinan 50l, michaeljung 25cr, Monkey Business 15tl, 63bc, 68, mountaintreks 74, MSA 99tr, muro 10cr, okinawakasawa 6 (beanbag), 6 (watch), Ruslan Olinchuk 99r, pat_hastings 27t, Pavel 101cl, PHB. cz 67r, pressmaster 51tl, Proma 72r, rangizzz 25b, Alexander Raths 37b, Rawpixel 97t, raywoo 10tl, robysaba 26bl, M. Rosenwirth 84c, Sabphoto 102 (Ben), sanjagrujic 50r, schwabenblitz 30cl, 30cr, 30br, Vlastimil Šesták 101tc, SG-design 84t, .shock 41b, stillkost 63bl, stockyimages 26tr, stokkete 91r, Syda Productions 10br, 14l, 14r, 44, teirin 99l, 99c, 99bl, ulchik74 5tr, VanderWolf Images 87tr, Diana Vyshnikova 92bl, WavebreakmediaMicro 20b, 51cr, yanlev 32, 72b, Lisa F. Young 51cl; **Getty Images:** AFP / Saeed Khan 103, Apic 66b, Barcroft Media 62r, Thomas Barwick 20t, Bongarts / Christof Koepsel 77r, Marco Di Lauro 30tr, Christofer Dracke 13b, Tom Dulat 80-81, Christopher Futcher 75, Mike Harrington 73, Erik Isakson 31, Chris Jackson 53r, Jetta Productions 63tr, Allison Joyce 60-61, 61t, LatinContent / Gabriel Rossi 77l, Rich Legg 12t, Michael Nichols 96b, Lucas Oleniuk 29l, PeopleImages.com 107c (right), Margie Politzer 39t, Putu Sayoga 71, Kristian Sekulic 33, Oliver Strewe 30bl, Ray Tamarra 53l, UK Press / Julian Parker 53c, Caroline von Tuempling 28, WireImage / Jim Smeal 66t, WireImage / Mychal Watts 66c; **Guardian News and Media Ltd.:** Martin Godwin 48b; **Pearson Education Ltd:** 79, Jon Barlow 69b, Gareth Boden 7c, Handan Erek 6c, Debbie Rowe 87l; **PhotoDisc:** Ryan McVay 69c; **Shutterstock.com:** Galyna Andrushko 107cr, auremar 50c, bikeriderlondon 36c, 63tl, blackboard1965 78t, Willyam Bradberry 97c, CandyBox Images 43b, elitravo 42b, goory 6 (T-shirt), graja 10 (controller), Hitdelight 8/1, HomeArt 6 (skateboard), Jessmine 93tr, Jetrel 102bl, Dmitry Kalinovsky 25cl, Kamira 78b, Kzenon 37cl, Cecilia Lim H M 107tr, Laura Lohrman Moore 101bl, Lubo 23, Maridav 8/4, MJTH 10tr, Monkey Business Images 21, 45, MrGarry 10 (tablet), Mike Norton 107bc, oliveromg 57cl, ollyy 57cr, Pavel L Photo and Video 69t, Pressmaster 47, 51br, Andrew Roland 101cr, Sculpies 92-93, Valery Shanin 97b, sheff 41t, Jason Stitt 57t, Studio 1One 107br, Tooykrub 107bl, Jan Martin Will 98, WilleeCole 102tl, Halina Yakushevich 55l, Zakharoff 10 (mp3 player); **Telegraph Media Group:** 90

Illustrations

(Key: b-bottom; c-centre; l-left; r-right; t-top)
Joanna Balicka p. 9l, 24, 91; WORD STORE booklet p. 5, 17; Tom Hughes p. 15, 22, 23, 52, 71, 89, 95; Ewa Olejnik p. 4bl, 11, 54; WORD STORE booklet p. 9; Magdalena Rudzińska p. 38; WORD STORE booklet p. 1; Virus Group p. 4r, 6, 7, 8, 9r
All other images © Pearson Education

Every effort has been made to trace the copyright holders and we apologise in advance for any unintentional omissions. We would be pleased to insert the appropriate acknowledgement in any subsequent edition of this publication.